Acta Universitatis Stockholmiensi

STOCKHOLM STUDIES IN ENGLISH

LXVII

ACTA UNIVERSITATIS STOCKHOLMIENSIS

Stockholm Studies in English
LXVII

REACTIONS TO NON-NATIVE ENGLISH

Native English-Speakers' Assessments
of Errors in the Use of English
Made by Non-Native Users of the
Language

Part 1
Acceptability
and
Intelligibility

by
Pär Hultfors

ALMQVIST & WIKSELL INTERNATIONAL

STOCKHOLM, SWEDEN

Doctoral dissertation
at the University of Stockholm
Department of English
S-106 91 STOCKHOLM

ABSTRACT

This study is intended as a contribution to ERROR EVALUATION,
i.e. the study of the relative gravity of errors. By submitting
samples of non-native English to native speakers of English living
in England their reactions to the errors represented were charted.
This was accomplished by means of written questionnaires,
containing 75 test sentences, 70 of which contained grammatical or
vocabulary errors typical of foreign users of English in general
and Swedish users of English in particular. The remaining five
sentences were examples of correct and idiomatic English, and
served as A-control sentences, testing the reliability of the
informants. The test subjects come from different age groups and
occupations and have different educational backgrounds. They have
also been classified according to a number of other social
criteria.

This study analyses the results of the experiments and it is
shown to what degree the errors give rise to foreign impressions
of the test sentences in which they occur and to what degree the
errors made the test sentences difficult to understand.
Differences between various groups of informants (age, sex, social
variables) in these respects are also revealed. The results throw
light on acceptability and indications of linguistic change are
also shown. The effects of the errors included are also compiled
in a number of rank lists, for easy reference.

The complete material has been computerized and subjected to a
number of different significance tests to show the reliability of
the results.

The results may give teachers of English a better guide as to
what errors should be considered serious from a communicative
point of view.

© Pär Hultfors 1986
ISBN 91-22-00806-3   ISSN 0346-6272
Gotab, Stockholm 1986

ACKNOWLEDGEMENTS

It is a great pleasure for me to express my sincere gratitude here to all those who have helped me in the course of my work.

Professor Magnus Ljung suggested the subject of the investigation, provided me with funds and gave me invaluable advice at various stages of my work. I thank him for this and for his kindly guidance and criticism through all the years this book was in the making. I also thank him and Professor Lennart Björk for including this book in the series Stockholm Studies in English.

Professor Stig Johansson, Oslo, also guided me and gave me a great deal of valuable advice in the early stages of my work, for which I owe him a great debt of gratitude.

I also particularly wish to thank Docent Nils-Lennart Johannesson for many stimulating discussions and comments. His guidance and thorough criticism have been invaluable, and his encouragement has meant a great deal to me.

My thanks are also due to Professor Sven Jacobson, Uppsala, for stimulating discussions, to Professor Mats Rydén, Umeå, and Docent Sverker Brorström for suggesting a number of sentences for inclusion in the questionnaires, to Lektor Vincent Petti for valuable comments and for giving me permission to use a few of the sentences he included in his Code of Errors, and to the members of the WIP (Work in Progress) seminars where the test sentences were discussed.

Quite obviously, I am also indebted to all my informants and helpers in England. I particularly wish to thank the following people, who helped and assisted me in the field work in England: Mr Brian Creese and members of the staff at the Thomas Peacocke School in Rye, East Sussex, where the very first experiments were carried out in June, 1983, Mr J.M. Hawe and members of the staff at Easthampstead Park School, Easthampstead Park, Berkshire, and

Mr J.R. Score and members of the staff at Sandhurst School, Camberley, Surrey. I should also like to thank all the pupils who took part in the investigations at these coeducational comprehensive secondary schools.

Further I wish to thank Philip Mercer and Christine Nicholson at the City Lit, London, Pam Howells at Surrey Heath Adult Education Institute, Surrey, and Lorna Crookall at Quintin Kynaston Adult Education Centre, London, as well as all my informants at these educational establishments.

I owe a particular debt of gratitude to Joan Davies, Senior Lecturer at the Royal Military Academy Sandhurst, Camberley, Surrey, who helped me in various ways and also approached a number of institutions and educational establishments on my behalf. I also thank all my informants from the Royal Military Academy Sandhurst.

I should like to thank Frances Woods at the Counsel and Care for the Elderly in London, who gave me the names and addresses of many residential homes for elderly people. I should also like to thank the residents and the staff of the following residential homes for elderly people in the London area: The Alice Waddilove Club, Clapham Common; Delves House, Queensgate Terrace; Hampstead Old People's Housing, Hampstead; Lyle Park, Putney Hill; Rydons, Wimbledon; and Vicarage Gate, Notting Hill.

My thanks are also due to the residents and the staff of Devon Port House residential home for elderly people, Rye, East Sussex, and to the following people and institutions in the London area: Jo Cooper, other members of the staff and the visitors at Earl's Court Drop-In Center, Ian Burgoyne, director of Chelsea Community Association, and their visitors, the staff and the visitors at the Ashmole Lunch Club, Lambeth, at Kensington Day Centre, Kensington, at Kingsgate Day Centre, Camden, and at the Paddington Bowling and Sports Club, London.

I also thank all my other informants who were questioned in various places in Berkshire, London, Surrey, and East Sussex.

I thank Ann Wallin for her patience with my intruding into her room to use her typewriter and word processor.

I thank Lars Hellvig at QZ, Stockholm University, for occasional assistance with some of the more intricate aspects of computer processing.

I also wish to thank the British and the Swedish Embassies for valuable assistance, and Dan Andrée, Technical Attaché at the Swedish Embassy in London, for letting me stay in his flat during my time in the London area.

Finally, I thank my family and friends for their unflagging support and assistance.

Stockholm, March 1986

Pär Hultfors

CONTENTS

1. INTRODUCTION

1.1 Aim of the study

This study is intended as a contribution to ERROR EVALUATION, i.e. the study of the relative gravity of errors, a largely neglected field of research in applied linguistics. Its theoretical framework is the research field of ERROR ANALYSIS. Few studies in this field have been concerned with how the results should be applied and what errors should be regarded as more serious than others and hence have not tackled the problem of error evaluation. This study describes the results of the first of three different investigations which were carried out in order to chart the reactions of native speakers of English living in England to various solecisms or errors[1] in the use of English often made by non-native users and by Swedes in particular. Its approach is communicative, as it concentrates on the communicative effect of errors, such as the intelligibility of deviant sentences and the degree of foreignness associated with them. The results may also throw light on linguistic change in current English.

The first investigation was carried out in order to make clear to what degree various errors cause sentences to be perceived as foreign and difficult to understand by native speakers of English and thus how serious the errors represented are from these points of view. In the study 'more serious' refers to an error which made a sentence score higher than did another error on the five-graded scales that accompanied each sentence in the questionnaires distributed to the informants. This investigation thus combines the study of acceptability with the study of intelligibility.

The second investigation was carried out in order to make clear how serious the language error in a sentence is judged to be by native speakers of English when made by different types of foreigners, viz. a foreign tourist visiting Great Britain, a foreigner working as a secretary in Great Britain, and a manager of a big firm who is on business in Great Britain. The aim of this investigation is to find out the importance of FOREIGNER ROLE as far as language is concerned, i.e. to what extent these foreigners are required to have a good command of English, according to native speakers of English. The results of this investigation will be dealt with in a forthcoming publication.

The third investigation was carried out in order to make clear how native speakers of English interpret the erroneous sentences tested in the former two investigations. This was accomplished by asking test subjects to correct the sentences. The aim of this investigation is to find out which of the errors give rise to misinterpretations of the sentences in which they occur or a total lack of comprehension, and which of the errors cause no such problems at all. This investigation also functions as a control investigation, since it also aims at finding out whether or not there are any unexpected interpretations of the test sentences and what is the most common interpretation of each sentence. The results of this investigation will be dealt with in this study passim, and in detail in a forthcoming publication.

All the informants who took part in the three investigations were informed that the term foreigner referred to non-native users of English. The term will therefore be used with this sense in this study.

1.2 Scope and method

What is new in these investigations, compared to most earlier investigations of a similar type, is that a larger number of test sentences and error types have been used, that a larger number of test subjects have been questioned^2, that the informants come from different age groups and generations (the age span is 82 years, cf. 1.3), represent a wide variety of occupations, and have different educational backgrounds. Moreover, the informants have been classified according to a number of social criteria, such as the amount of contact they have with foreigners, experience of living abroad, and knowledge of other languages; foreigner role has been considered, an attempt has been made to carry out a relatively sophisticated statistical analysis of the data, and the data have been subjected to data processing by computer.

1.2.1 The questionnaires

Each of the three investigations was carried out by means of a written questionnaire, containing exactly the same set of 75 test sentences. However, the questions asked about the test sentences were different in the three questionnaires. By using the same set of test sentences a comparison of the three investigations is possible.

Each of the three types of questionnaires came in two versions, each of which had the 75 test sentences in the reversed consecutive order compared to the other version. Test sentence 1 in version A thus was the same as test sentence 75 in version B, test sentence 2 in version A was the same as test sentence 74 in version B, and so on. This method of ordering the test sentences produced six different questionnaires (1A, 1B, 2A, 2B, 3A, 3B) and was used as a precautionary step in order to minimize the risk that some questions and sentences would be answered and commented on by more informants than would other questions and sentences. This might have happened if only one version of each questionnaire had been used. It was expected that some informants would give up after having completed about half of their questionnaires and in this way the effect of such half-answered questionnaires was spread out to affect a larger number of questions and sentences than would have been the case if only one version of the questionnaires had been used. This means that each question on a sentence has been answered by about the same number of informants. Statistical comparison of answers to different questions thus becomes more accurate.

Another reason for the inversion of the consecutive order of the test sentences in the two versions of each questionnaire was that the possible influence of the preceding sentence on the answers given to the following sentence ought to be eliminated. By reversing the consecutive order of the test sentences, such possible influence was largely neutralized, as half of the informants had read and judged one test sentence before test sentence X and the other half of the informants had read and judged another test sentence before test sentence X, assuming, of course, that the informants read the test sentences and answered the questions in the order these were presented in the questionnaires, which virtually everybody actually did in fact do. I was able to confirm this myself in a number of cases and my helpers and assistants at the various institutions and places where the investigations were carried out reported likewise.

In order to test the utility and quality of the questionnaires, a try-out was conducted among Englishmen living in Sweden, in February and March, 1983, after which some modifications and alterations of the questionnaires were undertaken. The large-scale investigations were then carried out in England in June and July of the same year.

For reasons of limited financial resources and hence limited time, a planned total of 800 printed questionnaires was reduced to 600, 444 of which were then actually answered, completely or partly, by informants of differing age, sex, social background, residential background, and educational background. An overwhelming majority of the informants answered all the questions in the questionnaires and those who did not, usually missed only a few of the questions. Failure to answer some of the questions on page one of the questionnaires rendered the questionnaires invalid, and such questionnaires were therefore excluded from the subsequent statistical analysis. These obligatory questions were no. 1 (sex) and no. 2 (age) (cf. appendix 3).

Out of the 75 test sentences, common to all the questionnaire types, five were A-control sentences, i.e. sentences which contained no errors. These sentences served the purpose of testing the reliability of the informants, as the only 'normal' answers to the questions asked about these sentences would be answers which indicated that these sentences were faultless. The questionnaires of informants who failed to give such answers for two or more of the five A-control sentences were excluded from the subsequent statistical analysis, as these informants were obviously not attentive enough or were unreliable in some other way when answering their questionnaires.

There were also five pairs of B-control sentences among the 75 test sentences. The two sentences in each pair were all but identical with one another, or very similar, from a syntactic point of view, and tested exactly the same type of error. Unlike the A-control sentences, these control sentences thus contained errors, just like the rest of the test sentences, and were inserted in different places in the questionnaires with the dual purpose of testing the effects of the errors contained in them and being still another check on the reliability of the informants, as the 'normal' thing here would be to give very similar, if not identical, answers to each of the two very similar B-control sentences constituting a pair. The two B-control sentences in each pair were placed far away from each other in the questionnaires with many other test sentences between them, in an attempt to render comparison of the two similar B-control sentences more difficult for the informants, and thereby make this reliability test more effective. The questionnaires filled in by informants who failed to give identical or very similar answers to the two B-control sentences of each pair were not, however, excluded from the subsequent statistical analysis, provided that these informants had been found reliable in the case of the A-control sentences. The reason for this is that the B-control sentences are probably not as safe a test of the reliability of the informants as are the A-control sentences, as the informants might have a reason for giving different answers even to two very similar sentences. This is hardly the case with the A-control sentences, however, as these are examples of what is generally considered to be normal English usage. The results corroborate this, as the answers of nearly all the informants to the questions on the five A-control sentences indicate that these sentences were regarded as perfectly normal English, which clearly sets them apart from the rest of the test sentences. This is a good indication of the reliability of the informants, whose questionnaires were included in the subsequent statistical analysis. The answers to the questions on the B-control sentences of each pair are, however, very similar indeed, which is still another good indication of the reliability of the informants.

After the exclusion of questionnaires filled in by unreliable informants and informants who had failed to answer the first two questions on page one, 369 questionnaires remained. These had been filled in by informants who had all been found reliable in the A-control tests, and these questionnaires were all included in the subsequent statistical analysis. Out of these remaining 369 informants, 113 have answered questionnaire 1 (51 version A, and 62 version B), 118 have answered questionnaire 2 (59 for each version), and 138 have answered questionnaire 3 (71 version A, and 67 version A). Questionnaire 3 will be referred to as form 3 or the control form.

1.2.2 Methods for studying native speakers' reactions

The intention of this study is to examine the reactions of a fairly large group of informants (earlier studies of a similar type, as well as many linguistic investigations in general, have often used considerably fewer informants[2]), composed of as many different types of people as possible living in the south of England, in an attempt to make the informant group as heterogeneous as possible (earlier studies of a similar type have mainly used university students as test subjects and have therefore comprised very homogeneous informant groups), as this will make the test sample more likely to be representative of people living in the south of England. The method chosen to obtain this is usually called RANDOM SAMPLING, or, more specifically, STRATIFIED RANDOM SAMPLING[3].

From lists of names of coeducational comprehensive secondary schools, adult education centres, day centres, athletic associations, lunch clubs, and residential homes for elderly people, located in the counties of Berkshire, London, Surrey, and Sussex, some names were chosen at random. The schools and various other institutions with these names were then approached about their willingness to participate in these investigations. Very few declined to take part and most of these randomly selected places are therefore included in these investigations.

Two fundamentally different types of investigation can be made in the study of native speakers' reactions to foreign English, viz. the SUBJECTIVE METHOD and the OBJECTIVE METHOD. These methods correspond to JUDGEMENT TESTS and OPERATION TESTS, respectively, in Quirk-Svartvik (1966).

The subjective method means that informants are asked to give judgements about linguistic deviance and the objective method means that they are asked to perform various tasks, such as repeating erroneous sentences or reading texts with different types of errors. In the former situation informants are conscious of grading errors, whereas in the latter case the measure of error gravity is arrived at indirectly by studying informant behaviour.

Johansson (1975:34ff) found that there was a surprising amount of agreement between the results of judgement tests and performance tasks but he concluded that judgement tests seemed to have greater discriminatory power. Johansson calls the correspondence between subjective and objective techniques 'remarkable' and goes on to say that this 'could perhaps be taken as an indication that, through frequent experience in communication, the language user has developed an intuitive sense of communicative efficiency' (1975:50). He concluded that the agreement between subjective and objective testing techniques when studying the collective behaviour of a group of subjects means that the problem of establishing error gravity 'is reduced to manageable proportions, as the study could be based mainly on judgement tests. Such tests are easy to construct, administer and score, whereas the objective experiments require elaborate preparation, are time-consuming and difficult to evaluate' (1978:48).

Johansson thus found support for using mainly the judgement technique in the rest of his investigations. On the basis of these findings it was decided that the judgement technique should also be employed in the investigations for this study.

Johansson did, however, point out that there are certain problems concerning the judgement technique which show that it is important to have a check on comprehension for material to be judged. This is the purpose of the third investigation (cf 1.1), which will be referred to in various places throughout this study.

Just as in the case of some of Johansson's experiments, the most important limitation of the three investigations referred to in 1.1, is that isolated sentences are used without a real communicative context. As Johansson pointed out, however, this is a necessary limitation of the experimental technique (1978:29). Nevertheless, Johansson's impression was that most of his test sentences were clearly understood by the informants even without an explanatory context. That this is so in the case of the sentences tested in this study is corroborated by the results of investigation 3. Olsson (1977:42) also reported that three separate intelligibility investigations yielded similar results, whether disconnected sentences or a connected prose passage were used as test material. Petti (1979) also reported that native speakers of English seemed to be quite able to assess erroneous sentences out of context.

1.2.3 Statistical evaluation methods

The data of earlier studies of a similar type, as well as the data of many linguistic investigations in general, often have not been subjected to any thorough statistical analysis or evaluation, let alone data processing by computer[4]. However, it is always important to investigate one's data thoroughly in any analysis. An unwary user of computer systems for data analysis may also make serious errors, which may lead to deceptive information and false conclusions, unless he takes precautions and studies his data carefully.

All the various statistical tests and calculations described below have been carried out by means of the SAS computer system

(Statistical Analysis System), a powerful computer software system for data analysis, and run on a large IBM Amdahl V/7 computer at QZ, Stockholm University Computing Center for Higher Education and Research, in Stockholm, Sweden.

The statistical method used in testing for significant differences between means is the t-test. Moreover, differences have been cross-checked for significance by means of the advanced statistical GLM (General Linear Model) procedure in order to ensure accuracy and reliability in the results. The t-test is used to determine the probability that a difference between two sample means ($\bar{x}$ and $\bar{y}$) reflects a difference between the corresponding population means (μ_1 and μ_2). It is calculated by the formula

$$t = \frac{\bar{x} - \bar{y}}{\sqrt{\dfrac{s_1^2}{n_1} + \dfrac{s_2^2}{n_2}}}$$

for unequal population variances, and by the formula

$$t = \frac{\bar{x} - \bar{y}}{\sqrt{\dfrac{1}{n_1} + \dfrac{1}{n_2}} \; \sqrt{\dfrac{\Sigma x^2 - n_1 \bar{x}^2 + \Sigma y^2 - n_2 \bar{y}^2}{n_1 + n_2 - 2}}}$$

for equal population variances.

The GLM procedure uses the method of least squares[5] to fit general linear models. It performs analysis of variance and calculates significances, especially for experimental unbalanced data, i.e. when the subgroups of the data contain different numbers of observations, or when some subgroups contain no observations (the simpler ANOVA procedure should not be used in such cases). In the analysis of the data for this study GLM has also been used for regression[6] and analysis of variance procedures.

The PAIRED-COMPARISONS t TEST (henceforth abbreviated PCT) has been used for testing the significance of the difference between two means for the same group of test subjects (matched observations). This test has been based only on the answers of the informants who have answered both questions, i.e. the same question for the two sentences which are to be compared. This test is calculated by the formula

$$t = \frac{\bar{D}}{S_D} \sqrt{n} \quad .$$

The F-test has been used for estimating population variances. This test is used to determine the error probability for rejection of the null hypothesis, which says that the two population variances are equal (i.e. H_0: $\sigma_1^2 = \sigma_2^2$), and is calculated as the greater sample variance divided by the smaller sample variance, i.e.

$$F = \frac{s_1^2}{s_2^2} \qquad \text{(where } s_1^2 \geq s_2^2 \text{).}$$

The error probability has been set at $p \leq .05$ for t-tests, F-tests, GLM-tests, and PCT tests, which means that a weaker significance than $p = .05$ will not be accepted, and will therefore be marked by a dash in the significance columns.

Differences between two means, either for two different groups of test subjects (t-test) or for the same group of test subjects (PCT-test), will be said to be either not significant (dash), or significant on one of the following nine levels: A (.05 $\geq$ p > .025), B (.025 $\geq$ p > .01), C (.01 $\geq$ p > .005), D (.005 $\geq$ p > .0025), E (.0025 $\geq$ p > .001), F (.001 $\geq$ p > .0005), G (.0005 $\geq$ p > .00025), H (.00025 $\geq$ p > .0001), I (p $\leq$ .0001). On level A there are thus five chances in a hundred that the difference between the two sample means in question does not reflect a difference between the corresponding population means, and on level I there is one chance in ten thousand that this difference does not reflect a difference between the corresponding population means. To put it differently, on level A we have a 95 % chance of being right when we claim that the population mean is enclosed by the confidence interval, and on level I we have a 99.99 % chance of being right in doing so.

The value most often used as the representative of a group of observations is the ARITHMETIC MEAN, and this value will be employed as the most important statistical measure of location throughout this study. The value of the sample mean ($\bar{x}$), is the arithmetic average of all values of that variable in the sample, that is, the sum of the values of all the individual observations (Σxi) divided by the number of observations in the group (n), according to the following formula:

$$\bar{x} = \frac{\Sigma x i}{n}$$

As a further indication of how the informants have answered, the MODE, another statistical measure of location, is given both for the question on foreignness and for the question on intelligibility difficulty in all tables for the total number of informants, i.e. in all the tables under the heading of total sample. The mode is the value at which the density of the distribution is at a maximum. Some distributions have more than one mode. The sample mode is the value that occurs most often in the sample. For a distribution with multiple modes, the common convention is to select the lowest mode for reporting. However, here all modes will be reported in the case of such distributions, as the maximum number of modes is never more than three.

It is always a good rule not only to present arithmetic means, and modes, but also, whenever possible, the individual values from which such values are calculated. In this case, however, it is not possible to present all the individual values because of the great amount of such data. Therefore, the amount of variation within each group of informants will be indicated by means of the statistical measure of variability known as the SAMPLE STANDARD DEVIATION (s), the value of which is calculated as the square root of the sum of the squared differences between the sample mean and the value of each observation, divided by the number of observations minus one. Either of the following formulas can be used to illustrate this:

$$s = \sqrt{\frac{\Sigma(\bar{x} - x_i)^2}{n - 1}} \quad \text{or} \quad s = \sqrt{\frac{n\Sigma x_i^2 - (\Sigma x_i)^2}{n(n - 1)}}.$$

Another statistical method that has been carried out on the data of this study is CORRELATION[7], in order to get correlation coefficients between variables. This has been accomplished by means of the CORR procedure in SAS. The sample correlation estimates the true correlation. It is computed:

$$r_{xy} = \Sigma(x_i - \bar{x})(y_i - \bar{y}) / \sqrt{(\Sigma(x_i - \bar{x})^2 \Sigma(y_i - \bar{y})^2)}$$

(where $\bar{x}$ and $\bar{y}$ are the sample means of x and y).

1.2.4 Basic assumptions underlying the various computations

The arithmetic mean calculated for a randomly selected sample of informants, such as the sample in these investigations, may not be absolutely identical with the corresponding mean for the entire population (μ), but 'it will have a sufficient probability of being so close to the population mean that it can serve as an ESTIMATOR of the unknown population mean' (Johannesson 1986:110).

In the same way the sample standard deviation (s) functions as an estimator of the population standard deviation (σ).

The parameters studied are assumed to have a NORMAL DISTRIBUTION within the population. This is a prerequisite for a proper use of the t-test (cf 1.2.3). For practical purposes in linguistic investigations, 'if we can make a reasonable assumption about a parameter having (nearly) normal distribution, then we can feel justified in applying tests which presuppose a normal distribution. Only if it is quite unreasonable to assume a normal distribution should we refrain from applying such tests' (Johannesson 1986:111). In the case of the parameters under study in these investigations, it seems most reasonable to assume a normal distribution within the population. This situation is illustrated by the curve diagram in figure 1:1.

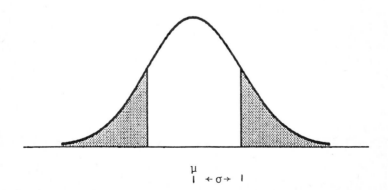

μ
| ←σ→ |

Fig. 1:1 A normal distribution curve.

The population values are thus assumed to cluster symmetrically round the population mean in such a way that there are ever fewer values the further away we move from μ.

1.3 The informants

The test subjects for the three investigations were chosen with a view to making the sample as heterogeneous as possible. This makes the sample more likely to be representative of the population of southern England than if only school children or university students had been used as test subjects. The following information on the informants applies to all the three investigations.

The informants were all chosen from the southern part of England, as the standard DIALECT[8] of this area is normally used as a model for foreign learners of English, just as RP[9] is often the model ACCENT[10] taught to foreign learners of English. The standard dialect of this area is often loosely called STANDARD ENGLISH. However, STANDARD ENGLISH (a better term is STANDARD BRITISH ENGLISH) refers to the dialect of educated people throughout the British Isles and is the dialect normally used in writing, for teaching in schools and universities, and heard on radio and television. Unlike RP, it exhibits some regional variation and it is not restricted to the speech of a particular social group. There are thus different standards of English in England, Scotland and Ireland, although variation between these standard dialects is quite limited. A better term for the English dialect of the area investigated is therefore STANDARD ENGLISH ENGLISH, employed in Hughes-Trudgill for the standard dialect of England and Wales (1979:8). As this standard English dialect is the one most often used as a model for foreign learners of English, it seems most appropriate to investigate the attitudes of the users of this dialect to errors made by foreign users of English. Comparing examples of Standard Scottish English and Standard English English, Hughes-Trudgill make the following comment: 'it goes without saying that it is usually the latter which is taught to foreign students' (1979:8).

The reason for using a rather limited area in the south of England for these investigations is that this will limit the differences between the non-standard English dialects spoken by some of the informants and Standard English English more than would be the case if one were to go further afield and include informants from a larger area of England, as the standard language developed out of the English dialects used in and around London, and as the southern area grammatically is a conservative one. This area may thus be regarded as the core of the Standard English English area[11].

Within this rather limited area of England, informants were questioned at randomly selected places, principally in some of the Home Counties (cf. 1.2.2). However, quite a few of the informants were born and grew up in other parts of the United Kingdom, for which reason other dialects are also represented. Some of the informants were born abroad or had lived abroad, either in English-speaking countries (i.e. countries where English is the official language or one of the official languages) or in non-English speaking countries, and thus sometimes represented still other varieties of English (cf. 19.4). This makes the group of informants still more heterogeneous. A foreigner who goes to England is, after all, likely to meet English-speaking people representing a great variety of dialects and varieties of English, even if he stays in the south of England.

However, all the informants have English as their mother tongue and most of the informants use Standard English English or a variety of English which is very similar to it. It should nevertheless be borne in mind that there is a slight predominance of southern English dialects, compared to other dialects, as the investigations were carried out in the south of England. These dialects (mainly Berkshire, Surrey, and Sussex), however, do not generally differ very much from Standard English English compared to many other dialects. The answers given by the informants to the question on their dialect show that about one third indicated that they did not know what dialect, or accent, they spoke or had missing answers to this question, whereas about 14 per cent indicated that they spoke no dialect or accent and 14 per cent indicated that they spoke Standard English. The remaining 39 per cent of the informants indicated that they spoke a dialect, the most common of which were Sussex (12 per cent) and London (6 per cent). The large number of informants who did not know what dialect they spoke or had missing answers to this question indicates that many informants were not aware of using any particular dialect. In actual fact many of these informants, too, proved to be using a variety of English that was very similar to Standard English English.

London is included in the area investigated, but only to a limited extent because of certain peculiarities sometimes associated with the language of large cities. The great majority of informants were thus found outside London and the London area, in counties such as Berkshire, Surrey, and Sussex. To exclude London altogether from the investigations would, however, be to go too far if one aims at heterogeneity, particularly in view of the importance of London and its very large population and also in view of the improved prestige of the English of the London region after the Second World War. Thus, London is rather underrepresented in the investigations. As far as the pensioners are concerned, however, this is not the case. Most of the pensioners were found in residential homes for elderly people, and as these usually do not house more than a very limited number of pensioners each, it was more or less necessary to stay in London, where many such homes can be found, in order to acquire a large enough sample of pensioners compared to the other groups of informants. The large drop-out rate of pensioners from the investigations, compared to the other groups of informants, made this even more necessary. However, many of the pensioners questioned were born and grew up in other parts of the country and only a few of them had lived all their lives in London or in the

London area, for which reason London usage seems to be no more common in the group of pensioners than in the other groups of informants, even though most of the pensioners happened to be questioned in London.

The age of the informants varied from 14 to 96 years of age, which means that the age range of the test subjects is 82 years. In the statistical analysis, the informants were assigned to three different age groups according to their age, in order to enable comparison of age groups containing a fairly large number of informants. Informants being at least 14 years old but less than 20 were thus assigned to the group of teen-agers, informants being at least 20 years old but less than 65 were assigned to the group of adults, and informants being at least 65 years old were assigned to the group of pensioners for statistical analysis. This is illustrated by the table below.

Age of test subject	Age group	No.	Mean age	Modal age
14 to 19 years	teen-agers	146	16	15
20 to 64 years	adults	141	40	33
65 years or older	pensioners	82	79	80
	Σ	369		
(Test subjects excluded from analysis		75)		
	Σ	444		

The age of the informants who indicated their age with decimals was rounded off to the nearest integer. A few of the border-line cases thus came to belong to a different age group than is shown by the table (e.g. 19.5 was rounded off to 20).

The average age of the informants was 39 years, the median age was 32, and the modal age 15. As for the teen-agers, pupils from the fifth and sixth forms of coeducational comprehensive secondary schools were used as test subjects, which means that most of them were between 15 and 18 years old. Fewer pensioners than either adults or teen-agers were included in the statistical analysis, as the number of questionnaires which had to be excluded from this analysis (cf. 1.2.1) was larger among the pensioners. Thus about 20 per cent of the informants whose answers were included in the statistical analysis were pensioners, whereas about 40 per cent were teen-agers and 40 per cent adults. However, the number of pensioners who took part in the investigations was roughly the same as the number of informants in each of the other two age groups (cf. note 3).

There are also fewer men than women represented in the investigations (about 65 % of the informants are female). The reason for this is that it was, on the whole, easier to persuade women to contribute to this research. This affects the group of adults most seriously, as the groups of teen-agers were fairly evenly balanced with regard to sex (where they were not, it was easy to alter the number of boys in proportion to girls), and the group of pensioners is unbalanced 'by nature', as women generally outlive men.

1.4 The testing situation

The informants were seated at random and each was given a different questionnaire (cf. 1.2.1) from those of the informants who were sitting next to him or her. No informants were allowed to choose which type of questionnaire to answer and each informant answered only one questionnaire. These precautionary steps were taken in order to minimize the risk of collaboration and the risk of an uneven distribution of informants on the six questionnaire types as regards differences in abilities, interests, opinions, and prejudices.

Before the informants were allowed to begin answering the questionnaires, they were informed about the nature of their task, what they were supposed to do, and why we wanted them to do it. The introduction at the top of page one of the questionnaires, which was identical for all the six questionnaire types, was then read aloud by the session leader in order to focus everybody's attention on the questionnaire. The informants were then asked to begin by answering the questions on page one of their questionnaires. These questions were the same for all the six versions of the questionnaire (cf. appendix 3). The informants were also asked to follow the instructions given by the session leader, question by question, when doing this.

The session leader read each question on page one aloud and gave the informants ample time to answer each question, after each reading. This was done because a renewed try-out had shown that there were a number of questions which the informants wanted to ask while completing page one. Question 6 ("How long have you lived where you live now?"), question 7 ("What dialect do you speak, if any?"), question 8 ("What is your mother tongue?"), and question 12 ("How often do you talk to foreigners?") were questions that often gave rise to uncertainty. By having all the informants simultaneously answer the questions on this page and allowing time for queries from the informants after each question had been read aloud, any uncertainty as to what was meant by the questions on this page was obliterated. The initial uncertainty shows, however, that some of the questions on page one were not clear enough and that a different wording might have made the meaning clearer.

When the first page had been completed by all the informants, they were asked to turn to page two and begin by carefully reading the instructions at the top of that page as well as the example given. For each of the six versions of the questionnaire an example was given after the initial instructions (cf. appendix 3), to show the informants exactly how to go about answering the questions in each questionnaire. When this had been done, the informants were asked if there was anything that they did not understand or felt hesitant about. In most cases, the instructions on page 2, which were of three different types (cf. 1.2.1), gave rise to very few questions. This may partly be due to the clarifying example, which was given immediately after the instructions.

Communication among the informants was not allowed during the answering session, which was always of about 45 minutes' duration. Some informants completed their questionnaires in about 20 minutes, whereas others needed the whole session to complete theirs. The informants who needed extra time were given this.

The informants were allowed to ask questions of the session leaders if there was anything about the answering technique that they did not understand. Most of the informants, however, did not have to ask any questions but declared, when asked, that they fully understood the instructions given in their questionnaires.

The informants were asked not to put their names or any other means of identification on their questionnaires. They were advised to go through the whole questionnaire again and check that they had answered all the questions before finishing. They were also asked not to leave the room before everybody had finished and all the questionnaires had been collected by the session leaders. These steps were taken in order to assure silence and thus avoid lack of concentration among the informants due to possible disturbances in the room.

1.5 <u>The</u> <u>test</u> sentences

It can always be discussed what sentences should be included in investigations of this type. Out of a corpus consisting of more than 400 erroneous sentences produced by foreign users of English in general and by Swedes in particular (mainly university and college students), 75 sentences were eventually chosen to be included in the questionnaires. Before this was done I had the opportunity of discussing the example sentences with several people at the English Department of the University of Stockholm, after which 90 sentences remained. These were then discussed at a WIP (Work In Progress) seminar, where the teachers and other attenders were also asked to contribute by proposing other suitable sentences, containing errors typical of foreign users of English. Some of the sentences under discussion had to be slightly changed compared to their original form in order to make them more suitable for the test situation. The Wippers were all agreed that the sentences represented common and typical errors, often made by Swedish users of English and also by foreign users of English in general.

It was decided that no mention should be made in the questionnaires as to whether the sentences were to be regarded as examples of spoken or written English. There were several reasons for this: 1. The sentences contain only errors that are common to both the spoken and written English of foreigners. 2. We do not want to compare the gravity of the errors in written English with the gravity of the same errors in spoken English (horizontal comparison), but rather the gravity of one error with the gravity of another (vertical comparison) (cf. fig. 1:2). 3. The sentences <u>were</u> to be administered to the test subjects in written form, and for that reason it would have been a bad method to present them as examples of anything else. 4. The variation of sentences and types of errors could be made greater if the informants did not have to think of each sentence either as an example of spoken English or as an example of written English.

It is important to bear in mind, however, that what the informants have been asked to react to <u>is</u> written material only, even if they may have thought of some of the sentences as first having been spoken and then transferred to paper, which actually was the case in many instances.

It is a well-known fact that errors in spoken English often are more indulgently met with by native speakers of English than are errors in written English, in equivalent styles and language situations, but the relative gravity of the errors can be presumed to be the same in both cases (cf. fig. 1:2).

What has been said so far about spoken English does, of course, exclude pronunciation, as a foreigner who makes the same error in both speech and writing may find that his written English is more indulgently met with by native speakers of English than is his spoken English, the reason being that he has a bad pronunciation, which makes him even more difficult to understand or even more foreign sounding.

	SPEECH	WRITING
error 1	'bad English'	'very bad English'
error 2	'rather bad English'	'bad English'
error 3	'very bad English'	'bad English'
error 4	'bad English'	'rather bad English'

Figure 1:2 Fictitious example of reactions to English sentences containing different errors. If the foreigner's pronunciation is perfect, the horizontal relationships may be as in the case of errors 1 and 2. If, on the other hand, the foreigner's pronunciation is faulty, the horizontal relationships may be more in accordance with those for errors 3 and 4. These investigations look at the vertical relationships of the errors, not the horizontal ones, without any consideration of the cumulative effect of faulty pronunciation or incorrect spelling, i.e. at the effects of the grammatical and lexical errors per se.

Consequently, what matters here is the relative importance of different grammatical and lexical errors per se, all of which are common to both the spoken and written English of many foreigners. Other types of errors, such as pronunciation errors, and so-called COVERT ERRORS (cf. Johansson 1978:53; and 1.6, and note 12 in this study), fall outside the scope of these investigations.

Most sentences contain only one error each. A few multi-error sentences were also included, however, since such sentences are very common indeed, both in the written and oral production of many foreign users of English. These multi-error sentences are authentic and of a very common type where one error may be regarded as more serious than the other/s/.

Many of the sentences in the corpus of sentences were ambiguous. Several of these were included in the questionnaires to investigate the effects of ambiguity, which seems to be a very common feature in the English produced by many foreigners, and sometimes also by native users of English. The results of investigation 3 will show which interpretations of these ambiguous sentences are the most common.

The aim has been to include as many different grammatical errors as possible and a few lexical errors. Thus, grammatical errors from most sections of a traditional English school grammar are represented. Errors involving all parts of speech are thus represented, as are errors in word order and errors in the use of certain idiomatic phrases. There are also examples of common lexical errors. This means that usually only one or two examples of each grammatical error could be included, as the questionnaires quite obviously could not be made too long or comprehensive. It was felt that 75 test sentences would be the maximum number of sentences that most test subjects would be able to judge in a reasonable length of time.

Owing to the rather limited number of sentences that can be included in questionnaires of this type, no attempt can be made at completeness. Even so, the number of sentences used in these investigations is considerably larger than in most previous investigations of a similar type.

1.6 Previous research

(Occasional references will be made to the present study for the sake of comparison).

A fairly extensive survey of previous research in the field of error gravity is made in Johansson (1978:8-28), for which reason only the research which has been carried out after 1978 will be dealt with here. However, one other work deserves to be mentioned as well, because of its relation to the present study.

Olsson (1977) carried out two oral intelligibility experiments with disconnected sentences, the majority of which were examples of incorrect use of the passive voice, and a written intelligibility experiment, consisting of three different versions of a continuous text, with inserted spelling errors, 'light errors', and 'serious errors' (Olsson's terms within quotes).

Her first oral experiment consisted of 36 erroneous sentences and 5 correct sentences, which were administered to students who had English as their first language and whose average age was 20. In one case a tape where Swedish school children spoke the deviant sentences was played to 69 students and in another case Olsson herself read the test sentences to 50 students. In both cases the tape was played twice. The first time the informants were asked to perform an operation on the sentences and the second time to correct them if they thought that they did not correspond to normal English usage. Only the results of the second playing of the tape (the correction or interpretation test) is dealt with by Olsson, as the operation test was originally designed to test acceptability and not comprehension, for which reason Olsson concluded that it was not relevant to her purpose.

Her second oral experiment consisted of 57 erroneous and 6 correct sentences plus 6 sentences of doubtful acceptability, which were all administered by means of a tape-recorder to students who had English as their first language. In one case a tape where an Englishman spoke the deviant sentences was played to 58 students whose average age was 27 and in another case a tape where Olsson herself spoke the sentences was played to 34 students whose average age was 19. In both cases the informants were asked to repeat in written form what they thought the speaker intended to say.

In Olsson's written intelligibility experiment 24 grammatical and lexical errors had been inserted in a continuous text, which was administered to students in England, Scotland, and the USA in the form of a cloze test, which was identical for all participating students. The test was to be completed by filling in 40 blanks after the students had seen one of the three versions of the text, which contained 419 words. The test material was sent by post to the various participating schools and was to be sent back after completion of the experiment. Olsson thus did not herself have control over the test situation. The number of students included in this experiment was 371. Olsson does not supply any information about the average age or the age range of these students.

Olsson's most important results showed that the degree of intelligibility of the erroneous utterances used in her investigations proved to be quite high and that the intelligibility of utterances seemed to be influenced by different degrees of deviance from well-formedness and by the relative plausibility of the competing interpretations of an utterance. All three of her experiments yielded similar results.

Johansson (1978) conducted a number of experiments within the framework of the project 'Fackspråk och kommunikationseffektivi-tet' (Technical language and efficiency of communication), initiated in 1975 by Professor Alvar Ellegård at the Department of English, Gothenburg University and financed by Statens Humanistiska Forskningsråd (the Swedish Council for Research in

the Humanities and Social Sciences). Johansson initiated a new
kind of research and broke new ground within the field of ERROR
ANALYSIS by focussing on ERROR EVALUATION and native-speaker
reactions to errors produced by foreign learners of English. His
approach is communicative, as he concentrates on the communicative
effect of errors by looking at, among other things, the
comprehensibility of deviant utterances and the degree of
irritation they give rise to in the receiver. He also outlines the
kind of research that is needed in the largely neglected area of
error evaluation in the years to come.

In his introduction, Johansson points out that error analysis is
currently a very active field of research. He goes on to say that
'the study of learners' errors is used as a means of revealing
what the learner has yet to know. As the analysis will normally
reveal a host of deficiencies, it may be difficult to know where
to start and what to emphasize in applying the results. This is
where error evaluation fits in, i e the study of error gravity'
(1978:1). He also points to the fact that most studies in error
analysis have not been concerned in detail with how the results
should be applied and hence have not tackled the problem of error
evaluation. Even though the need to establish error gravity has
occasionally been pointed out, e.g. by James (1972:76) and
Robinson (1973:192), and there have been occasional attempts to
establish error gravity in a systematic way, e.g. by Bansal
(1965/66, 1969), Engh (1971), Olsson (1972,1973), 'error
evaluation must be considered a largely neglected field of
research' (Johansson 1978:1).

As there is no single standard of correctness against which the
learner's utterances can be judged, the identification of
learners' errors is a difficult task and Johansson therefore
proposes that a combination of non-linguistic and linguistic
criteria be used, such as, for instance, irritation, and
communicative effect. He points out that not only OVERT ERRORS[12]
but also COVERT ERRORS[12] deserve to be regarded as errors, even
though serious problems of identification of errors arise if the
latter type of errors is subsumed under the notion of language
errors.

Rather than found a scale of errors on purely linguistic criteria, Johansson thinks it is more relevant to relate such a scale to the learners' communicative needs. Thus, 'the more the error interferes with communication, the more serious it seems from the point of view of the learner' (Johansson 1978:4).

According to the system of error evaluation outlined in Johansson (1975:22ff), the first thing which should be asked in evaluating an error is whether the erroneous utterance is fully comprehensible or not. 'If it is not, it is considered a more serious error. If the erroneous utterance is fully comprehensible, it could nevertheless have serious consequences from the point of view of communication, e g make the receiver tired or irritated or draw away his attention from the contents of the message. The further question must therefore be asked whether an error causes irritation or not. Erroneous utterances which are fully comprehensible and cause no irritation constitute the lowest grade of error' (Johansson 1978:4).

This system of error evaluation is employed by Johansson in the analysis of the results of his experiments, and will be used also in this study (cf. 1.8). Johansson points out that 'for errors which affect comprehensibility or cause irritation, there is a need to determine degrees of comprehensibility and irritation' (1978:6). This is one of the aims of the scales used in this study (cf. 1.8).

What is new in Johansson's work is the insistence that communicative efficiency does not mean comprehensibility in the strict sense. 'To be communicatively effective, the message must get across swiftly and unambiguously and without undue demands upon the receiver. Hence, the scheme of evaluation ---includes both comprehensibility and degree of irritation' (Johansson 1978: 6).

Johansson points to the need of establishing the communicative effect of different types of errors. 'This could be done by submitting samples of errors committed by foreign learners to groups of native speakers. A ranking of error types according to this criterion is in itself an enormous task' (1978:7).

A first step towards a more systematic and detailed ranking of error types according to this criterion is undertaken in the present study (cf. 20 and appendix 2).

However, Johansson also points out that error type is only one relevant factor. 'We must also consider that there may be differences depending upon such factors as: (1) receiver characteristics (e g the receiver's age, education, regional and social dialect, degree of association with foreigners), (2) the type of language situation (formal or informal, speech or writing, disturbed or undisturbed communication etc), (3) the role of the sender (whether the foreigner is a tourist, a visiting scientist, a secretary, an interpreter etc). All of these matters deserve detailed investigation. In particular, it seems relevant to examine the importance of the foreigner role(s).' (1978:7-8).

The present study, which primarily deals with the results of investigation 1 (cf. 1.1) will consider several of the characteristics of factor (1), suggested by Johansson, whereas investigation 2 (cf. 1.1) is primarily concerned with factor (3).

In his suggestions for further research, Johansson also comments on some of the above topics of research by saying that 'The present investigation does not exhaust the research programme outlined in Section 1.4. Such factors as differing reactions depending upon the type of receiver, the type of language situation, and, especially, foreigner role, need further investigation. Even the investigation of error type is incomplete' (1978:128).

Johansson's study thus deals with only a few of the central problems. He therefore hopes that his work will serve as a starting-point in further investigations of error gravity in the mentioned areas. The present investigations (cf. 1.1) serve to further examine some of the topics in the research programme outlined by Johansson.

Johansson's own contribution consists of eight experiments, exploring six important aspects of error gravity: subjective and objective measures of error gravity, overt vs. covert errors in written English, lexical and grammatical errors, foreign accent and speech distortion, types of phonological errors, and native vs. non-native judges. Most of his experiments were conducted in 1975 and 1976, and they are all based on errors typical of Swedish learners of English. Rather than use natural learner language he used constructed material containing specific error types, as samples of learner language often contain a mixture of error types, which makes it difficult to establish a correlation between specific error types and native speakers' reactions. Nevertheless, says Johansson, 'in producing the material we have been guided by observations of natural learner behaviour, more specifically by observations of the errors produced by Swedish learners of English' (1978:34) (A similar method has been employed in the present investigations, cf. 1.5).

In most cases the errors were presented in test batteries containing sequences of isolated words or disconnected sentences (cf. 1.2.2) and submitted for judgement by groups of about 25-44 university students, studying non-language subjects at the University of Lancaster, England. The students were all from the United Kingdom and were, with one exception 18-22 years old. (Apart from this information, information on the test subjects is scanty. There is, for instance, no information as to the the sex distribution of the test subjects). They were (unlike the test subjects in the investigations for the present study) paid to take part in the experiment. 'University students were chosen for reasons of availability; students of non-language subjects were selected as they are more representative of the type of receivers a foreigner will come in contact with and also because there is some evidence that untrained judges give more consistent responses than trained subjects' (Johansson 1978:30).

In Johansson's first experiment, 12 grammatically incorrect sentences were recorded by two native speakers of English (speakers of RP), whereas grammatically correct renderings of the

same sentences were recorded by two Swedish students of English
(with typical pronunciation errors). The tapes were played to
three groups of university students who were asked to repeat the
sentences in a form that seemed more natural to them and, in one
case, followed by a number sequence. After this perception test
the same test subjects were given a judgement task consisting of
the same material, where they were asked to rate each item by
putting a mark on a five-point scale with the poles 'native-like'
- 'very foreign' (this scale has also been used in one of the
investigations for the present study, but under slightly different
circumstances, cf. 1.8). The results of these experiments
indicated that certain kinds of phonological errors tended to
cause greater perception problems than the grammatical errors
represented and the results also confirmed earlier findings that
subjective judgements correlate well with more objective measures.
The conclusion drawn by Johansson is that the simpler judgement
technique can be relied on to a greater extent in future studies
of error gravity, and accordingly Johansson mainly employs this
technique in his other experiments (cf. 1.2.2). He points out,
however, that 'preferably, informants should be asked both to
interpret the material and to give a judgement of deviance. In
this way we do not need to speculate about the basis of the
informants' judgements. We can then also collect information on
the informants' own usage and on strategies of interpretation'
(1978:50) (cf. 1.1).

In Johansson's second experiment, designed to investigate the
relationship between overt and covert errors, 21 short essays,
written by Swedish students of English on the same subject ('A
Great Achievement') were rated by native judges (44 university
students) in original and corrected form. The papers were of
approximately the same length (100-150 words) and were selected so
as to represent a variety of possible treatments, both from the
point of view of form and content. Some informants were asked to
make a general assessment of the essays, without specific
instructions to concentrate on either form or content, whereas
others were instructed to concentrate on how successfully the
writer had handled the topic. In both cases a five-point scale was
used, with the poles 'very good' and 'very bad' for the first

group, and the poles 'The treatment of the topic is very successful and effective' and 'The treatment of the topic is very poor and ineffective' for the other group. The results showed that the presence of overt errors had a distinct effect on the ratings, but the type of instruction given also proved to be important. Johansson therefore concludes that the formal aspects are clearly important and that the results of an earlier investigation (by Landén & Trankell 1975) must not be generalized and taken as evidence that overt errors are unimportant under all circumstances.

Johansson's third and fourth experiments were designed to investigate the effects of grammatical and lexical errors. The test subjects (43 and 25 university students respectively) were asked to judge two short texts into which five errors (grammatical or lexical) had systematically been inserted, either by rewriting everything that seemed incorrect and putting a mark on a five-point scale with the poles 'very good' and 'very bad', or by underlining everything that seemed incorrect and putting a mark on a five-point scale with the poles 'very good' and 'very bad'. The 25 test subjects who took part in the fourth experiment had all taken part in the third experiment. For both experiments the results showed that the versions containing lexical errors had received lower ratings than those containing grammatical errors, that is, lexical errors were found to cause more serious problems of interpretation than grammatical errors. Five repetitions of the same error (whether lexical or grammatical) were judged to be less serious than five occurrences of different errors. The grammatical errors were shown to describe a scale of 'irritability', with article and spelling errors at the bottom, and certain prepositional and word-order errors at the top of the scale. Johansson ends his discussion of these experiments by saying that 'the present investigation has only included a limited number of examples of lexical and grammatical deviance. There is a need for further studies with a wider range of errors. In particular, there is a need for more systematic surveys of the different types of deviance' (1978:72). Investigation 1 of the present study (cf. 1.1) has been carried out as a first step towards meeting these needs.

Johansson also conducted a number of experiments devoted to various types of errors in the spoken language, such as the intelligibility of native and foreign-accent speech under increasing mechanical distortion, and various types of phonological errors characteristic of Swedish learners, such as phonemic, subphonemic and non-segmental errors, and in the two final experiments, Johansson showed that Swedish teachers of English were remarkably similar to native judges in their evaluation of corrected and uncorrected essays. However, as these experiments are less relevant to the investigations with which we are concerned here and for reasons of limited space, these experiments will not be summarized here.

Petti (1979) conducted an investigation based on assessments of errors by twenty Swedish, British, and American university teachers in 1973 and sixteen Swedish, British, and American university teachers in 1976. The teachers were asked to grade about four hundred errors. Each of the gradings was entered on a special list together with gradings from thirteen native English speakers, who received a list with a somewhat shorter number of errors. The thirteen were arbitrarily chosen from sixty lists returned from native English speakers in Britain, the U.S., Canada, and Australia. In his introduction Petti says 'I shall one day comment on interesting points found in these sixty lists and compare them with the lists compiled by my colleagues.' (1979:3).

In making a final grading of the errors Petti took note mainly of the assessments of his colleagues, 'since linguistic achievement in terms of the traditional contrastive grammar system as taught in Sweden was chiefly being measured. --- However, in a few significant instances, especially where there was doubt among my colleagues, the gradings of the thirteen (and sometimes the whole sixty) native English speakers were taken into consideration. An attempt was also made to preserve at least the semblance of relative balance in the list.' (1979:3).

Petti made no attempt at error analysis and he points out that the gradings in terms of so-called minus points were meant to assist in the marking of students' papers. Many of the errors were taken from examination papers, but some derived from 'other written material and some from spoken English' (1979:3).

The term ERROR 'was in some cases applied to what were hypothetically regarded as errors, but most items were assumed to be unacceptable, in different degrees, to native speakers who might have a fair degree of competence in handling such items. Thus the thirteen native English speakers (I am aware that this is a very small number) were: five students of linguistics, two research students, two university lecturers, a bank manager, a company director, a librarian, and a housewife.' (Petti 1979:3).

Lists of erroneous sentences were submitted to three groups of respondents, viz. to (A) native speakers of English (British, American, Canadian, Australian) who knew no Swedish, (B) native speakers of English who were all acquainted with Swedish, and (C) Swedish teachers of English (at school or university). Group A was expected to respond to different degrees of acceptability or intelligibility, group C to respond to different degrees of achievement in learning and to be aware of interlingual interference, and group B was expected to combine the responses of the other two groups. They were asked to put 0, 1, 2, or 3 against each item according to the following definitions:

'0 means that you find the item acceptable as English

1 means that you do not find the item acceptable as English BUT you think that the error included in it is a minor one

2 means that you do not find the item acceptable as English AND you think that the error is a serious one BUT you perfectly understand what was meant (i.e. it makes sense).

3 means that the item does not make sense

NOTE that a few items are not errors, but have had to be included for the sake of clarity.' (Petti 1979:4).

According to Petti, the gradings were elicited not only for practical teaching purposes, but also to ascertain whether there were significant differences between the groups. In the presentation of his investigation, Petti makes the 3-grading appear as a 4 in a 0, 1, 2, 4 scale, and sometimes a 3 in an alternative 0, 1, 2, 3, 4, scale. Petti explains that this has been done 'to single out the serious errors more clearly. Moreover the definition against 3 - is not reflected in the 4 (or 3) gradings in many cases, especially as Group B and Group C's assessments were in terms of achievement for this grading, rather than in intelligibility, in spite of the definition. Yet group A-gradings were consulted here too' (Petti 1979:4-5).

Just as Olsson and Johansson did in some of their experiments, Petti thus made use of disconnected sentences as test material. 'I was quite aware that presenting sentences out of context has defects, but on the whole the native speakers seemed to be quite able to assess them as items of English, and there was in fact a surprising degree of conformity between the assessments of all three groups on the whole, even more surprising when one considered that group A were considering the errors from the communicative angle.' (Petti 1979:4).

The results of Petti's investigation showed, among other things, that certain errors in the use of non-count nouns, verbs, pronouns, subjects, and word-order errors were given high gradings, whereas article errors and certain vocabulary errors were given rather low gradings. However, no systematic ranking of the gravity of the errors is undertaken in Petti's study.

Two books were published so recently that they can only be mentioned: Thagg Fisher (1985) analysed Swedish learners' concord problems in English, especially in the area of subject-verb agreement, and administered elicitation tests to Swedish and English students, nearly all of whom were between 18 and 26 years old. Her results showed that Swedish learners and native speakers have some concord problems in common. Linnarud (1986) showed the importance of lexis in composition evaluation and the need for composition tasks in the teaching and testing of foreign learners.

1.7 List of abbreviations

1.7.1 Error types

Abbreviation/label	Meaning
A-CONTROL	A-control sentence (correct sentence)
ADJ/ADV	Adjective substituted for adverb
ADJ^NOUN	Adjective used as noun with specific reference
ADJ-PHR	Attributive own substituted for predicatice own
ADV/ADJ	Adverb substituted for adjective
AUX	Incorrect use of modal auxiliary
COMP.ADJ	Incorrect comparison of adjective
COMP.ADV	Incorrect comparison of adverb
CONCORD	Incongruous sentence
DBL-NEG	Double negation
GENITIVE	Incorrect use of the genitive
IDIOM-PHR	Incorrect use of idiomatic phrase
ING/SIMPVF	ing-participle substituted for simple verb form (base form of verb)
INS.DEFART	Insertion of the definite article
INS.INDART	Insertion of the indefinite article
INS.PREP	Insertion of preposition
INS.RELPRO	Insertion of relative pronoun
IRREG-PLUR	Incorrect plural inflection of irregular noun
IRREG-VERB	Incorrect inflection of irregular verb
NUMB	Incorrect use of quantitative noun
OM.DEFART	Omission of the definite article
OM.DO-PPH	Omission of do-periphrasis
OM.INDART	Omission of the indefinite article
OM.PREP	Omission of preposition
PPRO/RFPRO	Personal pronoun substituted for reflexive pronoun
PRE/ATTADJ	Predicative adjective substituted for attributive
RFPRO/PPRO	Reflexive pronoun substituted for personal pronoun
SIMPVF/ING	Simple verb form (base form of verb) substituted for ing-participle
SUBJECT	Incorrect choice of grammatical subject
TENSE	Incorrect tense
TO-INF/B	to-infinitive substituted for bare infinitive
TO-INF/ING	to-infinitive substituted for ing-participle
UNC	Non-count noun used with s-plural
VOC	Incorrect choice of word
WORD ORDER	Incorrect word order
WR.ADVERB	Incorrect choice of adverb
WR.INDART	Incorrect form of the indefinite article
WR.INDPRO	Incorrect choice of indefinite pronoun
WR.PREP	Incorrect choice of preposition

1.7.2 Abbreviations and symbols used in the text

cf.	compare
e.g.	for example
no.	number
viz.	namely
Inc A-C	Inclusive of A-control sentences
Exc A-C	Exclusive of A-control sentences
F	foreignness
ID	intelligibility difficulty
T-A	teen-agers - adults
A-P	adults - pensioners
T-P	teen-agers - pensioners

Mathematics and statistics

D	difference between two matched values
$\bar{D}$	mean of the differences within a sample
F	F-value
H_0	null hypothesis
n	number of observations in a group
p	error probability
PCT	Paired Comparisons t test (see 1.2.3)
r	correlation
s	sample standard deviation
s^2	sample variance
SD	sample standard deviation (used in tables)
s_D	standard deviation of the differences within a sample
sign.	statistical significance of the difference between the means
t	t-value
x,y	variables
$\bar{x}$	sample mean
xi	individual observation
μ	population mean
σ	population standard deviation
σ^2	population variance
Σ	sum
$\sqrt{}$	square root
+	plus
-	minus
<	is less than
>	is greater than
$\leq$	is equal to or less than
$\geq$	is equal to or greater than
=	is equal to

1.8 Design of questionnaire 1
(cf. appendix 3)

Each of the 75 test sentences in questionnaires 1A and 1B (henceforth called questionnaire 1) was followed by two five-graded scales. The poles of the first scale were native-like (the left pole) and very foreign (the right pole). Each box in between the two extreme boxes represented a different degree of foreignness. The further to the right on the scale, the higher was the degree of foreignness represented by the box. A plus sign marked the left pole, as this was to be clearly regarded as the opposite of the right pole, which was marked by a minus sign. The plus sign was placed on the native-like pole because it is usually considered positive from a communicative point of view to conform to the language norm of native users of a language, and the minus sign was placed on the very foreign pole because it is usually considered negative from a communicative point of view to be very foreign in one's use of a language, thereby not conforming to the language norm of native users of the language (cf. fig 1:3 below).

It is important to bear in mind, however that simply being native-like in one's use of a language does not, by itself, assure communicative efficiency. Native speakers of a language often use ways of expression which are far from efficient from a communicative point of view. It is also important to bear in mind that being very foreign in one's use of a language does not, by itself, mean lack of communicative efficiency. A foreigner may be perceived by native speakers of a language as being very foreign in his use of the language but still he may be found to be easy to understand. Many of the answers to the questions on the test sentences in the questionnaires indicate this.

The first scale was designed to elicit the attitudes of the informants towards the test sentences by testing the ACCEPTABILITY[13] of the sentences and thus make the informants reveal whether or not they were likely to use or could think of using such sentences themselves. If a sentence is judged to be rather 'native-like' by one group of informants and rather 'foreign' by another group of informants, it seems reasonable to assume that the informants in the latter group are less likely to use such a sentence than are the informants in the former group, albeit there may be considerable individual differences within each group.

native-like + ■ ■ ■ ■ ■ - very foreign

very easy to ■ ■ ■ ■ ■ very difficult
understand to understand

Fig 1:3 The scales in questionnaire 1.

The poles of the second scale were very easy to understand (the left pole) and very difficult to understand (the right pole). Each box in between the two extreme boxes represented a different degree of INTELLIGIBILITY of the sentence. The further to the right on the scale the lower was the degree of intelligibility represented by the box. Unlike the first scale, the poles of this scale were not marked by plus and minus signs, as these poles were assumed to be more readily regarded as the opposites of one another. Just as for the first scale, the left pole could, however, be regarded as the positive pole and the right pole as the negative pole, as it is always positive from a communicative point of view if a sentence is very easy to understand, and it is always negative from a communicative point of view if a sentence is very difficult to understand (cf. fig 1:3 above). Unlike the question on 'foreignness', the question on the 'intelligibility difficulty' of a sentence was designed only to find out how the informants found the intelligibility of the sentence. The answers to this question cannot be expected to be indicative of the informants' own usage to the same extent as can the answers to the question on 'foreignness'. However, if a subgroup of the informants finds a test sentence both less foreign and easier to understand than does another subgroup, this may be an even stronger indication of different usages in the two groups than if a difference is found only for the question on 'foreignness', provided, of course, that the differences are found to be statistically significant (cf. 1.2.3).

The informants were carefully instructed how to use the scales. In addition to this, an example was given on the second page in the questionnaire to show the informants how to use the two scales (cf. 1.4 and appendix 3). The informants were asked to tick the box they thought best represented the degree of foreignness and intelligibility difficulty of each sentence. They were expressly told to tick only one box on each scale. In the very few cases where two boxes had been ticked, the answers were excluded from the subsequent statistical analysis.

The informants were also asked to indicate where they thought that the foreigners who produced the erroneous sentences came from, if they had any idea of this. However, very few informants did this, for which reason such answers have not been taken account of in this study.

When the answers given by the informants were coded to be keypunched onto data cards, it was decided that the boxes of each scale should be numbered from left to right. The extreme left box of each scale was thus called 1, and the extreme right box of each scale was called 5. This means that for both scales the higher the number of the box, the more negative from a communicative point of view is the scale degree it represents. This, of course, also applies to all the mean values calculated on the basis of the individual data for each question.

The errors tested in the present study will be evaluated on the basis of their communicative effect according to the system of evaluating language errors outlined in Johansson (1975:22f) (see 1.6).

It should be pointed out, however, that the scale measuring the degree of foreignness used here, may not be equated with a scale of irritation. However, from a purely communicative point of view, this seems not to be the case, as the more foreign an utterance or a sentence is judged to be, the more likely it seems that it will interfere with communication. The scale measuring the degree of foreignness may thus be said to be an indirect measure of the degree of irritation that an erroneous utterance or sentence gives rise to in the native receiver.

Two other principles of evaluation are, however, also quite important in a more detailed hierarchy of errors, viz. GENERALITY and FREQUENCY. 'An error involving a general rule reveals a weakness that may affect an indefinite number of cases and may therefore have more serious consequences for communication than errors involving individual items (words or grammatical exceptions). Likewise, an error involving frequent words or constructions may affect a larger number of cases in actual communication' (Johansson 1978:7). It is, of course, important to consider these principles as well, when evaluating language errors. Most of the errors exemplified by the test sentences in this study are errors involving general grammatical rules, and may therefore be regarded as quite serious from the generality point of view. This study will, however, concentrate on the previously neglected area (before Johansson) of establishing the communicative effect of different types of errors.

When differences in reactions to the test sentences are detected between the youngest informants (teen-agers) on the one hand and the other two age groups (adults and pensioners) on the other, this may or may not be indicative of a forthcoming general change in usage. If the teen-agers give significantly different answers, particularly on the question on 'foreignness', compared to the other two age groups and provided that the teen-agers will not later in life alter their opinions to become more similar, and eventually identical, to those of the adults and the pensioners, a change in general usage may be predicted. If, on the other hand, as the teen-agers grow older and cease being teen-agers, their opinions become more similar to and eventually identical to those of the pensioners, a general change in usage is not really at hand. In such a case there is only indications of different usages in different age groups, which may be age-grading differences of a type that are repeated in every generation rather than differences resulting from linguistic change (cf. Chambers-Trudgill 1980:88ff).

Only a diachronic language study can throw light on what actually happens with people's opinions and their language in the course of time. Absolute certainty in this respect can, of course, only be gained if the same individuals are questioned over again at a later point in time (studies in REAL TIME) but for most practical purposes such an arrangement seems uncalled for, provided that the population sample fulfils reasonable requirements of representativeness. If so, the alternative method of studying linguistic change in APPARENT TIME, i.e. comparing the language of older people with that of younger people, can be employed. The differences detected may be the result of linguistic change or age-grading differences. However, 'the hypothesis that apparent time can be equated to real time is by no means firmly supported, and the relationship between real and apparent time may be more complex than a simple equation of the two suggests.-- Nevertheless, studies in apparent time has several advantages. Since the investigator of both comparison groups is the same person, factors like methodology, transcription and analysis can easily be made comparable. The data is not limited in artificial and unnatural ways either, since the researcher can simply go back for more as it is required. For these reasons, studies of diffusion have focused on apparent time rather than real time differences in recent research.' (Chambers-Trudgill 1980:165-167).

The results of this study can be compared to the results of earlier and future studies to determine whether or not people's opinions about the grammatical and lexical matters here concerned really change as time goes by.

PART 1

RESULTS OF QUESTIONNAIRE 1

The first sentence number refers to the number of the sentence in
questionnaire 1A, whereas sentence numbers in brackets refer to
the number of the same sentence in questionnaire 1B.

2. IMPROPER USE OF THE INDEFINITE ARTICLE

2.1 Insertion of the indefinite article

Sentence 1 (75) ("What a dreadful weather!"), sentence 31 (45)
("It is a hard work to write a book"), and sentence 51 (25) ("What
an awful weather!") tested reactions to insertion of the
indefinite article before a non-count noun, premodified by an
adjective. Sentences 1 and 51 functioned as B-control sentences
(see 1.2.1).

Total sample

Sentence no.	Foreignness			Intelligibility difficulty		
	Mean	SD	Mode	Mean	SD	Mode
1	3.71	1.09	4	1.70	.86	1
31	3.20	1.41	4	1.53	.76	1
51	3.71	1.14	4	1.66	.89	1

Significance (PCT)

1-31:	G	A
31-51:	F	-
1-51:	-	-

The results indicate that these sentences made a fairly strong
foreign impression on the informants and that they were judged to
be fairly easy to understand. The differences between the means of
sentence 1 and sentence 31 and the means of sentence 31 and
sentence 51 for the question on foreignness are statistically
highly significant. These differences indicate that the two

sentences dealing with weather made a considerably more foreign impression on the informants than sentence 31. This may perhaps be due to the relatively high frequency of such weather sentences in the language of native users of English. When such a sentence deviates from normal English usage it probably therefore strikes the native speaker of English as more foreign than does a sentence which is not as frequently used and which exhibits signs of deviance from normal English usage.

The differences between the means for the question on intelligibility difficulty are not as great as for the question on foreignness. However, the difference between the means for sentence 1 and sentence 31 is statistically significant.

The two B-control sentences received almost exactly the same ratings, which means that neither of the differences are statistically significant. This is a good indication of the reliability of the informants.

Age differences

Sentence no.		Teen-agers		Adults		Pensioners		Significance		
		Mean	SD	Mean	SD	Mean	SD	T-A	A-P	T-P
	1	3.91	.68	3.59	1.23	3.52	1.47	-	-	-
F	31	3.51	1.32	3.09	1.31	2.79	1.72	-	-	-
	51	3.86	.95	3.66	1.16	3.44	1.59	-	-	-
	1	2.05	.79	1.48	.71	1.47	1.12	F	-	B
ID	31	1.84	.87	1.35	.61	1.24	.56	D	-	B
	51	2.05	.94	1.33	.61	1.44	1.03	I	-	A

The differences between the means of the teen-agers and the means of the other two age groups are statistically significant for all these three sentences as regards the question on intelligibility difficulty. These differences indicate that the teen-agers found these three sentences considerably more difficult to understand than did the other two age groups.

Sex differences

Sentence no.		Females		Males		Significance
		Mean	SD	Mean	SD	
	1	3.60	1.12	3.90	1.02	-
F	31	3.15	1.45	3.29	1.35	-
	51	3.64	1.18	3.83	1.07	-
	1	1.67	.93	1.76	.73	-
ID	31	1.52	.81	1.54	.67	-
	51	1.63	.85	1.71	.96	-

The male informants seem to have been more critical of these sentences than the female informants were, but none of the differences between the means of the two sexes are by themselves statistically significant.

2.2 Omission of the indefinite article

Sentence 40 (36) ("My sister is nurse") tested reactions to omission of the indefinite article before the name of a profession. This error is sometimes made by Swedish users of English as a result of interference from Swedish.

Total sample

Sentence no.	Foreignness			Intelligibility difficulty		
	Mean	SD	Mode	Mean	SD	Mode
40	3.54	1.16	4	1.62	.86	1

This sentence has similar means to the three sentences which tested the opposite case, viz. improper insertion of the indefinite article (cf 2.1). It made a rather strong foreign impression on the informants but was judged to be fairly easy to understand.

Age differences

		Teen-agers		Adults		Pensioners		Significance		
Sentence no.								T-A	A-P	T-P
		Mean	SD	Mean	SD	Mean	SD			
F	40	3.52	1.05	3.64	1.04	3.25	1.73	-	-	-
ID	40	1.93	.87	1.42	.70	1.29	.99	D	-	B

Just as for the three sentences testing the opposite case (cf. 2.1), the teen-agers apparently found this sentence more difficult to understand than did the other age groups. On the other hand, the amount of foreign impression caused by this sentence is largely the same for the various age groups.

Sex differences

		Females		Males		Significance
Sentence no.		Mean	SD	Mean	SD	
F	40	3.46	1.21	3.66	1.06	-
ID	40	1.54	.85	1.76	.86	-

Consistent with the results in 2.1 above, the male informants seem to be slightly more critical of this sentence than the female informants. However, the differences between the means of the two sexes are not statistically significant.

2.3 Incorrect form of the indefinite article

2.3.1 a for an

Sentence 62 (14) ("It took me a hour to get there") tested reactions to the use of the one-letter form of the indefinite article (a) in place of the two-letter form (an) required by the context.

Total sample

Sentence no.	Foreignness			Intelligibility difficulty		
	Mean	SD	Mode	Mean	SD	Mode
62	2.10	1.21	1	1.19	.44	1

Significance
(PCT) 62-48:   I   D

Obviously this error was not judged to be a particularly serious
one, as the sentence made only a slight foreign impression on the
informants and was judged to be very easy to understand. In fact
the highest value for intelligibility difficulty given by any one
informant was 3.

One reason for these very low scores may very well be that many
informants did not notice that a was used instead of an, as these
two forms of the indefinite article differ by one letter only. It
is therefore also quite likely that this would not have been
observed if the sentence had been spoken. Lack of attention may
thus have contributed to the low scores here. However, this
sentence represents an error which is also sometimes made by
people whose native tongue is English, which was also confirmed by
some of the informants, and the sentence cannot be misinterpreted
simply because the wrong form of the indefinite article is used,
for which reasons low means were expected.

Age differences

							Significance		
Sentence no.	Teen-agers		Adults		Pensioners		T-A	A-P	T-P
	Mean	SD	Mean	SD	Mean	SD			
F	62	2.12	1.14	2.14	1.19	2.06	1.51	-	-	-
ID	62	1.35	.57	1.10	.30	1.05	.23	B	-	C

The teen-agers apparently found this sentence slightly more
difficult to understand than did the other two age groups.
However, their mean is also very low, which indicates that they
generally found this sentence quite easy to understand.

Sex differences

Sentence no.		Females		Males		Significance
		Mean	SD	Mean	SD	
F	62	2.03	1.18	2.22	1.27	-
ID	62	1.15	.40	1.25	.49	-

The means of the female and the male informants are very similar for this sentence and neither difference between the means of the two sexes is statistically significant.

2.3.2 an for a

Sentence 48 (28) ("He is an useful member of the team") tested reactions to the use of the two-letter form of the indefinite article (an) in a context where the one-letter form (a) is normally required.

Total sample

Sentence no.	Foreignness			Intelligibility difficulty		
	Mean	SD	Mode	Mean	SD	Mode
48	2.79	1.23	3	1.43	.77	1

Significance
(PCT) 48-62:   I   D

Compared to sentence 62 (cf 2.3.1), which tested the opposite case, this sentence made a stronger foreign impression on the informants and it was also found to be slightly more difficult to understand. It is probably easier to spot a letter which should not be there than it is to notice that a letter which one expects to find actually is not there. This may be part of the reason for the different results of the two sentences.

Just as for sentence 62, low scores were expected for both
questions as the error exemplified by this sentence is also
occasionally made by native users of English, which was also
confirmed by some of the informants, and the sentence cannot be
misinterpreted simply because the wrong form of the indefinite
article is used. It is worth noticing, however, that the effects
were more serious when the two-letter form of the indefinite
article was used in place of the one-letter form than when the
opposite error was made.

The results of form 3 show that the potential risk of misreading
this sentence as He is an unuseful member of the team is virtually
non-existent, probably because of the great rarity of the word
unuseful, at least when used without a negative. This adjective
was very common in the 17th century but has now largely been
replaced by useless, for which reason this alternative
interpretation can, at most, have only a marginal bearing on the
results.

Age differences

		Teen-agers		Adults		Pensioners		Significance		
Sentence no.		Mean	SD	Mean	SD	Mean	SD	T-A	A-P	T-P
F	48	2.82	1.23	2.56	1.18	3.24	1.35	-	-	-
ID	48	1.57	.70	1.23	.53	1.53	1.26	B	-	-

This sentence made a much stronger foreign impression on the
pensioners than did sentence 62 (cf 2.3.1). This difference is
statistically significant on the B level (PCT). The other two age
groups do not show such a great difference between their
respective means for these two sentences.

The teen-agers found sentence 48 somewhat more difficult to
understand than did the adults. This difference is also
statistically significant.

<u>Sex</u> <u>differences</u>

Sentence no.		Females		Males		Significance
		Mean	SD	Mean	SD	
F	48	2.86	1.29	2.69	1.14	-
ID	48	1.40	.85	1.48	.63	-

Neither of the differences between the means of the female and the male informants is statistically significant for this sentence.

2.4 <u>Summary</u>

Improper use of the indefinite article in the six sentences discussed above caused no particular intelligibility difficulty but made a fairly strong foreign impression on the informants, with the exception of the two sentences exemplifying the use of the wrong form of the indefinite article. The latter sentences were also judged to be easier to understand than the other sentences.

The sentence with the highest mean for foreignness and for intelligibility difficulty exemplified insertion of the indefinite article before a non-count noun. The sentence with the lowest mean for foreignness also had the lowest mean for intelligibility difficulty and exemplified the use of the one-letter form in place of the two-letter form of the indefinite article. The means for this sentence are lower than for the sentence testing the opposite case.

For all the six sentences there are significant differences between the means of the age groups which show that the teen-agers found the sentences more difficult to understand than did the adults, and five of the sentences were judged to be more difficult to understand by the teen-agers than by either of the other age groups.

There are no statistically significant differences between the means of the male and the female informants for any of the sentences. However, the male informants seem to have been more critical of all the sentences, with the possible exception of sentence 48.

The results of two B-control sentences indicated that the reliability of the informants was very high.

3. IMPROPER USE OF THE DEFINITE ARTICLE

3.1 Insertion of the definite article

Sentence 56 (20) ("The most people would agree with you") tested reactions to improper insertion of the definite article. This is a fairly common feature in the English produced by foreigners, not least by Swedes, who sometimes do this even when writing official English.

Total sample

Sentence no.	Foreignness			Intelligibility difficulty		
	Mean	SD	Mode	Mean	SD	Mode
56	3.57	1.04	4	2.00	1.05	1

Significance
(PCT) 56-1:   -   B
      56-31:   A   I
      56-51:   -   F

These statistics indicate that this sentence made a rather strong foreign impression on the informants and that the error apparently caused some intelligibility difficulty. Compared to the sentences which tested reactions to insertion of the indefinite article (cf 2.1), this sentence was found to be somewhat more difficult to understand. These differences are statistically significant, as is the difference between the means for the foreign impression made by sentence 56 and sentence 31.

Age differences

								Significance		
Sentence no.		Teen-agers		Adults		Pensioners		T-A	A-P	T-P
		Mean	SD	Mean	SD	Mean	SD			
F	56	3.61	.89	3.60	1.00	3.33	1.54	-	-	-
ID	56	2.36	1.04	1.86	.94	1.47	1.07	B	-	D

The youngest informants found this sentence considerably more difficult to understand than did the other age groups. The same thing was observed with the sentences testing reactions to improper insertion of the indefinite article (cf. 2.1).

Sex differences

Sentence no.		Females		Males		Significance
		Mean	SD	Mean	SD	
F	56	3.58	1.08	3.56	.98	-
ID	56	1.92	1.04	2.12	1.05	-

Neither of the differences between the means of the female and the male informants is statistically significant at the accepted level.

3.2 Omission of the definite article

Sentence 10 (66) ("I am staying at Sheraton hotel for three days") tested reactions to improper omission of the definite article. Owing to a typing error in the original version of the

questionnaire, the word hotel was given a lower-case initial in
all the questionnaire versions. This does, in fact, mean that this
sentence contains two errors, as the word hotel normally takes a
an upper-case initial when immediately preceded by the proper
noun. In view of this the low mean values of the answers to the
two questions are perhaps even more interesting. The results of
form 3 show, however, that hardly any of the informants indicated
that they regarded the use of a lower-case initial in this case as
an error.

Total sample

Sentence no.	Foreignness			Intelligibility difficulty		
	Mean	SD	Mode	Mean	SD	Mode
10	2.13	1.29	1	1.23	.61	1

Significance
(PCT) 10-56:   I   I

Compared to the sentence which tested the opposite case, viz.
improper insertion of the definite article (cf. 3.1), this
sentence made a much less foreign impression on the informants and
was also judged to be a great deal easier to understand.

This result may be due to the fact that native speakers of
English themselves sometimes omit the definite article before the
names of hotels and thus may not regard this as foreign.

This result was expected and shows that omission of the definite
article before the name of a well-known hotel had hardly any
consequences at all as regards foreign impression and
intelligibility, probably because the common noun (hotel) was also
used. If the omission of the definite article in a case like this
is considered a mistake it may therefore be said to be a minor
one. The same thing may also be said about the use of a lower-case
initial of hotel when this word is preceded by the proper noun.
Even if spelling has no place in these investigations it was thus
inadvertently tested in this one case.

It is to be expected, however, that the means would have been higher if the common noun had not been used, as the absence of the definite article would then mean that there was no linguistic information whatsoever that the proper noun referred to a hotel.

Age differences

Sentence no.		Teen-agers		Adults		Pensioners		Significance T-A A-P T-P		
		Mean	SD	Mean	SD	Mean	SD			
F	10	1.72	1.05	2.58	1.30	1.95	1.51	E	-	-
ID	10	1.26	.49	1.30	.79	1.06	.24	-	-	A

There is an interesting difference between the means of the teen-agers and the adults for the question on foreign impression. The teen-agers found this sentence much less foreign than the adults did. This difference is statistically highly significant and may be indicative of different usages in these two age groups, which may eventually lead to a general acceptance of omission of the definite article before the names of hotels (cf 1.8).

This does not, however, explain the low mean for foreignness shown by the group of pensioners. However, due to the large standard deviation in this group, the differences between their mean and the means of either of the other two age groups are not statistically significant. On the other hand, there is a significant difference between the means of the pensioners and the teen-agers which shows that the pensioners found sentence 10 even easier to understand than the teen-agers did.

Sex differences

Sentence no.		Females		Males		Significance
		Mean	SD	Mean	SD	
F	10	1.93	1.23	2.46	1.32	A
ID	10	1.17	.45	1.34	.79	-

There is a statistically significant difference between the means of the female and the male informants for the question on foreign impression. This indicates that sentence 10 made a considerably stronger foreign impression on the male informants than it did on the female informants. It seems likely, therefore, that the male informants are less apt than the female informants to omit the definite article in sentences of this type.

Age and sex differences (broken down table)

Sentence no.	Teen-agers Females		Males		Sign	Adults Females		Males		Sign
	Mean	SD	Mean	SD		Mean	SD	Mean	SD	
F 10	1.67	1.07	1.81	1.05	-	2.29	1.27	2.86	1.28	-
ID 10	1.22	.50	1.31	.48	-	1.18	.50	1.41	1.01	-

	Pensioners Females		Males		Sign	Male adults		Others		Sign
	Mean	SD	Mean	SD		Mean	SD	Mean	SD	
F 10	1.75	1.39	3.00	2.00	-	2.86	1.28	1.94	1.23	E
ID 10	1.07	.27	1.00	0	-	1.41	1.01	1.19	.45	-

If the statistics are broken down further they reveal that it was, above all, the male adults and the male pensioners who found this sentence foreign. The mean for the male pensioners is uncertain because of the large standard deviation, but the difference between the means of the male adults and the other subgroups of informants taken together is statistically highly significant for the question on foreignness. The reason for the stronger foreign impression made on the male informants being 20 years of age or older is uncertain and can only be speculated upon. It can be seen from the table, however, that the means for these groups are still not very high and in the case of male adults more on the 'native-like' than on the 'very foreign' side of the scale.

The female teen-agers have the lowest mean for the question on foreignness of all the subgroups of informants. The difference between their mean for this question and the mean for all the other subgroups taken together (2.28) is statistically significant on the A level.

3.3 <u>Summary</u>

The two sentences exemplifying errors in the use of the definite article are really too different for a comparison of the results. In neither case, however, did the error cause any great amount of intelligibility difficulty.

The sentence with an inserted definite article has higher means for both questions than does the sentence where the definite article had been omitted. This is important to note for Swedish users of English, many of whom often make the former error as a result of interference from Swedish, sometimes even in official English.

The sentence where the definite article had been omitted before the name of a hotel was judged very leniently. This may be due to the fact that the common noun <u>hotel</u> was also used, that the proper noun referred to a well-known hotel and that native speakers of English themselves sometimes omit the definite article in such sentences. The definite article may be felt to be redundant in such contexts.

Statistically significant age differences were found in the case of both sentences. The teen-agers found both sentences more difficult to understand than did either one or both of the other age groups. However, the teen-agers found sentence 10 considerably less foreign than did the adults, which may indicate that the teen-agers omit the definite article before the names of hotels more often than the adults do. If so, this may perhaps lead to a future general usage without the definite article before the names of hotels.

Sentence 10 also made a significantly less foreign impression on the female informants than on the male informants. The female teen-agers were shown to have the lowest mean for this question of all the subgroups of informants in the broken down table. The difference between their mean and the mean for the other informants taken together was shown to be statistically significant. This may indicate that the female informants, and the female teen-agers in particular, omit the definite article before the names of hotels more often than the other informants do so.

4. IMPROPER USE OF NOUNS

4.1 <u>Regular plural inflection for irregular plural form</u>

Sentence 64 (12) ("The house was full of mouses") exemplifies an error which is fairly common both among foreign users of English and small children whose native language is English, viz. the overgeneralization of the regular plural inflection <u>s</u>.

<u>Total sample</u>

Sentence no.	Foreignness			Intelligibility difficulty		
	Mean	SD	Mode	Mean	SD	Mode
64	3.43	1.19	3	1.39	.71	1

Significance
(PCT) 64-38:   -   -
       64-66:   -   -
       64-70:   H   I

This sentence made a foreign impression on the informants but was found to be quite easy to understand. In view of the fact that the error exemplified by this sentence is also often made by small children who have English as their first language, the mean for foreignness may seem high. However, the informants were told that the sentences in the questionnaires were produced by foreigners. Also, the fact that a sentence is a 'possible' one for a small child whose mother tongue is English does not detract from the fact that the very same sentence can also be associated with foreigners.

Compared to the other three sentences exemplifying 'child language' (cf. 5.1, 7.1, and 8.3), this sentence has lower means for both questions. However, only the differences between the means for this sentence and the means for sentence 70 are statistically significant, although very highly so.

Age differences

		Teen-agers		Adults		Pensioners		Significance		
Sentence no.								T-A	A-P	T-P
		Mean	SD	Mean	SD	Mean	SD			
F	64	3.20	.93	3.42	1.26	3.83	1.50	-	-	-
ID	64	1.45	.50	1.19	.39	1.63	1.30	C	-	-

The oldest informants seem to have been more critical of this sentence, particularly where the question on foreignness is concerned. However, the only statistically significant difference to be found for this sentence is between the means of the teen-agers and the adults for the question on intelligibility difficulty. This difference indicates that the adults found sentence 64 even easier to understand than did the teen-agers.

Sex differences

Sentence no.		Females		Males		Significance
		Mean	SD	Mean	SD	
F	64	3.42	1.29	3.43	1.02	-
ID	64	1.40	.82	1.36	.48	-

The means for the female and the male informants are all but identical for this sentence.

4.2 Non-count noun used as count noun

Sentence 14 (62) ("She has very limited knowledges of German") tested reactions to the use of the non-count noun knowledge as a count noun. When this error is made by Swedish users of English, the cause is often interference from Swedish, where the corresponding noun is a count noun.

Total sample

Sentence no.	Foreignness			Intelligibility difficulty		
	Mean	SD	Mode	Mean	SD	Mode
14	3.06	1.36	4	1.56	.73	1

The mean for the question on foreign impression is almost exactly in the middle of the scale, which indicates that this sentence made a rather foreign impression on the informants. At the same time, however, it was found to be rather easy to understand. This result was largely expected, as the error involved can hardly give rise to any plausible alternative interpretations of the sentence.

Age differences

	Sentence no.	Teen-agers		Adults		Pensioners		Significance		
								T-A	A-P	T-P
		Mean	SD	Mean	SD	Mean	SD			
F	14	2.95	1.07	3.34	1.43	2.67	1.78	-	-	-
ID	14	1.84	.72	1.51	.77	1.00	0	A	I	I

The differences between the age groups are all statistically significant for the question on intelligibility difficulty, and in two cases highly significant. This indicates that the younger the informants were the more difficult to understand they found this sentence. However, for none of the three age groups is the mean for intelligibility difficulty particularly high.

Sex differences

Sentence no.		Females		Males		Significance
		Mean	SD	Mean	SD	
F	14	3.00	1.40	3.17	1.30	-
ID	14	1.57	.73	1.54	.74	-

The means of the two sexes are almost identical for this sentence.

4.3 Improper use of the group genitive

Sentence 45 (31) ("This is my brother's-in-law cap") tested reactions to incorrect use of the s-genitive of the word-group brother-in-law. Normal usage is to affix the s-suffix to the last element of the postmodification of the noun head. However, foreigners sometimes affix the inflection to the noun head instead, thus making the sentence deviate from normal English usage.

Total sample

Sentence no.	Foreignness			Intelligibility difficulty		
	Mean	SD	Mode	Mean	SD	Mode
45	3.17	1.34	4	1.77	1.10	1

The statistics show that this sentence made a rather foreign impression on the informants but was found to be rather easy to understand.

A potential risk with the error in this sentence is that one may get the impression that more than one brother is referred to, albeit this risk is probably lower when the following noun is singular, as in sentence 45. Generally speaking, this error might therefore give rise to misinterpretations in the spoken language, where the s may be conceived of as a plural inflection rather than as a genitive inflection. In the written language, however, there is no such risk as long as the apostrophe is not omitted. This may explain the low mean for the question on intelligibility difficulty.

Age differences

Sentence no.		Teen-agers		Adults		Pensioners		Significance T-A A-P T-P		
		Mean	SD	Mean	SD	Mean	SD			
F	45	3.39	1.08	3.09	1.39	2.81	1.76	-	-	-
ID	45	2.16	1.22	1.49	.77	1.58	1.30	D	-	-

The difference between the means of the teen-agers and the adults for the question on intelligibility difficulty is statistically highly significant. The teen-agers apparently found this sentence a great deal more difficult to understand than did the adults. This sentence also seems to have made a stronger foreign impression on the teen-agers than on the other age groups, but these differences are not statistically significant.

Sex differences

Sentence no.		Females		Males		Significance
		Mean	SD	Mean	SD	
F	45	3.16	1.36	3.19	1.33	-
ID	45	1.78	1.20	1.76	.93	-

The means of the female and the male informants are virtually identical for this sentence.

4.4 Summary

The three sentences exemplifying errors in the use of nouns all made a rather foreign impression on the informants but were found to be fairly easy to understand. The sentence with the highest mean for foreign impression was the one where the regular plural s-suffix was affixed to the noun mouse, instead of the use of the correct irregular mutation plural (mice). However, at the same time this sentence was found to be the easiest to understand of the three sentences. The sentence with the lowest mean for foreign impression was the one where the non-count noun knowledge was used in the same way as a count noun, i.e. with the regular plural s-suffix.

The sentence with the highest mean for intelligibility difficulty exemplified incorrect use of the group genitive. It might perhaps have been judged to be even more difficult to understand if it had been delivered to the informants in spoken form, as the s then might have been interpreted as a plural inflection rather than as a genitive inflection. If the apostrophe had been omitted, as it often is in normal everyday writing, this sentence may also have been considered to be even worse than it turned out to be here.

Statistically significant differences between the means of the various age-groups were found for all the three sentences as regards the question on intelligibility difficulty. These showed that the teen-agers found all the three sentences somewhat more difficult to understand than did either one or both of the other age-groups.

The female and the male informants gave so similar answers that the means for these two groups are virtually identical.

5. IMPROPER USE OF ADJECTIVES

5.1 Improper comparison

Sentence 66 (10) ("This is the goodest cake I have ever tasted!")
tested reactions to improper comparison of the adjective good,
viz. the use of the regular superlative inflectional suffix -est
rather than the correct irregular superlative form best (or an
alternative adjective in the superlative form, such as most
delicious, nicest, or finest). A sentence with this adjective was
chosen as it is fairly frequently used and errors such as this are
therefore often met with, even though they are usually made at a
very elementary stage of language learning, both where native and
foreign users of English are concerned. This sentence thus
exemplifies an error type which is typical not only of foreign
users of English, and may therefore also be regarded as an example
of 'child language', just as sentences 38, 64 and 70 (cf 4.1, 7.1,
and 8.3).

Total sample

Sentence no.	Foreignness			Intelligibility difficulty		
	Mean	SD	Mode	Mean	SD	Mode
66	3.58	1.07	4	1.50	.78	1

Significance
(PCT) 66-38:   -   -
      66-64:   -   -
      66-70:   H   I

The statistics show that this sentence made a rather strong
foreign impression on the informants but was found to be easy to
understand. The mean value for foreignness may seem high in view
of the fact that a sentence like 66 may also be produced by small
children whose native language is English. However, cf. what was
said about this in connection with sentence 64 (4.1). The
differences between the means for the latter sentence and the
corresponding means for this sentence are not statistically

significant, which indicates that these two sentences resulted in largely the same reactions of the informants. Compared to sentence 70 (cf. 7.1), which was also an example of 'child language', this sentence made a less foreign impression on the informants and was found to be considerably easier to understand. These differences are highly significant. However, compared to sentences 38 and 64, which were also examples of 'child language' this sentence made about the same amount of foreign impression and was judged to be about as easy to understand.

Age differences

Sentence no.		Teen-agers		Adults		Pensioners		Significance T-A A-P T-P		
		Mean	SD	Mean	SD	Mean	SD			
F	66	3.45	.82	3.60	1.14	3.79	1.47	-	-	-
ID	66	1.64	.61	1.44	.83	1.37	1.01	-	-	-

The figures indicate that this sentence made a stronger foreign impression on the older informants than on the younger informants and that the younger informants found it slightly more difficult to understand. However, none of the differences between the means of the age groups are statistically significant, but they are largely consistent with the differences between the means of the age groups which are found for sentences 38 (cf. 8.3), 64 (cf. 4.1), and 70 (cf. 7.1), which are also examples of 'child language'.

Sex differences

Sentence no.		Females		Males		Significance
		Mean	SD	Mean	SD	
F	66	3.54	1.11	3.64	1.03	-
ID	66	1.51	.86	1.50	.63	-

The female and the male informants have virtually identical means for this sentence.

5.2 Improper use of adjective as head of a noun phrase

Sentence 17 (59) ("I took the blind by the arm and led him across the street"), and sentence 63 (13) ("He has a blue car and I have a red") tested reactions to improper use of the adjectives blind and red, viz. as the head of a noun phrase without generic reference. When these errors are made by Swedish users of English the cause is often interference from Swedish, where the corresponding adjectives can be used as the head of a noun phrase without generic reference.

Total sample

Sentence no.	Foreignness			Intelligibility difficulty		
	Mean	SD	Mode	Mean	SD	Mode
17	3.45	1.29	4	1.91	1.02	1
63	2.03	1.09	1	1.31	.66	1

Significance
(PCT):   I   I

There is a highly significant difference between the means of these two sentences for each of the two questions. Sentence 17 made a rather foreign impression on the informants and was found to be rather easy to understand, whereas sentence 63 made a much less foreign impression and was found to be a great deal easier to understand. The latter sentence was thus much more favourably met with, which is also indicated by the modes.

The error exemplified by sentence 63 may thus be regarded as a minor one, at least when compared to the error in sentence 17. The difference between the means of the two sentences for the question on foreignness indicates that it is more likely that native speakers of English themselves omit either a pro-form (one) for the noun phrase head or the noun-phrase head itself in sentences like 63 where the noun-phrase head has been previously mentioned, than that they do this in a sentence like 17 where the noun-phrase head has not been previously mentioned. This is further indicated by the fact that many informants expressed surprise about sentence 63, saying that they found nothing wrong with it.

Unlike sentence 63, sentence 17 thus is an example of a sentence-type where the omitted noun-phrase head (man, boy, or person) has not been previously mentioned, which obviously makes the reference of the adjective unclear. The use of an adjective as a noun-phrase head probably therefore seems less attractive. The way the adjective is used in sentence 17 may initially even evoke thoughts of the homonymous substantive. It is therefore not surprising that the two sentences above show such large differences between their means for the two questions.

Age differences

Sentence no.		Teen-agers		Adults		Pensioners		Significance T-A	A-P	T-P
		Mean	SD	Mean	SD	Mean	SD			
F	17	3.43	1.25	3.57	1.19	3.35	1.69	-	-	-
	63	2.20	1.09	2.02	1.05	1.65	1.17	-	-	-
ID	17	2.29	1.13	1.77	.81	1.45	1.00	B	-	C
	63	1.52	.70	1.25	.72	1.00	0	-	A	I

The means show that the teen-agers found sentence 17 considerably more difficult to understand than the other two age groups did.

The pensioners found sentence 63 significantly easier to understand than did either of the other two age groups. This sentence also seems to have made a less foreign impression on the pensioners than on either of the other two age groups, even though the latter differences are not statistically significant.

Sex differences

Sentence no.		Females		Males		Significance
		Mean	SD	Mean	SD	
F	17	3.24	1.38	3.80	1.04	A
	63	1.95	1.16	2.14	.98	-
ID	17	1.78	.97	2.13	1.07	-
	63	1.19	.50	1.50	.83	A

Sentence 17 made a considerably more foreign impression on the male informants than on the female informants. This may indicate that the male informants are even less apt than the female informants to omit the head of a noun phrase in a sentence where the noun-phrase head has not been previously mentioned. The means for intelligibility difficulty also indicate that the male informants were less tolerant than the female informants as regards sentence 17. This difference, however, is not statistically significant.

The male informants found sentence 63 somewhat more difficult to understand than did the female informants. They also seem to have found it slightly more foreign than the female informants. Unlike the first difference, however, the latter difference is not statistically significant.

For these sentences there are thus slight indications that the male informants prefer to use the replacive one as an anaphoric substitute for a singular count noun, or to use the count noun itself, more often than the female informants prefer to do so.

5.3 Predicative adjective used in attributive position

Sentence 53 (23) ("He is a very alone man") tested reactions to the use of the predicative adjective alone in attributive position, where the corresponding adjective lonely normally is required. Alone does not belong to the group of the most common predicative adjectives, which refer to the health or lack of health of an animate being (such as faint, ill, unwell, well). However, this sentence nevertheless exemplifies an error which seems to be frequently made by many foreign users of English.

Alone is described by Quirk et al. (1972:237) as being 'perhaps a marginal adjective', among other things because it is not acceptable to all speakers with the premodifying adverb very. It is important to bear in mind that this may have made some of the informants even more critical of this sentence, as some of them may have found two reprehensible things about it, whereas others may have found only one point worth criticizing. The sentence was nevertheless included in the questionnaires as an authentic example of a sentence which can be criticized from more than one point of view, which is very often the case with sentences produced by foreign users of English.

Total sample

Sentence no.	Foreignness			Intelligibility difficulty		
	Mean	SD	Mode	Mean	SD	Mode
53	3.71	1.15	4	2.02	1.12	1

The means show that this sentence made a rather strong foreign impression on the informants and that it was not judged to be very easy to understand. In view of the fact that this sentence can be criticized from more than one point of view the means do not seem particularly high. The reason for this seems to be that many of the informants did not realize that more than one thing could be debated but rather seem to have regarded the use of <u>alone</u> simply as a wrong choice of adjectives, mentally rectifying the sentence by replacing <u>alone</u> by any other adjective which can freely be used attributively and also be premodified by <u>very</u>, the latter quality of which is generally considered to be a characteristic of adjectives. The results of the control form corroborate these assumptions.

Age differences

Sentence no.		Teen-agers		Adults		Pensioners		Significance		
		Mean	SD	Mean	SD	Mean	SD	T-A	A-P	T-P
F	53	3.75	1.08	3.64	1.14	3.73	1.49	-	-	-
ID	53	2.23	1.03	1.86	1.15	2.00	1.27	-	-	-

There are no substantial differences between the means of the various age groups for this sentence.

Sex differences

Sentence no.		Females		Males		Significance
		Mean	SD	Mean	SD	
F	53	3.58	1.30	3.90	.86	-
ID	53	2.06	1.18	1.95	1.02	-

Neither of the differences between the means of the female and the male informants is statistically significant for this sentence.

5.4 Improper use of adjective phrase

Sentence 2 (74) ("He has an own company") tested reactions to the use of the adjective own in attributive position without a preceding noun in the genitive case or a possessive pronoun. This error is frequently made by many Swedish users of English, as a result of interference from Swedish, where the corresponding adjective can be used attributively without a preceding noun in the genitive case or a possessive pronoun. The phrase intended is therefore most often of his own (or alternatively any other possessive pronoun or a noun in the genitive case). It was expected, however, that most of the informants would get the impression that the error committed in sentence 2 consisted of a replacement of a possessive pronoun by the indefinite article. Quite obviously, this is the most natural interpretation, as it is the easiest. The results of the control form show that this surmise was correct, as a vast majority of the informants indicated that they interpreted sentence 2 in the following way: He has his own company.

One of the problems with this error is that it may rather easily give rise to the impression that the sentence is emphatic, as the interpretation given to the sentence by most of the informants is more emphatic than is often the intention of the speaker or writer.

Total sample

Sentence no.	Foreignness			Intelligibility difficulty		
	Mean	SD	Mode	Mean	SD	Mode
2	4.11	.97	5	2.65	1.17	2

This sentence made a strong foreign impression on the informants and it was also found to be somewhat difficult to understand, even though the mean is slightly more on the easy side than on the difficult side of the scale.

Improper use of the adjective own apparently makes a very awkward impression on the informants, as both means are comparatively high. This error may therefore be regarded as a serious one, particularly as it may also rather easily give rise to an interpretation which emphatically is slightly different from what is often the intention of the speaker or writer.

Age differences

		Teen-agers		Adults		Pensioners		Significance T-A A-P T-P		
Sentence no.		Mean	SD	Mean	SD	Mean	SD	T-A	A-P	T-P
F	2	4.26	.69	3.91	1.12	4.19	1.12	-	-	-
ID	2	2.98	1.06	2.48	1.06	2.42	1.50	A	-	-

The statistics indicate that the teen-agers found this sentence significantly more difficult to understand than did the adults. It also seems that this sentence made a slightly less foreign impression on the adults than on the other two age groups, but the differences in this respect are not statistically significant.

Sex differences

		Females		Males		Significance
Sentence no.		Mean	SD	Mean	SD	
F	2	4.09	1.05	4.15	.82	-
ID	2	2.70	1.24	2.58	1.03	-

The differences between the means of the female and the male informants are very small for this sentence.

5.5 Adjective used as adverb

Sentence 15 (61) ("He speaks French quite good") tested reactions to the use of the adjective good instead of the adverb well, a usage which is rather common among foreign users of English and also in American English. This sentence therefore also tested how native speakers of British English hold their own against the influence of American English usage in this respect.

As British English is constantly under the influence of American English, it was expected that this sentence would not make a very foreign impression on the informants. This assumption was borne out by the results, which can be seen from the table below.

Total sample

Sentence no.	Foreignness			Intelligibility difficulty		
	Mean	SD	Mode	Mean	SD	Mode
15	2.53	1.28	2	1.26	.50	1

Significance		
(PCT) 15-6:	I	F
15-30:	I	I

This sentence made a less foreign impression on the informants than most of the other test sentences included in the questionnaires, and it was also judged to be very easy to understand. Compared to the two sentences (nos 6 and 30) which tested the opposite case, viz. the use of the adverb well instead of the adjective good (cf. 7.2), this sentence made a much less foreign impression on the informants and it was judged to be a great deal easier to understand. These differences are statistically highly significant.

Age differences

Sentence no.		Teen-agers		Adults		Pensioners		Significance		
		Mean	SD	Mean	SD	Mean	SD	T-A	A-P	T-P
F	15	2.17	1.06	2.65	1.21	3.05	1.68	-	-	A
ID	15	1.26	.54	1.32	.52	1.11	.32	-	-	-

The differences between the means of the age groups for the question on foreign impression are quite striking and probably reflect the effects of the influence of American English on British English, as the youngest informants more readily accepted this sentence as native-like, whereas the two groups of older informants and the group of pensioners in particular apparently associated it more with foreigners. However, the difference between the means of the teen-agers and the pensioners is the only one which is statistically significant for this question. The difference between the means of the teen-agers and the adults is just slightly too weak to be statistically significant (viz. p= .053 instead of the required p= .05). It nevertheless seems likely that the teen-agers themselves can think of using good in contexts where well is normally required in British English more often than the adults and the pensioners can think of doing so, and that they are influenced in doing so by American English. This may eventually lead to a general acceptance of adjectives with adverbial function in sentences of this type in British English.

Sex differences

Sentence no.		Females		Males		Significance
		Mean	SD	Mean	SD	
F	15	2.72	1.37	2.23	1.05	-
ID	15	1.26	.54	1.25	.44	-

This sentence seems to have made a less foreign impression on the male informants than on the female informants, even though the difference between the means for this question is not statistically significant. However, the difference is only fractionally too weak for statistical significance (viz. p= .0535 instead of the required p= .05). This may indicate that the male informants use the adjective good with an adverbial function more often than the female informants do, perhaps because the former group is more easily influenced by American English than the latter is.

Age and sex differences (broken down table)

Sentence no.	Teen-agers Females		Males		Sign	Adults Females		Males		Sign
	Mean	SD	Mean	SD		Mean	SD	Mean	SD	
F 15	2.30	1.17	1.93	.80	-	2.95	1.24	2.36	1.14	-
ID 15	1.26	.59	1.27	.46	-	1.36	.58	1.27	.46	-

	Pensioners Females		Males		Sign	Male teen-agers		Others		Sign
	Mean	SD	Mean	SD		Mean	SD	Mean	SD	
F 15	3.13	1.75	2.67	1.53	-	1.93	.80	2.63	1.32	C
ID 15	1.13	.34	1.00	0	-	1.27	.46	1.26	.51	-

A further statistical breakdown of the figures reveals that the means for the question on intelligibility difficulty are very similar over the various subgroups of informants but that the means for the question on foreign impression vary all the more.

The most positive attitude towards this sentence as regards foreignness was shown by the male teen-agers (mean 1.93) and the most negative attitude was shown by the female pensioners (mean 3.13). The difference between the means of the male teen-agers and the other informants taken together is statistically highly significant for this question. This may very well be indicative of a language change in progress, consisting of a more frequent use of adjectives with adverbial function at the cost of traditional adverbs, picked up by young males in particular and working its way into British English primarily through the male population. The reason for the lower means for the male informants and for the male teen-agers in particular may be that young males are more easily influenced by American English than are other people.

5.6 Summary

Most of the six sentences exemplifying errors in the use of adjectives made a rather strong foreign impression and were found to be rather easy to understand. The sentence with the highest mean for foreign impression also had the highest mean for intelligibility difficulty. This sentence was an example of improper use of the adjective phrase of his own. The sentence with the lowest mean for foreign impression was an example of the omission of the prop-word one as an anaphoric substitute for the noun-phrase head, which had previously been mentioned.

The sentence with the lowest mean for intelligibility difficulty was an example of the use of the adjective good with adverbial function. It was shown that there are indications that this usage is gaining ground in British English, primarily among male teen-agers, probably as a result of the influence of American English.

Significant differences between the means of the age groups were found for four of the six sentences. These indicated that the teen-agers found three of the six sentences more difficult to understand than did either one or both of the other age groups, that the pensioners found one sentence easier to understand than did the other two age groups, and that the teen-agers found one sentence a great deal less foreign than did the pensioners.

Significant differences between the means of the female and the male informants were found for two of the six sentences. These indicated that one sentence made a less foreign impression on the female informants and that the male informants found one sentence more difficult to understand.

6. IMPROPER USE OF PRONOUNS

6.1 Personal pronoun for reflexive pronoun

Sentence 46 (30) ("She was standing alone, beside her with rage") tested reactions to the use of an objective personal pronoun (her) instead of a reflexive pronoun (herself), i.e. an incorrect choice from among the various subclasses of pronouns. A reflexive pronoun is generally considered obligatory after the preposition beside in the phrase which is incorrectly used in sentence 46 and which means 'at the end of one's self control'. When errors such as this are made by foreign users of English the cause is probably most often unfamiliarity with this phrase or an exaggerated application of the prescriptive grammar rule which says that objective personal pronouns should be used in prepositional adverbial phrases expressing spatial relationship despite co-reference with the subject.

Total sample

Sentence no.	Foreignness			Intelligibility difficulty		
	Mean	SD	Mode	Mean	SD	Mode
46	4.19	.96	5	3.04	1.35	2,3*

Significance
(PCT) 46-58:   I   I

* There are two modes for this question.

The results of the questions show that this sentence made a strong foreign impression on the informants and that it was judged to be rather difficult to understand. In fact, this sentence was judged to be the third most difficult to understand of all the sentences in the questionnaire (cf appendix 1).

These results indicate that the error in sentence 46 deserves to

be regarded as a very serious one. The use of an objective
personal pronoun instead of a reflexive pronoun in sentences like
46 may give the impression that there is no co-reference with the
subject and accordingly that another girl or woman is also
referred to (i.e. a spatial relationship between concretes). This,
and the fact that the adverb <u>alone</u> was also used may explain the
high mean for the question on intelligibility difficulty. The high
mean for the question on foreign impression reveals that this type
of error is probably very seldom, if ever, made by native users of
English. In view of these results it seems essential that foreign
learners of English are taught how to use phrases where the
reference is metaphorical and emotionally to a person's self[14],
such as in the phrase incorrectly used in sentence 46.

Compared to sentence 58, which tested the opposite case, viz. the
use of a reflexive pronoun instead of a personal pronoun (cf 6.2),
this sentence made a considerably stronger foreign impression and
was judged to be much more difficult to understand. These
differences are statistically very highly significant.

<u>Age differences</u>

		Teen-agers		Adults		Pensioners		Significance		
Sentence no.								T-A	A-P	T-P
		Mean	SD	Mean	SD	Mean	SD			
F	46	4.25	.89	4.09	.92	4.22	1.22	-	-	-
ID	46	3.52	1.19	2.77	1.27	2.67	1.64	C	-	A

The means for the question on foreignness are very similar for
the three age groups. As regards the question on intelligibility
difficulty, however, there is a striking difference between the
mean of the teen-agers on the one hand and the means of either of
the other two age groups on the other. Apparently the teen-agers
found this sentence a great deal more difficult to understand than
did the other two age groups. This may, perhaps, be due to less
experience of foreign English in general on the part of the teen-
agers.

Sex differences

Sentence no.		Females		Males		Significance
		Mean	SD	Mean	SD	
F	46	4.29	.96	4.02	.95	-
ID	46	3.03	1.44	3.05	1.23	-

The means of the female and the male informants are very similar for this sentence.

6.2 Reflexive pronoun for personal pronoun

Sentence 58 (18) ("She had her radio beside herself") tested reactions to the use of a reflexive pronoun (herself) for an objective personal pronoun (her), i.e. an incorrect choice from among the various subclasses of pronouns. An objective personal pronoun is generally considered to be the correct choice in prepositional adverbial phrases expressing spatial relationship, even if there is co-reference with the subject. When this error is made by Swedish users of English, the cause is often interference from Swedish, where a reflexive pronoun is used in such cases.

As there is considerable vacillation even among native users of English in the use of objective personal pronouns versus reflexive pronouns in prepositional adverbial phrases expressing spatial relationship, it was expected that this sentence would not meet with as much criticism as sentence 46, which tested the opposite case (cf 6.1), as the latter sentence involved a phrase in which a reflexive pronoun is generally considered obligatory.

Total sample

Sentence no.	Foreignness			Intelligibility difficulty		
	Mean	SD	Mode	Mean	SD	Mode
58	3.61	1.12	4	2.02	1.02	1

Significance
(PCT) 58-46:   I   I

The results of the questions show that this surmise was correct.
This sentence made a considerably less foreign impression on the
informants than sentence 46 and it was also judged to be much
easier to understand. However, the mean for the former question
indicates   that this sentence still made a rather foreign
impression on the informants and the mean for the latter question
indicates that the error caused some intelligibility difficulty.
Even though vacillation occurs in this area, it still seems likely
that most native users of English today prefer an objective
personal pronoun rather than a reflexive pronoun in sentences of
this type. The results of the control form further indicate this.
The differences between the means for this sentence and the means
for sentence 46 are statisticall very highly significant.

Age differences

							Significance		
Sentence no.	Teen-agers		Adults		Pensioners		T-A	A-P	T-P
	Mean	SD	Mean	SD	Mean	SD			
F	58	3.41	1.04	3.60	1.09	3.95	1.35	-	-	-
ID	58	2.11	.89	1.88	.99	2.11	1.37	-	-	-

The younger informants seem to have found this sentence less
foreign than the older informants and the adults seem to have
found this sentence slightly easier to understand compared with
the other age groups. However, none of the differences between the
means of the age groups is statistically significant.

Sex differences

Sentence no.		Females		Males		Significance
		Mean	SD	Mean	SD	
F	58	3.66	1.12	3.52	1.13	-
ID	58	2.12	1.09	1.85	.88	-

The male informants seem to have found this sentence slightly easier to understand compared with the female informants, but neither of the differences between the means is statistically significant.

6.3 Insertion of relative pronoun

Sentence 13 (63) ("I don't know what improvements that are being planned") tested reactions to insertion of a relative pronoun (that) in an indirect interrogative clause. When this error is made by Swedish users of English the cause is often interference from Swedish, where a relative pronoun is normally used in such clauses.

Total sample

Sentence no.		Foreignness			Intelligibility difficulty		
		Mean	SD	Mode	Mean	SD	Mode
	13	3.18	1.27	4	2.02	1.00	1,2*

* There are two modes for this question.

This sentence made a foreign impression on the informants and it was found to be fairly easy to understand.

Age differences

Sentence no.		Teen-agers		Adults		Pensioners		Significance T-A	A-P	T-P
		Mean	SD	Mean	SD	Mean	SD			
F	13	3.33	1.08	3.07	1.25	2.89	1.68	-	-	-
ID	13	2.60	1.05	1.74	.80	1.29	.47	I	B	I

The means seem to indicate that the older informants found this sentence less foreign than did the younger informants. However, these differences are not statistically significant.

The differences between the means of the age groups for the question on intelligibility difficulty are statistically highly significant. The means indicate that the teen-agers found this sentence a great deal more difficult to understand than did the adults and the pensioners, and that the pensioners found it easiest to understand of all the three age groups. This may, once again, be due to less experience of foreign English on the part of the younger informants. The difference between the means of the teen-agers and the pensioners for the question on intelligibility difficulty is quite striking, being so great. The difference between the means of these age groups for the question on foreignness is also considerable but not statistically significant. These differences taken together seem to indicate that the pensioners had a more positive attitude towards this sentence than did the teen-agers.

Sex differences

Sentence no.		Females		Males		Significance
		Mean	SD	Mean	SD	
F	13	3.18	1.37	3.17	1.09	-
ID	13	2.00	1.05	2.05	.92	-

The means for the female and the male informants are virtually identical for this sentence.

6.4 Incorrect choice of indefinite pronouns

Sentence 8 (68) ("None of my two brothers knew about my plans")
and sentence 26 (50) ("I haven't heard something from him for a
long time") tested reactions to the use of none instead of
neither and something instead of anything, respectively. Both
these errors are fairly common in the English of many foreigners.

Total sample

Sentence no.	Foreignness			Intelligibility difficulty		
	Mean	SD	Mode	Mean	SD	Mode
8	2.19	1.22	1	1.28	.53	1
26	3.06	1.21	4	1.75	.87	1

Significance
(PCT):   I   I

The statistics show that these sentences were judged in very
different ways. The differences between the means are quite large
and statistically highly significant. The means indicate that
sentence 8 was considerably more acceptable to the informants than
was sentence 26. The use of none instead of neither with reference
to two people apparently made a much less foreign impression on
the informants than did the use of something instead of anything
in a negated sentence. In fact, some of the informants declared
that they themselves sometimes use none rather than neither with
reference to two people or to two objects. This seems to explain
very well the particularly large difference between the means of
the two sentences for the question on foreign impression. Sentence
26, on the other hand, made a much more foreign impression on the
informants and was judged to be less easy to understand than
sentence 8. The error exemplified by sentence 8 may therefore be
said to be a minor one, at least when compared with the error in

sentence 26. The sentence in which the former error ocurred was not judged to be particularly foreign and it was judged to be very easy to understand. It should, perhaps, be pointed out that the correct form of sentence 8, according to the rules of a prescriptive grammar, is Neither of my brothers knew about my plans, as the use of both neither and two would be tautological.

Sentence 26 could, as is often the case with English sentences produced by foreigners, be given an alternative but perhaps more far-fetched interpretation, viz. I haven't heard him say the word 'something' for a long time. The rather high mean for the question on foreign impression and the rather low mean for the question on intelligibility difficulty as regards this sentence indicate, however, that this interpretation did not occur to very many of the informants. If it had, one would have expected a lower mean for foreign impression, as the sentence with this interpretation is both possible and grammatical, and a higher mean for intelligibility difficulty, as this interpretation, which probably seems less plausible than the one previously mentioned, would probably give rise to uncertainty as to which of the two interpretations the person producing the sentence actually had in mind. It is, however, not possible to test this error, and many other types of errors, without allowing for another interpretation, however far-fetched it may ever seem. Even sentences like I didn't do something, I didn't buy something, or I didn't hear something can be given other, and more far-fetched, interpretations, some of which may seem less plausible than others (e.g. if something for some reason is used as a substitute word for another noun phrase, such as my homework, an article, e.g. coffee, and a door-bell, respectively).

The rather low mean for the intelligibility difficulty of sentence 26 is therefore consistent with Olsson's finding (1977:141-142) that the intelligibility of an utterance seems to be influenced not only by different degrees of deviance from wellformedness but also by the relative plausibility of the competing interpretations of an utterance (cf 1.6).

Age differences

		Teen-agers		Adults		Pensioners		Significance T-A A-P T-P		
Sentence no.		Mean	SD	Mean	SD	Mean	SD			
F	8	2.05	1.02	2.36	1.28	2.11	1.53	-	-	-
	26	2.84	1.11	3.14	1.09	3.32	1.67	-	-	-
ID	8	1.40	.58	1.28	.55	1.06	.24	-	A	E
	26	1.81	.88	1.67	.79	1.79	1.08	-	-	-

The pensioners found sentence 8 significantly easier to understand than did the other age groups. However, the means for the intelligibility difficulty of this sentence are so low for all the three age groups that no real intelligibility difficulty seems to have existed.

Sentence 26 seems to have made a less foreign impression on the teen-agers than on the other age groups, but these differences are not statistically significant.

Sex differences

		Females		Males		Significance
Sentence no.		Mean	SD	Mean	SD	
F	8	2.28	1.28	2.02	1.11	-
	26	3.09	1.27	3.00	1.12	-
ID	8	1.30	.58	1.24	.43	-
	26	1.76	.93	1.73	.78	-

The female informants seem to have been slightly more critical of both aspects of these sentences than the male informants, particularly of sentence 8, but none of the differences between the means of the female and the male informants is statistically significant.

6.5 <u>Summary</u>

The means for the five sentences exemplifying errors in the use of pronouns differ a great deal. The sentence with the highest mean for foreign impression also had the highest mean for intelligibility difficulty. This sentence was an example of the use of the objective personal pronoun <u>her</u> instead of the reflexive pronoun <u>herself</u> in a phrase where the reference was emotionally to the person's self. The sentence with the lowest mean for foreign impression also had the lowest mean for intelligibility difficulty. This sentence was an example of incorrect choice of indefinite pronouns, viz. the choice of <u>none</u> instead of <u>neither</u> with reference to two people.

Statistically significant differences between the means of the age groups were found for three of the five sentences. In each case the teen-agers found the sentence more difficult to understand than did either one or both of the other age groups. The pensioners found two of these three sentences significantly easier to understand than did the other age groups.

The means of the female and the male informants did not differ significantly for any of the five sentences.

7. IMPROPER USE OF ADVERBS

7.1 Improper comparison

Sentence 70 (6) ("He drives badlier than his brother") tested reactions to improper comparison of the adverb badly, viz. the use of the regular inflectional suffix -er instead of the normal irregular comparative form worse. A sentence with this adverb was chosen to be included in the questionnaires because of the rather high frequency of this adverb in the language, although errors in the comparison of this adverb are usually made at a very elementary stage of language learning, both where foreign and native users of English are concerned. Sentence 70 is thus a possible one for a small child whose mother tongue is English.

Total sample

Sentence no.	Foreignness			Intelligibility difficulty		
	Mean	SD	Mode	Mean	SD	Mode
70	3.91	1.02	4	2.03	1.03	2

Significance			
(PCT) 70-38:	F		I
70-64:	H		I
70-66:	H		I

This sentence made a strong foreign impression on the informants but was found to be rather easy to understand. Compared with sentences 38, 64 and 66, which are also examples of 'child language' (cf. 8.3, 4.1 and 5.1 respectively), this sentence made a considerably stronger foreign impression and was judged to be considerably more difficult to understand. These differences are statistically highly significant.

Age differences

Sentence no.		Teen-agers		Adults		Pensioners		Significance
		Mean	SD	Mean	SD	Mean	SD	T-A A-P T-P
F	70	3.82	.84	3.84	1.04	4.26	1.33	- - -
ID	70	2.34	.94	1.74	.90	1.83	1.34	D - -

The teen-agers apparently found this sentence more difficult to understand than did the adults. This difference is statistically highly significant. The differences between the means of the age groups are consistent with the differences which were found for sentences 38, 64, and 66, which were also examples of 'child language'.

Sex differences

Sentence no.		Females		Males		Significance
		Mean	SD	Mean	SD	
F	70	3.93	1.11	3.88	.89	-
ID	70	2.03	1.02	2.02	1.05	-

The means for the female and the male informants are almost identical for this sentence, just as for the other three sentences which were examples of 'child language'.

7.2 Adverb used as adjective

Sentence 6 (70) ("This soup tastes well!") and sentence 30 (46) ("This cake smells well!") tested reactions to the use of the adverb well instead of the adjective good. An adjective is normally required as complement after the verbs taste and smell in standard English usage. Errors like this are not infrequent in the English produced by many foreigners, who may not always be aware of the fact that certain verbs are COPULAS and require a noun or an adjective as subject complement. These sentences also served the purpose of being B-control sentences (cf 1.2.1).

Total sample

Sentence no.	Foreignness			Intelligibility difficulty		
	Mean	SD	Mode	Mean	SD	Mode
6	3.51	1.22	4	1.58	.88	1
30	3.67	1.20	4	1.83	1.02	1

Significance		
(PCT) 6-30:	-	E
6-15:	I	F
30-15:	I	I

The means indicate that these sentences were judged in a very similar way, sentence 30 having only slightly higher means than sentence 6, which is a good indication of the reliability of the informants. Sentence 30 was judged to be slightly more difficult to understand than sentence 6, which is indicated by the fact that the difference between the means for intelligibility difficulty is statistically highly significant. However, the difference between the means of the answers to this question is still very small. Whether this difference is due to the fact that different subjects were used in the two sentences or that different verbs were used seems unclear.

Compared to sentence 15, which tested the opposite case, viz. the use of the adjective good instead of the adverb well (cf. 5.5) these two sentences made a much stronger foreign impression on the informants but were judged to be only slightly more difficult to understand. The reason for these differences may be that the use of an adverb with reference to a verb in these sentences, which have inanimate subjects, creates a rather odd impression, as it can make the subject seem animated, and the fact that sentence 15 was an example of a usage which is fairly frequent in American English and in certain cases also in British English.

Age differences

Sentence no.	Teen-agers		Adults		Pensioners		Significance		
							T-A	A-P	T-P
	Mean	SD	Mean	SD	Mean	SD			
F 6	3.65	1.11	3.30	1.24	3.61	1.46	-	-	-
30	3.91	1.15	3.50	1.13	3.53	1.50	-	-	-

Significance
(PCT):   -   -   -

| ID   6 | 1.88 | .93 | 1.40 | .73 | 1.24 | .97 | C | - | B |
| 30 | 2.19 | 1.10 | 1.60 | .88 | 1.56 | 1.04 | C | - | A |

Significance
(PCT):   -   -   A

None of the differences between the means of the age groups are statistically significant for the question on foreignness. However, for the question on intelligibility difficulty there are several statistically significant differences between the means. These show that the teen-agers found both sentences more difficult to understand than did the other two age groups. In no case, however, was the amount of intelligibility difficulty particularly high.

Another statistically significant difference indicates that the pensioners found sentence 30 slightly more difficult to understand than sentence 6.

Sex differences

Sentence no.		Females		Males		Significance
		Mean	SD	Mean	SD	
F	6	3.59	1.24	3.39	1.18	-
	30	3.59	1.26	3.80	1.08	-
Significance (PCT):		-		C		
ID	6	1.57	.95	1.59	.77	-
	30	1.85	1.13	1.80	.84	-
Significance (PCT):		C		-		

There are no statistically significant differences between the means of the female and the male informants for either of the two questions on these sentences. However, there are two highly significant differences between the means of the two sentences, which indicate that sentence 30 made a stronger foreign impression on the male informants than sentence 6 and that the female informants found sentence 30 slightly more difficult to understand than sentence 6.

7.3 Incorrect choice of adverbs

Sentence 44 (32) ("He works very hardly") tested reactions to the the use of the adverb hardly instead of the adverb hard, when the latter adverb is required by the context or intended. The cause of this error may be an exaggerated application of the common adverb suffix -ly. As the adverb which means 'with great exertion' does not take this adverb suffix, this error may give rise to the interpretation that hardly is synonymous with barely. On the other hand, hardly is usually not preceded by the adverb very.

Total sample

Sentence no.	Foreignness			Intelligibility difficulty		
	Mean	SD	Mode	Mean	SD	Mode
44	4.07	1.10	5	2.47	1.28	2

The means indicate that this sentence made a strong foreign impression on the informants and that the error did indeed cause some intelligibility difficulty. This error therefore deserves to be regarded as a serious one, particularly as it can give rise to misinterpretations. It thus seems essential that foreign learners of English are taught the difference between hard and hardly.

Age differences

		Teen-agers		Adults		Pensioners		Significance		
Sentence no.								T-A	A-P	T-P
		Mean	SD	Mean	SD	Mean	SD			
F	44	4.02	1.05	4.16	1.08	4.00	1.37	-	-	-
ID	44	2.64	1.18	2.71	1.33	1.61	1.14	-	D	D

The means indicate that this sentence made a strong foreign impression on all the three age groups. As for the question on intelligibility difficulty, the statistics indicate that there are two highly significant differences. These indicate that the pensioners found sentence 44 much easier to understand than did either of the other two age groups. This seems rather surprising in view of the fact that this sentence made about as strong a foreign impression on the pensioners as it did on the other two age groups. It may be, however, that the pensioners are more familiar with the old usage, where hardly too could be used in the sense 'with energy, force or strenuous exertion; vigorously, forcibly, violently'[15], i.e. where hard is normally used today. This usage is now obsolete and is listed as such by the Oxford English Dictionary (volume 5, 1970), which also gives some examples of its use, the latest known instance of which is in the 1865 edition of <u>Frankenstein</u> (1818) by Mary W. Shelley: "My pulse beat so quickly and hardly, that I felt the palpitation of every artery"[16].

It is possible that the pensioners are more familiar with this older usage from literature and thus may find it easier to understand than the other two age groups do. This may perhaps explain the much lower mean for the pensioners where intelligibility difficulty is concerned.

The fact that the pensioners apparently found this sentence about as foreign as the other two age groups did may be due to the fact that the use of <u>hardly</u> in this sense is now obsolete and therefore no longer associated with the English of native users of the language. The sentence can nevertheless be easy to understand for the pensioners.

Sex differences

Sentence no.		Females		Males		Significance
		Mean	SD	Mean	SD	
F	44	3.99	1.20	4.21	.90	-
ID	44	2.34	1.34	2.67	1.18	-

Neither of the differences between the means of the female and the male informants is statistically significant for this sentence. However, the male informants seem to have been slightly more critical of it than do the female informants.

7.4 <u>Summary</u>

The four sentences exemplifying errors in the use of adverbs made a rather strong foreign impression on the informants but their intelligibility varied a great deal. The sentence with the highest mean for foreign impression also had the highest mean for intelligibility difficulty and was an example of incorrect choice of adverbs, viz. <u>hardly</u> instead of <u>hard</u>, with the sense of 'with energy'.

The sentence with the lowest mean for foreign impression also had the lowest mean for intelligibility difficulty. This sentence was an example of the use of <u>well</u> instead of <u>good</u> as complement of the copula <u>taste</u>, which was preceded by the inanimate subject <u>soup</u>.

Statistically significant differences between the means of the age groups were found for all four sentences. In all cases the teen-agers found the intelligibility difficulty higher than did either one or both of the other age groups. The pensioners found one sentence much easier to understand than the other two age groups did.

The means for the female and the male informants were not significantly different from one another for any of the questions as regards these four sentences.

The results of two B-control sentences showed that these were judged in a very similar way, which is a good indication of the reliability of the informants.

8. IMPROPER USE OF VERBS

8.1 Incorrect tense

Sentence 3 (73) ("I am born in 1945"), sentence 16 (60) ("I didn't saw him today"), sentence 29 (47) ("Things have went too far"), and sentence 61 (15) ("The firm is established in 1970") tested reactions to the use of the wrong tense of the verbs be, see, and go.

Total sample

Sentence no.	Foreignness			Intelligibility difficulty		
	Mean	SD	Mode	Mean	SD	Mode
3	3.86	1.08	4	1.68	.79	1
16	3.90	1.13	5	1.91	.94	1
29	4.05	1.04	5	2.17	1.00	2
61	3.23	1.12	3	1.51	.68	1

Significance
(PCT) 3-61:   I   A

The statistics show that most of these sentences made a strong foreign impression and that they were judged to be fairly easy to understand. Sentence 29 has the highest means for both questions, indicating that the use of a preterite form of the verb go instead of the required past participle form of the same verb was judged to be the worst of the errors. This type of construction is, however, found in certain non-standard English dialects, where went is used both as the past tense and the past participle form.

The differences between the means of the two rather similar sentences testing reactions to the use of the present tense of the verb be instead of the required past tense are interesting and statistically significant. Sentence 3 involved an animate (and personal) subject and sentence 61 involved an inanimate subject. The former sentence made a considerably stronger foreign impression on the informants and it was also found to be slightly more difficult to understand than the latter sentence. It seems unlikely that these differences have anything to do with the fact that the two subjects require different present tense forms of the verb <u>be</u> (the subject in the former sentence is first person and the subject in the latter sentence is third person). It may be, however, that a person's birth in most people's minds is more associated with the past than is the establishing of a firm. Comments given by some of the informants indicate that this is the case. Use of the historic present may also be more common with other verbs than <u>be born</u>.

Sentence 16 is a 'possible' one if one accepts its rather absurd meaning (<u>I</u> <u>didn't</u> <u>cut</u> <u>him</u> <u>with</u> <u>a</u> <u>saw</u> <u>today</u>). However, none of the informants indicated that they interpreted the sentence in that way. This sentence is an example of a very common type of error among many foreign users of English, viz. a grammatical error which may give rise to ambiguity. The sentence made a strong foreign impression on the informants but was found to be fairly easy to understand despite the ambiguity, which seems to indicate that the ambiguity was not very obvious because of the unlikeliness of the alternative meaning. This result is consistent with Olsson's finding (Olsson 1977:141-142) that the intelligibility of utterances seems to be influenced not only by different degrees of deviance from wellformedness but also by the relative plausibility of the competing interpretations of an utterance (cf 1.6).

<u>Age</u> <u>differences</u>

Sentence no.		Teen-agers		Adults		Pensioners		Significance T-A	A-P	T-P
		Mean	SD	Mean	SD	Mean	SD			
F	3	3.91	.92	3.75	1.18	4.00	1.25	-	-	-
	16	4.00	.88	3.80	1.25	3.84	1.38	-	-	-
	29	4.23	.81	3.84	1.18	4.06	1.16	-	-	-
	61	3.07	.97	3.21	1.09	3.65	1.50	-	-	-
ID	3	1.84	.75	1.53	.70	1.65	1.04	-	-	-
	16	2.21	.78	1.72	.85	1.68	1.29	C	-	-
	29	2.60	.93	1.86	.80	1.94	1.30	H	-	A
	61	1.77	.74	1.40	.54	1.15	.49	B	-	E

The means for the question on foreign impression are fairly similar for the various age groups, except for sentence 61, which seems to have made a stronger foreign impression on the pensioners than on the other two age groups. However, these differences are not statistically significant.

For the question on intelligibility difficulty, however, there are five significant differences. These indicate that the teen-agers found three of the four sentences more difficult to understand than did either one or both of the other age groups. The differences between the means for sentence 3 also indicate this, but these differences are not statistically significant. The most striking difference in this respect is shown by the means for sentence 29, which the teen-agers judged to be a great deal more difficult to understand than did the other two age groups.

Sex differences

Sentence no.		Females		Males		Significance
		Mean	SD	Mean	SD	
F	3	3.85	1.14	3.88	.98	-
	16	3.82	1.15	4.03	1.10	-
	29	4.09	1.07	3.98	.99	-
	61	3.25	1.10	3.19	1.15	-
ID	3	1.74	.87	1.59	.63	-
	16	1.88	.48	1.95	.88	-
	29	2.23	1.08	2.07	.88	-
	61	1.46	.70	1.60	.63	-

The differences between the means of the female and the male informants are fairly small for both questions where these four sentences are concerned.

8.2 Omission of the periphrastic auxiliary do

Sentence 7 (69) ("Became he a dentist?"), sentence 72 (4) ("Came he to the party yesterday?"), and sentence 34 (42) ("He thinks not that they know what to do") tested reactions to omission of the periphrastic auxiliary do in POLAR QUESTIONS[17] and in a negated sentence. Sentences 7 and 72 served as B-control sentences (cf. 1.2.1).

Total sample

Sentence no.	Foreignness			Intelligibility difficulty		
	Mean	SD	Mode	Mean	SD	Mode
7	4.33	.90	5	2.21	1.17	1
34	4.53	.70	5	3.50	1.33	5
72	4.17	.97	5	2.17	1.13	1

Significance		
(PCT) 7-34:	B	I
34-72:	H	I
7-72:	-	-

The means indicate that these sentences made a strong or very strong foreign impression on the informants and that they were found to be rather easy to understand, with the exception of sentence 34, which was found to be difficult to understand.

Sentence 34 made the strongest foreign impression on the informants of all the test sentences in the questionnaires and it was also found to be the most difficult to understand of all the test sentences in the questionnaires. The use of the do-periphrasis in negated sentences is clearly one of the most important points there is to teach to foreign users of English. It seems clear that if errors are made in this respect they may cause serious intelligibility difficulty and also make the sentence give a very strong foreign impression. The correct version of sentence 34 is He does not think that they know what to do, which is usually synonymous with He thinks that they do not know what to do.

The two B-control sentences were examples of omission of a do-periphrasis in polar questions. These sentences also made a strong foreign impression on the informants but were found to be considerably easier to understand than sentence 34. These differences are statistically highly significant. The differences between the means of the two B-control sentences, however, are so small that neither difference is statistically significant. This is, once again, a good indication of the reliability of the informants.

Age differences

Sentence no.		Teen-agers		Adults		Pensioners		Significance T-A	A-P	T-P
		Mean	SD	Mean	SD	Mean	SD			
F	7	4.37	.85	4.27	.97	4.35	.93	-	-	-
	34	4.53	.74	4.57	.66	4.47	.77	-	-	-
	72	4.09	.94	4.26	.90	4.21	1.27	-	-	-
ID	7	2.44	1.10	2.09	1.19	2.00	1.33	-	-	-
	34	3.90	1.21	3.51	1.24	2.65	1.54	-	A	E
	72	2.61	1.10	2.00	1.05	1.44	1.04	B	-	G

The statistics indicate that the three age groups all found these three sentences foreign or very foreign and that the differences between the means of the age groups for this question are very small. This is an indication of the fact that this usage is no longer associated with the English of native users of the language and that a do-periphrasis is required in such cases in current English.

For the question on intelligibility difficulty, however, there are several significant differences between the means of the age groups. These indicate that the pensioners found sentence 34 much easier to understand than did the other age groups and that the teen-agers found sentence 72 a great deal more difficult to understand than did the other age groups. The reason for these differences may be that the older informants are perhaps more familiar with the old usage with no periphrastic auxiliary do in negated sentences and in polar questions. This usage can be met with in old English literature, e.g. Shakespeare, and it is possible that the older informants are more used to reading this kind of literature than are the younger informants and thus may find this usage easier to understand.

Sex differences

Sentence no.		Females		Males		Significance
		Mean	SD	Mean	SD	
F	7	4.32	.90	4.34	.91	-
	34	4.49	.68	4.61	.74	-
	72	4.16	1.07	4.19	.80	-
ID	7	2.15	1.21	2.29	1.12	-
	34	3.38	1.42	3.70	1.16	-
	72	2.11	1.16	2.26	1.11	-

The male informants seem to have been slightly more critical of these sentences compared with the female informants, particularly of the intelligibility of sentence 34, but none of the differences between the means of the female and the male informants is statistically significant.

8.3 Irregular verb used as regular verb

Sentence 38 (38) ("They fighted bravely in the war") tested reactions to incorrect choice of preterite conjugation of the verb fight. This error, which seems to be fairly frequently made by foreign users of English and by small children whose mother tongue is English, appears usually to be caused by an exaggerated application of the -ed suffix of regular verbs. This sentence is thus still another example of what might be called 'child language' (cf. 4.1, 5.1, and 7.1).

Total <u>sample</u>

Sentence no.	Foreignness			Intelligibility difficulty		
	Mean	SD	Mode	Mean	SD	Mode
38	3.50	1.31	5·	1.53	.80	1

Significance

(PCT) 38-64:	-			-		
38-66:	-			-		
38-70:	F			I		

This sentence made a rather strong foreign impression on the informants but was found to be fairly easy to understand. These results are consistent with the results of two of the other three sentences which were also examples of 'child language'. Compared to sentence 70, however, this sentence made a less foreign impression and was judged to be considerably easier to understand.

Age <u>differences</u>

	Sentence no.	Teen-agers		Adults		Pensioners		Significance T-A A-P T-P		
		Mean	SD	Mean	SD	Mean	SD			
F	38	3.07	1.30	3.70	1.13	4.06	1.57	B	-	B
ID	38	1.59	.69	1.45	.80	1.53	1.07	-	-	-

The means indicate that this sentence made a much less foreign impression on the teen-agers than on the older informants. These differences are consistent with the differences which were found between the means of the age groups for the three other sentences exemplifying 'child language', although the differences between the means were not statistically significant in those cases (cf. 4.1, 5.1, and 7.1).

Sex differences

Sentence no.		Females		Males		Significance
		Mean	SD	Mean	SD	
F	38	3.58	1.32	3.37	1.30	-
ID	38	1.53	.87	1.54	.67	-

Consistent with the results for sentences 64, 66, and 70, there are no statistically significant differences between the means of the female and the male informants for this sentence.

8.4 Improper use of modal auxiliaries

Sentence 39 (37) ("Can you French?") and sentence 55 (21) ("He needs not come") tested reactions to improper use of the modal auxiliaries can and need, the latter one of which is often regarded as a marginal modal auxiliary, as it can be constructed either as a modal auxiliary or as a lexical verb.

Sentence 39 is an example of a grammatical error which can give rise to ambiguity. The sentence can be interpreted as meaning either Do you know French? or Can you speak French?. There are, in fact, several other possible interpretations of this sentence, but these two, and the latter one in particular, were expected to be the most common ones. The answers given to the control form show that a majority of the informants did indeed interpret the sentence exactly in this way. However, when sentence 39 is produced by Swedish users of English, the intended meaning is actually just as often Do you know French? as Can you speak French?. This means that they often use the wrong verb, viz. the modal auxiliary can instead of the lexical verb know (with an accompanying do-periphrasis). This erroneous way of expressing oneself can thus lead to misinterpretations. The foreigner might just want to inquire whether or not the person he is addressing (in speech or writing) has a general knowledge of French but instead he is interpreted as meaning <u>Can</u> <u>you</u> <u>speak</u> <u>French</u>?. He may then get the reply <u>No,</u> <u>but</u> <u>I</u> <u>can</u> <u>understand</u> <u>it</u>, which must seem rather bewildering to him if what he really meant was <u>Do</u> <u>you</u> <u>know</u> <u>French</u>?.

Other possible, but probably less likely, interpretations of sentence 39 are <u>Can</u> <u>you</u> <u>read</u> <u>French</u>?, <u>Can</u> <u>you</u> <u>understand</u> <u>French</u>?, <u>Can</u> <u>you</u> <u>write</u> <u>French</u>?, and <u>Can</u> <u>you</u> <u>communicate</u> <u>in</u> <u>French</u>?. In some cases the foreigner producing sentence 39 can even be interpreted as meaning something completely different, viz. <u>Can</u> <u>you</u> <u>practise</u> <u>fellatio/cunnilingus</u>? (to <u>French</u> = to practise fellatio or cunnilingus (with)[18]), which was shown by some of the comments on this sentence. It should, perhaps, be pointed out that this verb does have a capital initial.

<u>Total</u> <u>sample</u>

Sentence no.	Foreignness			Intelligibility difficulty		
	Mean	SD	Mode	Mean	SD	Mode
39	4.45	.80	5	3.19	1.28	3
55	3.73	1.13	4	2.22	1.28	1

Significance
(PCT):   I   I

The statistics indicate that sentence 39 made a very strong foreign impression on the informants and that it was judged to be rather difficult to understand. In fact, only one sentence in the questionnaires (no. 34, cf. 8.2) had higher mean values for the two questions. This indicates that the error in sentence 39 definitely deserves to be regarded as a very serious one, the avoidance of which is essential and ought to be paid a great deal of attention in the teaching of English to foreigners, particularly as this error is fairly frequently made by, among others, Swedish users of English.

Sentence 55 did not meet with nearly as much criticism as sentence 39. However, the means for the two questions are serious enough in view of the fact that only one letter makes the sentence ungrammatical (the s in needs).

The general conclusion to be drawn from the results of the two sentences exemplifying improper use of these modal auxiliaries is that the teaching of the proper use of these modal auxiliaries seems very important, as improper use may result in a strong or very strong foreign impression and considerable or serious intelligibility difficulty.

Age differences

Sentence no.		Teen-agers		Adults		Pensioners		Significance		
		Mean	SD	Mean	SD	Mean	SD	T-A	A-P	T-P
F	39	4.43	.73	4.50	.70	4.35	1.22	-	-	-
	55	3.95	.78	3.51	1.18	3.63	1.71	A	-	-
ID	39	3.34	1.18	3.16	1.36	3.00	1.32	-	-	-
	55	2.59	1.15	2.00	1.33	1.88	1.36	A	-	A

The results indicate that the three age groups had very similar opinions about the foreign impression and the intelligibility difficulty of sentence 39. As regards sentence 55, however, the teen-agers were apparently the most critical age group. The statistics indicate that this sentence made a significantly stronger foreign impression on them than on the adults and that the teen-agers found it considerably more difficult to understand than did the other two age groups. These differences may indicate that the teen-agers are more apt to employ the periphrastic auxiliary do with need in negatives than are the other age groups. If so, this is consistent with the results of previous investigations of auxiliaries, which indicate that the modal auxiliaries <u>ought to</u> and <u>used to</u> are being reclassified as full verbs by younger speakers in negative and interrogative constructions (cf. Hughes-Trudgill, 1979:23).

<u>Sex differences</u>

Sentence no.		Females		Males		Significance
		Mean	SD	Mean	SD	
F	39	4.45	.86	4.44	.71	-
	55	3.63	1.22	3.88	.98	-
ID	39	3.16	1.31	3.24	1.24	-
	55	2.08	1.22	2.45	1.36	-

The male informants seem to have been slightly more critical of sentence 55 than do the female informants, particularly of the intelligibility of this sentence. However, none of the differences between the means of the female and the male informants is statistically significant.

8.5 <u>Improper use of the -**ing** participle/the base form of a verb</u>

8.5.1 <u>Use of the -**ing** participle with stative verb</u>

Sentence 74 (2) ("He is meaning this book, not that one") tested reactions to the use of the -ing participle with the usually stative verb <u>mean</u>. This error seems to be a fairly common one, as many foreign users of English tend to exaggerate the use of the -ing participle.

<u>Total</u> <u>sample</u>

Sentence no.	Foreignness			Intelligibility difficulty		
	Mean	SD	Mode	Mean	SD	Mode
74	3.62	1.10	4	1.85	1.08	1

The means indicate that this sentence made a rather strong foreign impression on the informants and was judged to be fairly easy to understand. The use of the wrong form of the verb here does not seem to have given rise to any competing interpretations of sufficient plausibility. If this had been the case, the mean for the question on intelligibility difficulty would perhaps have been higher, as this would probably make the informants feel hesitant about which interpretation was the intended one.

<u>Age</u> <u>differences</u>

						Significance			
Sentence no.	Teen-agers		Adults		Pensioners		T-A	A-P	T-P
	Mean	SD	Mean	SD	Mean	SD			
F	74	3.59	1.09	3.49	1.12	3.94	1.20	-	-	-
ID	74	2.34	1.16	1.48	.67	1.60	1.27	I	-	B

Whereas the means of the answers to the question on foreign impression are fairly similar for the three age groups, the means of the answers to the question on intelligibility difficulty vary all the more. There are two significant differences which indicate that the teen-agers found this sentence a great deal more difficult to understand than did the other two age groups. However, the teen-agers' mean for this question is still not very high.

Sex differences

Sentence no.		Females		Males		Significance
		Mean	SD	Mean	SD	
F	74	3.54	1.15	3.74	1.04	-
ID	74	1.79	1.08	1.95	1.08	-

The male informants have slightly higher means than do the female informants but neither of the differences between their means is statistically significant.

8.5.2 Use of the base form of a verb after a preposition

Sentence 35 (41) ("I am used to get up early in the morning") and sentence 52 (24) ("I look forward to hear from you") tested reactions to the use of the base forms of the verbs get and hear, instead of the -ing forms of the same verbs, after the preposition to, which seems to be a particularly difficult preposition to learn for many foreigners, who frequently confuse it with the infinitive marker to, and thus sometimes make this error.

Two sentences with the preposition to were chosen to be included in the questionnaires, as this type of error very often occurs after this preposition, and in order to find out whether or not the two prepositional verbs exemplified differ in any respect with regard to the opinions of native users of English.

Total sample

Sentence no.	Foreignness			Intelligibility difficulty		
	Mean	SD	Mode	Mean	SD	Mode
35	3.54	1.22	4	1.86	1.02	1
52	2.89	1.28	4	1.38	.62	1

Significance
(PCT):   I   I

The means indicate that these sentences were judged very differently. Sentence 35 apparently made a much stronger foreign impression on the informants and was judged to be somewhat more difficult to understand than sentence 52. These differences are statistically highly significant, and may probably be explained in terms of a possible ambiguity where sentence 35 is concerned. If the prepositional verb phrase be used to is used without a following -ing form of the verb it can rather easily be confused with used to, which has a different meaning, as the latter phrase is never used with a following -ing form of the verb. The prepositional verb phrase look forward to, on the other hand, cannot as readily be confused with any other phrase. This seems to be the probable reason for the greater disapproval of sentence 35.

These results were expected and indicate that it is more acceptable to use the base form of a verb after the prepositional verb phrase look forward to than to do this after the prepositional verb phrase be used to. The correct use of the latter phrase may therefore be said to be higher on the priority scale for foreign users of English than the correct use of the former phrase.

Age differences

		Teen-agers		Adults		Pensioners		Significance		
Sentence no.								T-A	A-P	T-P
		Mean	SD	Mean	SD	Mean	SD			
F	35	3.77	1.09	3.43	1.13	3.24	1.75	-	-	-
	52	2.66	1.26	3.23	1.05	2.33	1.68	B	-	-

Significance
(PCT):　　　　　I　　　　　　-　　　　　　A

ID	35	2.26	1.03	1.70	.91	1.28	.96	C	-	F
	52	1.50	.63	1.37	.66	1.12	.49	-	-	A

Significance
(PCT):　　　　　I　　　　　A　　　　　　-

The statistics indicate that sentence 52 made a significantly stronger foreign impression on the adults than on the teen-agers. This may perhaps indicate that the teen-agers themselves use the base form of a verb after the prepositional verb phrase look forward to more often than the adults do so. The pensioners also have a low mean for the question on foreign impression, but the difference between their mean and the mean of the adults is not statistically significant owing to the large standard deviation for the group of pensioners. However, sentence 52 was judged to be significantly easier to understand by the pensioners than by the teen-agers. The mean for the teen-agers, however, is also very low.

Sentence 35 was judged to be considerably more difficult to understand by the teen-agers than by the other two groups of informants. These differences are statistically highly significant.

The teen-agers show the most significant and greatest differences between the means of the two sentences, which may be still another indication that they sometimes use the base form instead of the -ing form of a verb following the prepositional verb phrase look forward to. If so, this may eventually lead to a more general use of the base form of verbs after this prepositional verb phrase.

Sex differences

Sentence no.		Females		Males		Significance
		Mean	SD	Mean	SD	
F	35	3.44	1.31	3.71	1.05	-
	52	2.78	1.39	3.05	1.09	-

Significance
(PCT):   I   C

ID	35	1.73	1.02	2.07	1.01	-
	52	1.35	.67	1.44	.55	-

Significance
(PCT):   C   I

The means are slightly higher for the male informants than for the female informants for both questions as regards these sentences. However, none of the differences between the means of the female and the male informants is statistically significant.

The female informants show the most significant difference between the means of the two sentences for the question on foreign impression and the male informants show the most significant difference between the means of the sentences for the question on intelligibility difficulty. The female informants also seem to have found the two sentences more different as regards their foreignness than as regards their intelligibility, whereas the male informants seem to have found both aspects as different between the two sentences.

8.5.3 Use of the **to**-infinitive instead of the **-ing** participle after a verb which takes only the participle construction as object.

Sentence 59 (17) ("Many cities have stopped to expand") tested reactions to the use of the to-infinitive after the verb stop, which takes only the -ing participle construction as object. This is still another sentence which can be given another, though unlikely, interpretation. It can thus give rise to ambiguity. This is the case with a great many English sentences frequently produced by foreigners, and sometimes also by native users of English, and this sentence was therefore included in the questionnaires to test for the reactions to such sentences. The most plausible and 'natural' interpretation of sentence 59 seems to be Many cities have ceased to expand, and the less plausible or 'unnatural' interpretation Many cities have stopped walking (or doing something else) in order to expand. It should be pointed out that under the latter interpretation sentence 59 is perfectly grammatical, on the surface, but it violates the semantic rule which says that a non-animate subject cannot walk or do something with a view to doing something else.

Total sample

Sentence no.	Foreignness			Intelligibility difficulty		
	Mean	SD	Mode	Mean	SD	Mode
59	3.83	1.20	5	2.86	1.38	3

The results indicate that this sentence made a rather strong foreign impression on the informants and that it was also judged to be rather difficult to understand. The error in sentence 59 may thus be said to be a serious one. It is unlikely, however, that the intelligibility difficulty is a result of the possible ambiguity of this sentence, because of the implausibility of the 'unnatural' interpretation. It rather seems from some of the comments and the results of the control form that the use of the to-infinitive in this sentence may give the impression that the 'expansion' has not yet taken place. Cf. 1.6 for a discussion of the effects of the relative plausibility of competing interpretations on the intelligibility of an utterance.

Age differences

	Sentence no.	Teen-agers		Adults		Pensioners		Significance		
		Mean	SD	Mean	SD	Mean	SD	T-A	A-P	T-P
F	59	3.63	1.16	4.00	1.18	3.89	1.41	-	-	-
ID	59	3.35	1.19	2.69	1.33	2.22	1.59	B	-	D

The means indicate that the teen-agers found this sentence a great deal more difficult to understand than did the other two age groups.

Sex differences

	Sentence no.	Females		Males		Significance
		Mean	SD	Mean	SD	
F	59	3.86	1.23	3.79	1.18	-
ID	59	2.97	1.41	2.69	1.32	-

The female informants have slightly higher means than the male
informants for both questions on this sentence, but neither of the
differences between the means of the female and the male
informants is statistically significant.

8.6 **to**-infinitive for bare infinitive

Sentence 33 (43) ("They made me to do it") also exemplifies an
error which can give rise to ambiguity and which seems to be
fairly frequently made by many foreign users of English. If this
sentence is considered to be grammatical, it means something like
They gave birth to me in order that I should do it (for them).
Unlikely though this interpretation may seem, it is a possible
one. However, the meaning intended by the foreigner who used
sentence 33 is probably more likely to be They forced me to do it.

Total sample

Sentence no.	Foreignness			Intelligibility difficulty		
	Mean	SD	Mode	Mean	SD	Mode
33	3.72	1.16	4	2.08	1.11	1

The means indicate that this sentence made a rather strong
foreign impression on the informants but was found to be fairly
easy to understand. The fairly low mean for intelligibility
difficulty indicates that the less plausible interpretation was
probably not considered by very many informants. If it had been,
the amount of intelligibility difficulty would probably have been
higher than is reflected by the mean and the mode for this
question, as this interpretation would probably cause uncertainty
as to which interpretation was the intended one. The results of
form 3 corroborate this.

Age differences

Sentence no.		Teen-agers		Adults		Pensioners		Significance T-A A-P T-P		
		Mean	SD	Mean	SD	Mean	SD			
F	33	3.93	.89	3.50	1.27	3.89	1.32	-	-	-
ID	33	2.48	1.04	1.79	1.04	1.94	1.29	D	-	-

The means for the question on foreign impression are fairly similar for the three age groups. However, the teen-agers apparently found this sentence a great deal more difficult to understand than did the adults.

Sex differences

Sentence no.		Females		Males		Significance
		Mean	SD	Mean	SD	
F	33	3.63	1.18	3.88	1.14	-
ID	33	2.11	1.10	2.03	1.14	-

The means for the female and the male informants are very similar for this sentence.

8.7 Summary

Most of the fifteen sentences exemplifying errors in the use of verbs made a rather strong foreign impression on the informants and were not judged to be altogether easy to understand.

The sentence with the highest mean for foreign impression also had the highest mean for intelligibility difficulty and exemplified omission of the do-periphrasis in a negated sentence.

This sentence made an exceptionally strong foreign impression on the informants and was also judged to be difficult to understand. It had, in fact, the highest means for both foreign impression and intelligibility difficulty of all the 75 test sentences in the questionnaires.

The other two sentences exemplifying omission of the do-periphrasis also have considerably higher means for both questions than most of the other 74 test sentences.

The sentence with the second highest mean for foreign impression also had the second highest mean for intelligibility difficulty and exemplified improper use of the modal auxiliary can. This sentence also made an exceptionally strong foreign impression on the informants and was judged to be rather difficult to understand. Compared to the other 74 test sentences, this sentence made the third strongest foreign impression and was the second most difficult to understand.

Of the fifteen sentences exemplifying errors in the use of verbs the sentence with the lowest mean for foreign impression also had the lowest mean for intelligibility difficulty and exemplified the use of the base form instead of the -ing form of the verb following the prepositional verb phrase look forward to. This sentence is found near the bottom of the rank lists of the test sentences (cf. appendix 1).

Significant age differences were found for 12 of the 15 sentences, 11 of which were found to be more difficult to understand by the teen-agers than by either one or both of the other age groups. There is no significant difference where the reverse is true.

One sentence, an example of what might be called 'child language' (no. 38), made a stronger foreign impression on the older informants than on the teen-agers, and another sentence (no. 52) made a stronger foreign impression on the adults than on the teen-agers. This sentence was an example of the use of the base form instead of the -ing form of the verb following the prepositional verb phrase <u>look</u> <u>forward</u> <u>to</u>. It was argued that this result may indicate that the teen-agers more often than the adults use the base form instead of the -<u>ing</u> form of verbs following this phrase. This was further indicated by the fact that the teen-agers showed a greater difference between the means for this sentence and the means for another sentence with a prepositional verb phrase, viz. <u>be</u> <u>used</u> <u>to</u>, than did either of the other two age groups. If usage really differs between these age groups in this way it may eventually lead to a more general use of the base form of verbs after the prepositional phrase <u>look</u> <u>forward</u> <u>to</u>. The opposite was found to be the case for another sentence (no. 55), which made a stronger foreign impression on the teen-agers than on the adults. This sentence was an example of improper use of the modal auxiliary <u>can</u>.

There are no statistically significant differences between the means of the female and the male informants, for either of the two questions on any of the fifteen sentences.

The results of two B-control sentences indicated that the reliability of the informants was very high.

9. INCONGRUITY

Sentence 4 (72) ("I don't know much people in this town"), sentence 18 (58) ("Here are the money I owe you"), sentence 22 (54) ("My brother have worked for this company for many years"), sentence 47 (29) ("We have a great deal of problems"), and sentence 69 (7) ("There is one chair too much") tested reactions to the use of incongruous elements within the same sentence. This is a very common feature in the English produced by many foreigners.

Total sample

Sentence no.	Foreignness			Intelligibility difficulty		
	Mean	SD	Mode	Mean	SD	Mode
4	3.66	1.10	4	1.80	.94	1
18	3.92	1.00	4	1.82	.95	1
22	3.38	1.27	4	1.58	.76	1
47	2.02	1.24	1	1.28	.54	1
69	3.03	1.20	3	1.48	.68	1

Significance
(PCT):   The differences between the means are all statistically significant, with the exception of the differences between the means for the intelligibility difficulty of sentences 4 and 18, and sentences 22 and 69.

The foreign impression made by these five incongruous sentences varies a great deal, but they were all judged to be rather easy to understand.

The means for sentence 47 deviate a great deal from the means for the other sentences, particularly as regards foreign impression. It made a much less foreign impression on the informants than any of the other four sentences and it was also judged to be the easiest to understand. This indicates that the use of the expression a great deal of with a following noun in the plural is not associated with the English of foreigners to any great degree. This may in fact mean that this type of expression is sometimes employed by native users of English as well (cf. age differences below).

Sentence 18 seems to have been regarded as the worst of the five sentences. This indicates that money is hardly ever treated as a plural noun by native users of English (cf. however monies) and that errors such as this make a strong foreign impression and also make the sentence slightly more difficult to understand.

Sentence 4 also met with about the same kind of disapproval, which indicates that people is hardly ever treated as a singular noun by native users of English.

Sentence 22 is an obvious example of an ambiguous sentence. It can be given either of the following interpretations: My brother has worked for this company for many years, or My brothers have worked for this company for many years. Either way, the sentence is ungrammatical as administered to the informants. The results of the control form indicate that it was more common to interpret sentence 22 as referring to only one brother. In view of the fact that this sentence is clearly an ambiguous one, the mean for intelligibility difficulty seems rather low. This may, however, indicate that only a few informants realized that it was indeed ambiguous. If this is so, it means that the error in this sentence is even more serious than indicated by the means above, as many informants may have taken for granted that the sentence referred to only one brother and thus may have missed the opportunity to ask the foreigner for clarification. Thus we here have an example of an error which can be serious from a communicative point of view.

Sentence 69 was found to be the least serious but one of the five sentences as regards foreign impression. It still made a rather foreign impression on the informants, but was found to be easy to understand.

Age differences

Sentence no.		Teen-agers		Adults		Pensioners		Significance		
								T-A	A-P	T-P
Mean	SD	Mean	SD	Mean	SD	Mean	SD			
F	4	3.62	1.01	3.63	1.11	3.75	1.37	-	-	-
	18	3.98	.78	3.73	1.11	4.20	1.20	-	-	-
	22	3.60	1.07	3.23	1.29	3.11	1.68	-	-	-
	47	1.48	.76	2.40	1.29	2.35	1.62	I	-	A
	69	2.68	1.01	3.23	1.11	3.35	1.69	B	-	-
ID	4	2.07	.92	1.64	.89	1.60	1.05	A	-	-
	18	2.14	.84	1.60	.89	1.61	1.20	D	-	-
	22	1.98	.83	1.40	.66	1.11	.32	G	B	I
	47	1.23	.52	1.32	.56	1.29	.59	-	-	-
	69	1.61	.58	1.40	.63	1.32	.95	-	-	-

The statistics show that there are eight statistically significant differences between the means of the age groups here. Perhaps the most interesting of these are the ones for the question on foreign impression. These indicate that the teen-agers found sentence 47 much less foreign than did the other two age groups and that they also found sentence 69 a great deal less foreign than did the adults. The differences between the means for the former sentence are quite dramatic as the mean for the teen-agers is exceptionally low, which may indicate that the teen-agers use the expression a great deal of with a following noun in the plural more often than the other age groups do. The difference between the means for the latter sentence is not as great, and the mean for the teen-agers is considerably higher than for sentence 47, but it may still indicate that the teen-agers use much instead of many with reference to count nouns more often than the adults do. The fact that the teen-agers did not find either of these sentences significantly more difficult to understand than one or both of the other age groups, unlike the other three sentences, further indicates that usage may differ between the age groups in these cases. If this is so, this may eventually lead to a general usage change, the effects of which will be a more general acceptance of a plural noun after the expression a great deal of and of the use of much with reference to count nouns.

The remaining five significant differences between the means of the age groups indicate that the teen-agers found sentence 4 and sentence 18 considerably more difficult to understand than did the adults, that they found sentence 22 considerably more difficult to understand than did either the adults or the pensioners and that the pensioners found sentence 22 even easier to understand than the adults did.

Sex differences

Sentence no.		Females		Males		Significance
		Mean	SD	Mean	SD	
F	4	3.63	1.12	3.70	1.09	-
	18	3.86	1.02	4.03	.97	-
	22	3.22	1.32	3.63	1.16	-
	47	1.95	1.20	2.12	1.31	-
	69	2.97	1.24	3.12	1.15	
ID	4	1.81	.99	1.78	.86	-
	18	1.88	1.03	1.72	.79	-
	22	1.52	.75	1.68	.79	-
	47	1.23	.52	1.36	.58	-
	69	1.47	.73	1.50	.59	-

These sentences seem to have made a slightly stronger foreign impression on the male informants than on the female informants. However, none of the differences between the means of the female and the male informants is statistically significant either for the question on foreign impression or for the question on intelligibility difficulty.

10. IMPROPER USE OF PREPOSITIONS

10.1 Incorrect choice of prepositions

Sentence 9 (67) ("I met him in the stairs"), sentence 32 (44) ("I met him in the steps"), and sentence 37 (39) ("She is married with a German") tested reactions to the use of the prepositions in and with instead of on and to, respectively. Sentence 9 and sentence 32 also served as B-control sentences (cf. 1.2.1).

Total sample

Sentence no.	Foreignness			Intelligibility difficulty		
	Mean	SD	Mode	Mean	SD	Mode
9	3.53	1.16	4	1.81	.90	1
32	3.69	1.12	4	2.10	1.08	1
37	3.56	1.13	4	1.60	.78	1

Significance		
(PCT) 9-32:	-	E
32-37:	-	I
9-37:	-	B

The three sentences all made a rather strong foreign impression on the informants but were found to be fairly easy to understand. The differences between the means of the sentences for the question on foreign impression are very small and not statistically significant. The differences between the means of the sentences for the question on intelligibility difficulty, however, are somewhat greater and all statistically significant.

It turns out that the two B-control sentences were judged to be rather different as regards intelligibility. Sentence 32 was judged to be somewhat more difficult to understand than sentence

9. This result may possibly be due to the fact that <u>stairs</u> usually refers to a series of fixed steps indoors and <u>steps</u> usually, but not always, refers to a series of fixed steps outdoors. It may therefore be felt to be more 'natural' to use the preposition <u>in</u> in the former case than in the latter. The means for foreignness indicate, however, that this is hardly ever done by native users of English. It may nevertheless be found to be easier to understand a sentence where the preposition <u>in</u> refers to <u>stairs</u> than when it refers to <u>steps</u>. However, the difference between the means of sentences 9 and 32 as regards intelligibility difficulty is rather small.

Sentence 37 also made a rather strong foreign impression on the informants but was found to be significantly easier to understand than the other two sentences.

Age differences

Sentence no.		Teen-agers		Adults		Pensioners		Significance T-A A-P T-P		
		Mean	SD	Mean	SD	Mean	SD			
F	9	3.63	1.09	3.34	1.20	3.72	1.32	-	-	-
	32	3.84	.95	3.61	1.13	3.44	1.54	-	-	-
	37	3.40	1.03	3.58	1.14	3.94	1.39	-	-	-
ID	9	2.14	.86	1.56	.73	1.72	1.18	E	-	-
	32	2.28	.88	2.02	1.17	1.94	1.35	-	-	-
	37	1.79	.77	1.49	.70	1.41	1.00	-	-	-

The only statistically significant difference here is between the means of the teen-agers and the adults for the question on the intelligibility difficulty of sentence 9. This difference indicates that the teen-agers found sentence 9 considerably more difficult to understand than did the adults. The differences between the means for the other sentences indicate the same thing but are not statistically significant.

Sex differences

Sentence no.		Females		Males		Significance
		Mean	SD	Mean	SD	
F	9	3.52	1.15	3.54	1.21	-
	32	3.54	1.22	3.93	.91	-
	37	3.44	1.19	3.75	1.01	-
ID	9	1.80	.95	1.83	.83	-
	32	2.06	1.01	2.17	1.20	-
	37	1.55	.86	1.68	.69	-

The differences between the means of the female and the male informants are small for these sentences and none of them is statistically significant.

10.2 Insertion of preposition

Sentence 5 (71) ("I was here for two years ago"), sentence 50 (26) ("Smell on these flowers!"), sentence 54 (22) ("Have you ever seen the river of Ganges?), sentence 60 (16) ("I am sure of that he will come"), and sentence 68 (8) ("She was here for two years ago") tested reactions to insertion of the prepositions for, of, and on. Sentences 5, 50, 60, and 68 are examples of errors which, when made by Swedes, are usually caused by interference from Swedish, where prepositions are used in such cases, whereas sentence 54 is an example of an error whose cause probably is an exaggerated use of the preposition of as an appositive indicator, linking a geographical common noun with the proper noun. Sentence 5 and sentence 68 served as B-control sentences.

Sentence 54 is a multi-error sentence, as it contains two errors, which is very often the case with English sentences produced by foreigners. The other error is that the common noun is not preceded by the proper noun, which, according to some grammar books, is the normal word order with the names of most non-European rivers (the preposition of is then obliterated). Alternatively, the common noun and the appositive indicator can be omitted and the proper noun be used alone, preceded by the definite article.

When the common noun precedes the proper noun, as it does in sentence 54, it may have either an upper-case or a lower-case initial. If an upper-case initial had been used in this sentence, this might have influenced the informants to think of the correct usage where the common noun is preceded by the proper noun (which usually means that the common noun has an upper-case initial). A lower-case initial was used, however, as this was used in the original sentence produced by a foreign learner of English, making sentence 54 an authentic one.

Total sample

Sentence no.	Foreignness			Intelligibility difficulty		
	Mean	SD	Mode	Mean	SD	Mode
5	4.05	1.05	5	2.69	1.37	1
50	3.89	1.11	4	2.21	1.16	1
54	3.13	1.29	4	1.61	.97	1
60	3.83	1.37	5	2.14	1.19	1
68	4.09	.95	4	2.93	1.37	2,4*

Significance
(PCT): 5-68:   -   -

* There are two modes for this question.

The two B-control sentences made the strongest foreign impression on the informants and were also found to be the two most difficult sentences to understand out of these five sentences. The means indicate that they made a strong foreign impression and were judged to be rather difficult to understand. This was expected, as the error involved in both these sentences can make the meaning ambiguous. The differences between the means for the B-control sentences are very small and neither of the differences is statistically significant, which is a good indication of the reliability of the informants.

Sentence 50 and sentence 60 also have very similar means. They made a rather strong foreign impression and the errors caused some intelligibility difficulty.

The means for sentence 54 are very significantly different from the means of the other four sentences. In spite of the fact that this sentence was the only multi-error sentence out of the five sentences, it apparently made a much less foreign impression on the informants and was also judged to be considerably easier to understand. However, the results of the control form show that hardly any of the informants indicated that they were aware of the fact that the name of a non-European river, according to some grammar books, should precede and not follow the common noun river. It also turns out that the informants who indicated that they wanted to delete only the preposition outnumbered those who indicated that they wanted to delete both the preposition and the common noun. This makes the results even more interesting, as they indicate that the word-order error in sentence 54 is a minor one, the importance of which can be seriously questioned. The error which is mainly responsible for the rather mild negative reactions to sentence 54 thus seems to be the insertion of the preposition of and not the word-order error.

Age differences

Sentence no.		Teen-agers		Adults		Pensioners		Significance T-A	A-P	T-P
		Mean	SD	Mean	SD	Mean	SD			
F	5	4.23	.78	4.00	1.10	3.75	1.45	-	-	-
	50	4.07	.90	3.73	1.15	3.81	1.52	-	-	-
	54	2.64	1.26	3.48	1.02	3.67	1.54	E	-	B
	60	3.66	1.48	4.09	1.05	3.56	1.76	-	-	-
	68	4.05	.75	4.21	.86	3.95	1.51	-	-	-
ID	5	3.12	1.18	2.65	1.43	1.94	1.39	-	-	E
	50	2.66	1.01	1.93	1.18	1.81	1.22	D	-	C
	54	1.75	.99	1.41	.76	1.82	1.33	-	-	-
	60	2.59	1.30	1.90	.96	1.58	1.07	C	-	D
	68	3.30	1.13	2.88	1.45	2.32	1.49	-	-	C

The means indicate that the teen-agers found sentence 54 much less foreign than did the other two age groups. These differences are statistically significant and may indicate that the teen-agers themselves possibly make use of constructions like the one in sentence 54 more often than the other two age groups do. This is further indicated by the fact that this sentence is the only one of the five sentences which the teen-agers did not judge to be significantly more difficult to understand than one or both of the other age groups did.

For four of the five sentences there are statistically significant differences between the means of the teen-agers and one or both of the other age groups for the question on intelligibility difficulty. These differences show that the teen-agers judged these four sentences to be considerably more difficult to understand than did either one or both of the other age groups. The differences are especially pronounced for sentences 5, 60 and 68. Sentence 54, however, is an exception in this respect (cf. above).

Sex differences

Sentence no.		Females		Males		Significance
		Mean	SD	Mean	SD	
F	5	3.94	1.14	4.22	.88	-
	50	3.92	1.10	3.83	1.14	-
	54	3.08	1.36	3.22	1.19	-
	60	3.79	1.39	3.90	1.36	-
	68	4.04	1.02	4.17	.82	-
ID	5	2.67	1.48	2.73	1.18	-
	50	2.12	1.14	2.34	1.20	-
	54	1.61	1.06	1.61	.80	-
	60	2.15	1.22	2.12	1.15	-
	68	2.93	1.35	2.93	1.40	-

The differences between the means of the female and the male informants are very small and for two of the sentences their means are identical for the question on intelligibility difficulty.

10.3 Omission of preposition

Sentence 27 (49) ("This room smells food, doesn't it?"), sentence 42 (34) ("I was operated last week"), and sentence 71 (5) ("We have just come back from the island Rhodes") tested reactions to omission of the prepositions of and on. When this error is made by Swedish users of English, the cause is often interference from Swedish, where no prepositions are used in such sentences.

Total sample

Sentence no.	Foreignness			Intelligibility difficulty		
	Mean	SD	Mode	Mean	SD	Mode
27	4.26	.99	5	2.61	1.29	3
42	4.05	1.08	5	2.89	1.33	2,3*
71	2.64	1.30	2	1.35	.71	1

Significance
(PCT) 27-42:   -   -
       42-71:   I   I
       27-71:   I   I

* There are two modes for this question.

Compared with most of the sentences which tested the opposite case, viz. insertion of a preposition, these sentences made a stronger foreign impression on the informants and were judged to be somewhat more difficult to understand, which shows the importance in meaning carried by the prepositions in the phrases exemplified by these sentences, the one exception being sentence 71.

Sentence 27 made a strong foreign impression on the informants and the error gave rise to considerable intelligibility difficulty. This is understandable, as the omission of the preposition of in this sentence makes the sentence violate either a grammatical rule, which says that the preposition of is to be used between the verb smell and an object when the verb has the sense 'give out a smell', or the semantic rule which says that a non-animate subject cannot smell something, depending upon how the sentence is interpreted. This sentence is therefore likely to make a very awkward impression on most native users of English. As this sentence can be interpreted in two ways it is still another example of an ambiguous sentence. Such sentences seem to be very common in the English produced by many foreigners.

Sentence 42 is also an example of an ambiguous sentence. The interpretation which presupposes that the sentence is a grammatical one may seem less plausible than the other one, which presupposes that the sentence is ungrammatical. The results of the control form corroborate this, as virtually all the informants interpreted the sentence in the following way: I <u>was</u> <u>operated</u> <u>on</u> <u>last</u> <u>week</u>. The less plausible interpretation, I <u>was</u> <u>put</u> <u>to</u> <u>work</u> <u>last</u> <u>week</u>, which could be the one intended if the sentence were produced by, for instance, a foreign agent or a private investigator, was thus largely rejected in favour of the more plausible one.

The means for sentence 71 differ very significantly from the means of the other two sentences. This sentence apparently made a much less foreign impression on the informants and the error seems to have caused virtually no intelligibility difficulty at all. It turns out, however, that the use of <u>Rhodes</u> as a place name was not very good, as some informants were not sure what this word referred to and some even misinterpreted it altogether, as they thought that it referred to Rhode Island, i.e. the smallest state in the United States, rather than to the Greek island (which, in fact, is visited by many people from Great Britain). This misinterpretation was discovered thanks to the use of the control form, where the informants were asked to correct the sentences, thereby revealing how they interpreted them (cf. 1.1).

The fact that sentence 71 was misinterpreted by some of the informants does, in fact, mean that it contains 'covert' intelligibility difficulty, contrary to the low mean for this question. The direct cause of this difficulty was not the fact that the sentence is ungrammatical, but rather ignorance on the part of some of the informants. However, as the informants had no way of knowing for sure exactly what constituted the error in the sentence, some informants may incorrectly have assumed that the error consisted in the use of <u>the</u> <u>island</u> <u>Rhodes</u> instead of <u>Rhode</u> <u>Island</u>. If this is taken into consideration, the sentence can thus have an ambiguous <u>effect</u>. However, unlike the other two sentences, this one is not inherently ambiguous, which is probably one reason for the low means for the question on intelligibility difficulty. The foreigner who used this sentence was, in fact, referring to the island with the name of <u>Rhodes</u>.

Of the three sentences with omitted prepositions two are thus inherently ambiguous, albeit the competing alternative interpretations may seem implausible, and one is not. The differences between the means of the first two sentences and the mean of sentence 71 for the question on intelligibility difficulty seem to reflect this fact very well. The two inherently ambiguous sentences are more likely to have been experienced as ambiguous by the informants than sentence 71, the ambiguous effect of which was probably concealed from the informants as they themselves were the direct cause of this ambiguous effect.

Age differences

Sentence no.		Teen-agers		Adults		Pensioners		Significance T-A	A-P	T-P
		Mean	SD	Mean	SD	Mean	SD			
F	27	4.63	.62	3.98	1.11	4.11	1.20	E	-	-
	42	4.27	.69	3.95	1.11	3.81	1.64	-	-	-
	71	2.18	1.13	3.00	1.13	2.76	1.79	E	-	-
ID	27	3.45	1.11	2.10	1.07	1.94	1.20	I	-	I
	42	3.34	1.12	2.69	1.37	2.24	1.48	B	-	E
	71	1.41	.82	1.30	.64	1.21	.54	-	-	-

The means indicate that sentence 27 made a considerably stronger foreign impression on the teen-agers than on the adults and that the teen-agers also judged this sentence to be much more difficult to understand than did either of the other age groups. These differences are statistically highly significant. The teen-agers' mean for the foreignness of this sentence is extremely high, and their mean for the intelligibility difficulty of this sentence is also very high compared to the means for this question for most of the other 74 test sentences. In fact, this sentence made the strongest foreign impression on the teen-agers of all the 75 test sentences in the questionnaires and it was found to be the third most difficult to understand. The differences between their mean and the means of the other two groups of informants for the question on intelligibility difficulty are quite remarkable as they are very great.

Sentence 42 was also judged to be more difficult to understand by the teen-agers than by the other two age groups. However, the differences between the means for intelligibility difficulty are not as great for this sentence as they are for sentence 27.

Perhaps the most interesting result is in the reactions to sentence 71. This sentence apparently made a much less foreign impression on the teen-agers than on the adults. This difference is highly significant. The difference between the means of the teen-agers and the pensioners for the question on foreignness indicates that the teen-agers also found this sentence considerably less foreign than the pensioners did, but this difference is not statistically significant. This may indicate that the teen-agers find omission of the preposition of in such appositive phrases more acceptable than at least the adults do and possibly therefore themselves omit this preposition in such sentences more often than the adults, and possibly also the pensioners, do. The very fact that this sentence was the only one of the three with omitted prepositions which was not judged to be significantly more difficult to understand by the teen-agers than by the other two age groups further indicates that this may be the case. If this is really so, and if the teen-agers continue to omit this preposition in such sentences as they grow older, we may expect a general change in usage in this respect. Such a change has, in fact, already taken place in the case of the common noun river, which is normally not linked by the preposition of with a following proper noun. It does not seem very unlikely therefore that an analogous change in usage may come with the common noun island, particularly in view of the fact that the appositive indicator (of) is no more semantically required with this common noun than it is with the common noun river. However, it was also found above (10.2) that the teen-agers were more favourable than the other age groups towards the use of the appositive indicator as a link between river and the proper noun. These disparate findings may also indicate that the teen-agers are less consistent in their use of appositive indicators than the other age groups.

Sex differences

Sentence no.		Females		Males		Significance
		Mean	SD	Mean	SD	
F	27	4.28	1.08	4.22	.82	-
	42	4:09	1.16	3.98	.95	-
	71	2.62	1.33	2.69	1.26	-
ID	27	2.75	1.33	2.38	1.21	-
	42	2.82	1.36	3.00	1.30	-
	71	1.34	.73	1.36	.69	-

The means of the female and the male informants are very similar for both questions for these sentences. The largest difference between the means of the two sexes is found for the question on the intelligibility difficulty of sentence 27. However, none of the differences is statistically significant.

10.4 Summary

Of the eleven sentences testing reactions to prepositional errors, the one which made the strongest foreign impression on the informants was sentence 27, exemplifying omission of the preposition of after the verb smell in a sentence with an inanimate subject. This sentence also had a rather high mean for the question on intelligibility difficulty. The sentence which was found to be the most difficult to understand exemplified insertion of the preposition for in a sentence with ago. Two B-control sentences were used to test this, and the means for these sentences were found to be very similar, which is a good indication of the reliability of the informants. The reason for the high means for these three sentences may very well be that the errors exemplified by them can make the sentences ambiguous.

The sentence which made the least foreign impression on the informants was also judged to be the easiest to understand. It was an example of omission of the preposition of as an appositive indicator, linking the common noun island with the proper noun.

Compared to the sentences exemplifying the common error of omitting the prepositions of and on, the sentences exemplifying the common error of inserting the same prepositions made a less foreign impression on the informants and were found to be easier to understand. The reason for this is probably that the insertion of these prepositions did not make the sentences ambiguous as easily as the omission of the same prepositions in the three sentences discussed above.

Of the sentences exemplifying incorrect choice of prepositions, the most difficult to understand was the sentence where in was used instead of on to indicate location on a surface. This error was tested in two different sentences, which also served the purpose of being B-control sentences. The most difficult to understand of these sentences was the one where the surface referred to (steps) was most likely to be located outdoors. However, the differences between the means of the two sentences are small and statistically significant only for the question on intelligibility difficulty, which is a good indication of the reliability of the informants.

The overall results thus show that improper use of prepositions in these sentences most often made a rather strong foreign impression on the informants, caused some intelligibility difficulty, and could sometimes also give rise to ambiguity. Prepositions therefore merit an important place in grammar books, in language exercises, and in the teaching of English in general.

Significant age differences were found for nine of the eleven sentences exemplifying prepositional errors. Seven sentences were judged to be more difficult to understand by the teen-agers than by either one or both of the other age groups and there is no significant difference where the reverse is true. Two sentences made a less foreign impression on the teen-agers than on either one or both of the other age groups and one sentence made a stronger foreign impression on the teen-agers than on the other age groups. In two cases indications were found that the teen-agers possibly have a slightly different usage than the older informants, as they were altogether more favourable towards insertion of _of_ as an appositive indicator between _river_ and the proper noun, and they were also altogether more favourable towards omission of the same appositive indicator between _island_ and the proper noun. These disparate findings may indicate that the teen-agers are less consistent in their use of appositive indicators than are the other two age groups. If either of these possible usage differences will lead to a general usage change, it seems likely that the appositive indicator will eventually be omitted between _island_ and the proper noun, as an analogous change has already taken place with the appostive indicator in the case of _river_ and as the appositive indicator is no more semantically required with the former common noun than with the latter.

No statistically significant differences were found between the means of the female and the male informants for any of the eleven test sentences.

11. IMPROPER USE OF SUBJECTS

Sentence 24 (52) ("It was little else to do") and sentence 57
(19) ("There's a long time since I saw her") tested reactions to
incorrect choice between the prop subject it and the existential
subject there. Many Swedes often use the wrong English equivalent
of the Swedish det, which corresponds to both it and there. In
particular there seems to be a tendency to exaggerate the use of
it at the cost of there, as in sentence 24.

Total sample

Sentence no.	Foreignness			Intelligibility difficulty		
	Mean	SD	Mode	Mean	SD	Mode
24	3.65	1.15	4	2.47	1.24	2
57	3.91	1.05	4	2.07	1.01	1

Significance
(PCT):   -   E

The statistics indicate that both these sentences made a rather
strong foreign impression on the informants and that sentence 24
was judged to be somewhat more difficult to understand than
sentence 57. This difference is statistically highly significant
and particularly worth noticing for Swedish learners of English,
as the error in sentence 24 seems to be more frequent in the
English produced by Swedes than the error in sentence 57.

Age differences

Sentence no.	Teen-agers		Adults		Pensioners		Significance		
							T-A	A-P	T-P
	Mean	SD	Mean	SD	Mean	SD			
F	24	3.49	1.14	3.73	1.11	3.75	1.33	-	-	-
	57	4.02	.85	3.80	1.02	3.89	1.52	-	-	-
ID	24	2.79	1.21	2.38	1.23	2.00	1.24	-	-	B
	57	2.39	.97	1.95	.92	1.63	1.12	A	-	C

The means for the question on foreignness are fairly similar over the various age groups. The means for the question on intelligibility difficulty, however, vary considerably and three of the differences between the means are statistically significant. These differences indicate that the teen-agers found sentence 24 a great deal more difficult to understand than did the pensioners, and that the teen-agers found sentence 57 more difficult to understand than did either of the other age groups.

Sex differences

Sentence no.		Females		Males		Significance
		Mean	SD	Mean	SD	
F	24	3.65	1.17	3.63	1.11	-
	57	3.91	1.13	3.90	.93	-
ID	24	2.40	1.21	2.59	1.28	-
	57	1.99	1.04	2.21	.95	-

The means of the female and the male informants are very similar for these two sentences and none of the differences between the means is statistically significant.

12. IMPROPER USE OF QUANTITATIVE NOUN

Sentence 23 (53) ("He had to pay five hundreds of pounds") tested reactions to the use of the s-plural of the quantitative noun hundred when this was premodified by the numeral five and followed by an of-construction. The quantitative noun hundred, like thousand and usually million, normally have zero plurals when premodified by numerals.

Total sample

Sentence no.	Foreignness			Intelligibility difficulty		
	Mean	SD	Mode	Mean	SD	Mode
23	3.77	1.17	4	1.75	.95	1

The means indicate that this sentence made a rather strong foreign impression on the informants but that it was judged to be fairly easy to understand. The reason for the rather low mean for intelligibility difficulty is probably that the error in sentence 23 cannot very well give rise to any competing interpretations of the sentence with any reasonable degree of plausibility.

Age differences

Sentence no.	Teen-agers		Adults		Pensioners		Significance		
							T-A	A-P	T-P
	Mean	SD	Mean	SD	Mean	SD			
F	23	4.00	1.02	3.60	1.16	3.63	1.54	-	-	-
ID	23	1.98	.99	1.60	.86	1.58	1.07	-	-	-

The means of the adults and the pensioners are almost identical for both questions, whereas the means of the teen-agers are considerably higher for both questions. However, these differences are not statistically significant but consistent with the findings for the questions on most of the other test sentences in the questionnaires.

Sex differences

Sentence no.		Females		Males		Significance
		Mean	SD	Mean	SD	
F	23	3.66	1.25	3.95	1.02	-
ID	23	1.77	1.00	1.71	.87	-

The means of the female and the male informants are very similar, particularly for the question on intelligibility difficulty, and neither difference between the means is statistically significant.

13. IMPROPER WORD ORDER

Sentence 20 (56) ("He told me to not worry") and sentence 73 (3) ("When I five years ago visited London, I didn't realize how big it was") tested reactions to improper word order, viz. the use of the SPLIT INFINITIVE[19] where there exists a satisfactory alternative ordering[20], and the placing of an adverbial clause of time between the subject and the verb in the subordinate clause rather than in initial or final position in the subordinate clause.

Total sample

Sentence no.	Foreignness			Intelligibility difficulty		
	Mean	SD	Mode	Mean	SD	Mode
20	2.29	1.33	1	1.35	.64	1
73	3.59	1.19	4	1.84	.98	1

Significance
(PCT):   I   I

The differences between the means for these two sentences are statistically highly significant. The differences indicate that the sentence with a split infinitive made a much less foreign impression on the informants and was considerably easier to understand than the sentence with the improper placing of the adverbial clause of time. The former sentence did not make a very foreign impression on the informants and it was judged to be easy or very easy to understand, whereas the latter sentence made a rather strong foreign impression on the informants and was only found to be reasonably easy to understand.

These results are interesting and reflect the fact that the split infinitive is sometimes also used by many native users of English. Teaching foreign learners of English how to avoid the split infinitive seems justified in many cases, particularly at higher levels of language learning, but it does not seem to be very important from a mere intelligibility point of view. The fact that many native users of English also sometimes use the split infinitive means that this use does not in itself make the foreigner appear very foreign in his use of English. For the same reason, a sentence with a split infinitive cannot usually be very difficult to understand for native users of English, provided that the sentence is not deviant in some other respects as well.

Age differences

Sentence no.		Teen-agers		Adults		Pensioners		Significance T-A	A-P	T-P
		Mean	SD	Mean	SD	Mean	SD			
F	20	2.38	1.36	2.26	1.20	2.22	1.59	-	-	-
	73	3.41	1.21	3.79	.99	3.58	1.57	-	-	-
ID	20	1.40	.59	1.31	.52	1.35	1.00	-	-	-
	73	2.32	1.16	1.60	.69	1.28	.57	F	-	I

The most striking difference between the means of the age groups is found for the question on the intelligibility difficulty of sentence 73. The teen-agers apparently found this sentence a great deal more difficult to understand than did the adults and much more difficult to understansd than did the pensioners. These differences are statistically highly significant.

It should be noted that the teen-agers did not judge sentence 20 to be significantly more difficult to understand than the other age groups did, unlike most of the other test sentences in the questionnaires.

Sex differences

Sentence no.		Females		Males		Significance
		Mean	SD	Mean	SD	
F	20	2.17	1.30	2.50	1.38	-
	73	3.63	1.18	3.52	1.21	-
ID	20	1.31	.69	1.40	.55	-
	73	1.65	.89	2.14	1.05	B

The means of the female and the male informants are fairly similar for both questions as regards these sentences, with the exception of the question on the intelligibility difficulty of sentence 73. This sentence was judged to be a great deal easier to understand by the female informants than by the male informants. This difference is statistically significant and may seem rather surprising in view of the fact that the means of the two sexes hardly differ at all for the question on the foreign impression made by this sentence.

Age and sex differences (broken down table)

Sentence no.	Teen-agers Females Mean	SD	Males Mean	SD	Sign	Adults Females Mean	SD	Males Mean	SD	Sign
F 20	2.22	1.28	2.67	1.50	-	2.24	1.14	2.27	1.28	-
73	3.67	1.11	3.00	1.27	-	3.67	.97	3.91	1.02	-
ID 20	1.33	.55	1.53	.64	-	1.30	.57	1.32	.48	-
73	2.04	1.09	2.76	1.15	A	1.38	.59	1.82	.73	A

	Pensioners Females Mean	SD	Males Mean	SD	Sign	Male teen-agers Mean	SD	Others Mean	SD	Sign
F 20	2.00	1.56	3.33	1.53	-	2.67	1.50	2.23	1.30	-
73	3.56	1.63	3.67	1.53	-	3.00	1.27	3.70	1.15	A
ID 20	1.36	1.08	1.33	.58	-	1.53	.64	1.31	.63	-
73	1.33	.62	1.00	0	-	2.76	1.15	1.67	.84	I

A further breakdown of the statistics reveals that it was the male teen-agers in particular that found sentence 73 difficult to understand. The difference between their mean and the mean of the other informants taken together is statistically highly

significant for the question on intelligibility difficulty. The
table also shows that the difference between the means within the
group of teen-agers is statistically significant for this
question, indicating that the female teen-agers found sentence 73
a great deal easier to understand than did the male teen-agers.
Another statistical significance for the question on
intelligibility difficulty indicates that the female adults found
sentence 73 considerably easier to understand than did the male
adults. The mean of the female informants is very low for this
question.

With the exception of the male pensioners, these results may
indicate that the male informants, and the male teen-agers in
particular, find it more difficult to understand sentences where
an adverbial clause of time is placed between the subject and the
verb in a subordinate clause than do the female informants.

The fact that the male teen-agers found sentence 73 significantly
less foreign than did the other informants taken together may seem
contradictory in view of what was found about the means for the
intelligibility difficulty of this sentence. However, the male
teen-agers may have found sentence 73 to be an example of bad and
not very intelligible English without necessarily associating it,
to a very high degree, with the English of foreigners.

14. MULTIPLE NEGATION

Sentence 67 (9) ("I didn't buy nothing at the supermarket") tested reactions to the use of MULTIPLE NEGATION or NEGATIVE CONCORD, that is where two or more negatives are used but the meaning is that of a single negative, a phenomenon which is quite common also among large groups of native users of English[21]. It is, in fact, used in most non-standard English dialects[22]. This pleonastic use of negatives, which is thus not limited to two negatives only[23], can therefore just as well be associated with a native as with a foreign user of English. Consequently, it was expected that this sentence would not make a very strong foreign impression on the informants.

Total sample

Sentence no.	Foreignness			Intelligibility difficulty		
	Mean	SD	Mode	Mean	SD	Mode
67	2.56	1.28	2	1.63	.99	1

The mean and the mode for the question on foreign impression turned out to be fairly low compared to these statistics where most of the other 74 test sentences are concerned. This is probably due to what has been said above. The above assumption was thus borne out by the experiment.

The mean for the question on intelligibility difficulty is also rather low, which seems to reflect quite well the fact that this type of error is too often met with to cause any real intelligibility difficulty, in spite of the fact that this type of sentence is illogical in its most commonly intended sense.

Age differences

Sentence no.		Teen-agers		Adults		Pensioners		Significance T-A A-P T-P		
		Mean	SD	Mean	SD	Mean	SD			
F	67	2.41	1.13	2.47	1.22	3.11	1.66	-	-	-
ID	67	1.89	1.06	1.47	.88	1.39	1.04	A	-	-

The statistics show that the difference between the means of the teen-agers and the adults for the question on intelligibility difficulty is statistically significant. This difference indicates that the teen-agers judged sentence 67 to be slightly more difficult to understand than did the adults.

This sentence seems to have made a stronger foreign impression on the pensioners than on the other two age groups. However, the differences between the means of the pensioners and the other age groups are not statistically significant, owing to the large standard deviation in the group of pensioners.

Sex differences

Sentence no.		Females		Males		Significance
		Mean	SD	Mean	SD	
F	67	2.69	1.33	2.36	1.19	-
ID	67	1.74	1.13	1.45	.71	-

Neither difference between the means of the female and the male informants is statistically significant but it seems that the female informants are more critical of the use of multiple negation than are the male informants, as their means are higher for both questions.

15. IMPROPER USE OF CERTAIN IDIOMATIC PHRASES

Sentence 19 (57) ("I shouted to him to look up for the car when I saw that it was going to hit him") and sentence 41 (35) ("Excuse me, what is the clock, please?") tested reactions to improper use of the idiomatic phrasal-prepositional verb look out for and the idiomatic phrase what is the time, respectively. These errors are sometimes made by Swedish users of English, as a result of interference from Swedish.

Total sample

Sentence no.	Foreignness			Intelligibility difficulty		
	Mean	SD	Mode	Mean	SD	Mode
19	3.38	1.32	4	2.25	1.25	1
41	4.50	.85	5	2.42	1.28	1

Significance
(PCT):   I

The statistics indicate that sentence 41 made a very strong foreign impression on the informants and a much stronger foreign impression than sentence 19. This difference is statistically highly significant. It also seems that sentence 41 was slightly more difficult to understand than sentence 19, but this difference is not statistically significant. Sentence 41 did, in fact, make the second strongest foreign impression on the informants of all the 75 test sentences included in the questionnaires. As far as intelligibility difficulty is concerned, however, it was found to be only the 13th most difficult sentence to understand (cf. Appendix 1.1).

The reason for the large difference between the means of the two sentences for the question on foreign impression may be that the error in sentence 41 consists in an incorrect choice of nouns

(clock instead of time), whereas the error in sentence 19 consists
in an incorrect choice of verb particles (up instead of out), with
less lexical meaning than nouns. The fact that, in sentence 41, a
noun from the semantic class of concrete nouns has been chosen
instead of a noun from the semantic class of abstract nouns may
also have a bearing on the results. It seems less likely that a
native user of English should make a semantic error like the one
in sentence 41 than that he should happen to use the wrong verb
particle. Sentence 41 may have struck the informants as more
foreign for this reason.

On the other hand, the error in sentence 41 does not seem to have
caused as much intelligibility difficulty as might have been
expected in view of the strong foreign impression it caused. This
probably has to do with the fact that clock is semantically
related to time, even though the former noun is concrete and the
latter abstract.

Age differences

Sentence no.		Teen-agers		Adults		Pensioners		Significance T-A	A-P	T-P
		Mean	SD	Mean	SD	Mean	SD			
F	19	3.07	1.42	3.32	1.09	4.15	1.39	-	B	C
	41	4.53	.74	4.59	.66	4.24	1.44	-	-	-
ID	19	2.50	1.31	1.86	.89	2.67	1.61	B	-	-
	41	2.63	1.22	2.37	1.25	2.06	1.57	-	-	-

As can be seen from the table above, statistically significant
differences between the means of the age groups were found only
for sentence 19. These differences indicate that the pensioners
found sentence 19 a great deal more foreign than did the other two
age groups and that the adults found this sentence a great deal
easier to understand than did the teen-agers and possibly also the
pensioners, although the latter difference is not statistically
significant.

Sex differences

Sentence no.		Females		Males		Significance
		Mean	SD	Mean	SD	
F	19	3.43	1.37	3.28	1.26	-
	41	4.53	.89	4.45	.78	-
ID	19	2.32	1.34	2.13	1.09	-
	41	2.31	1.30	2.60	1.26	-

The differences between the means of the female and the male informants are very small for both questions where these sentences are concerned.

16. VOCABULARY ERRORS

Sentence 12 (64) ("I always tried to make my best at school"), sentence 21 (55) ("The car was badly injured in the accident"), sentence 28 (48) ("Who learnt you Spanish?"), sentence 43 (33) ("Yesterday's accident depended on the bad weather"), and sentence 75 (1) ("You do good coffee!") tested reactions to incorrect choice of verbs, viz. <u>make</u> instead of <u>do</u>, <u>injured</u> instead of <u>damaged</u>, <u>learnt</u> instead of <u>taught</u>, <u>depended</u> <u>on</u> instead of <u>was</u> <u>due</u> <u>to</u> (or <u>was</u> <u>caused</u> <u>by</u>), and <u>do</u> instead of <u>make</u>, respectively. These incorrect choices of verbs are fairly frequent in the English of many foreigners. In order not to make the questionnaires too long, the number of sentences testing each error type had to be limited, and in this case it was decided that the vocabulary errors to be tested should be limited to these commonly confused verbs.

Total sample

Sentence no.	Foreignness			Intelligibility difficulty		
	Mean	SD	Mode	Mean	SD	Mode
12	3.70	1.05	4	2.04	1.00	2
21	3.64	1.33	5	1.89	1.15	1
28	3.50	1.42	5	1.85	.96	1
43	3.61	1.20	5	2.65	1.27	3
75	3.09	1.28	2,4*	1.48	.78	1

Significance
(PCT): The differences between the means for sentence 75 and all the other sentences are the only ones that are statistically significant for the question on foreignness. For the question on intelligibility difficulty, all the differences between the means are statistically significant, with the exception of the differences between the means for sentences 12 and 21, 21 and 28, and 12 and 28.

* There are two modes for this question.

The table shows that four of these five sentences made a rather strong foreign impression on the informants, and thus were judged in a rather similar way where this question is concerned. The only exception is sentence 75, which made a considerably less foreign impression on the informants than any of the other four sentences. This sentence was also judged to be the easiest to understand of the five sentences. These differences are statistically significant. The reason for the lower means for sentence 75 is probably that this sentence is perfectly grammatical if it refers to a paying situation. In such cases the verb do is often preferred (e.g. We do good coffee, i.e. for a living), whereas the verb make seems to be the more common verb in non-paying situations (e.g. We make good coffee, i.e. have a habit of doing so). However, the way sentence 75 is written (indicating that somebody is telling somebody else something in the form of an exclamation) probably makes the paying interpretation seem less plausible. It is probably for this reason that sentence 75 got as high means as it did.

Sentence 43 was judged to be the most difficult to understand of the five sentences. It thus seems particularly important to make clear to learners of English that due to and owing to have the sense of causality, whereas depend on does not.

Sentence 28 is an example of a usage which is found in nearly all non-standard English dialects. In view of this, the mean for foreignness may seem high. However, this may perhaps also be taken as an indication of the fact that most of the informants use Standard British English rather than non-standard English (cf. 1.3).

Age differences

Sentence no.		Teen-agers		Adults		Pensioners		Significance T-A A-P T-P		
		Mean	SD	Mean	SD	Mean	SD			
F	12	3.79	.94	3.61	1.04	3.67	1.41	-	-	-
	21	3.57	1.33	3.70	1.12	3.68	1.70	-	-	-
	28	3.81	1.35	3.09	1.33	3.82	1.55	B	-	-
	43	3.73	.95	3.67	1.21	3.16	1.68	-	-	-
	75	2.84	1.16	3.00	1.20	3.84	1.54	-	B	C
ID	12	2.40	.93	1.90	.96	1.53	1.07	B	-	D
	21	2.10	1.28	1.79	1.01	1.71	1.21	-	-	-
	28	1.98	.89	1.77	.95	1.78	1.17	-	-	-
	43	3.14	1.09	2.56	1.28	1.72	1.18	A	B	I
	75	1.61	.69	1.26	.45	1.60	1.27	C	-	-

It can be seen from the table above that there are nine significant differences between the means of the age groups. As for the question on foreignness, these differences indicate that sentence 28 made a considerably stronger foreign impression on the teen-agers than on the adults and that sentence 75 made a much stronger foreign impression on the pensioners than on the other two age groups. As for sentence 28, this result may be due to the fact that the teen-agers were going to school, in which Standard British English is enforced as the norm, and therefore found the non-standard use of learn for teach more unnatural and foreign. On the other hand, influence from the standard language has been shown to be relatively weak where younger speakers are concerned (cf. Chambers-Trudgill 1980:92), which seems to contradict this assumption. However, the teen-agers did not judge the intelligibility difficulty of this sentence significantly differently than did either of the other age groups, which may reflect the fact that this usage is too often met with in non-standard dialects to cause any serious intelligibility difficulty for any of the three age groups. As for sentence 75, the result may perhaps indicate that the younger informants use do instead of make with reference to non-paying situations more often than the pensioners do so. However, the teen-agers found this sentence slightly more difficult to understand than did the adults, which makes this result less conclusive.

As for the question on intelligibility difficulty, the significant differences between the means indicate that the teen-agers found sentence 12 more difficult to understand than did either of the other age groups, that sentence 43 was more easily understood by the older informants and that sentence 75 was judged to be somewhat more difficult to understand by the teen-agers than by the adults. The difference between the means of the teen-agers and the pensioners for sentence 43 is quite remarkable, being so large. The pensioners apparently found this sentence quite easy to understand, whereas the teen-agers found it difficult to understand. Compared with the teen-agers and the adults, the pensioners also have a considerably lower mean for the foreignness of this sentence, but these differences are not statistically significant.

Sex differences

Sentence no.		Females		Males		Significance
		Mean	SD	Mean	SD	
F	12	3.67	1.09	3.76	1.00	-
	21	3.55	1.37	3.78	1.25	-
	28	3.58	1.46	3.39	1.36	-
	43	3.61	1.31	3.62	1.01	-
	75	3.15	1.30	3.00	1.27	-
ID	12	1.98	1.03	2.12	.95	-
	21	1.82	1.16	2.00	1.15	-
	28	1.85	1.00	1.85	.91	-
	43	2.73	1.28	2.52	1.25	-
	75	1.51	.88	1.43	.59	-

Here too, the female and the male informants seem to have very similar opinions, as the differences between the means of the two sexes are so small that none of them are statistically significant.

17. A-CONTROL SENTENCES

The following five sentences served the purpose of being A-control sentences (cf. 1.2.1): no. 11 (65) ("He has lived in London all his life"), no. 25 (51) ("She prefers walking to cycling"), no. 36 (40) ("They were badly shaken by the news"), no. 49 (27) ("Why did he leave so early?"), and no. 65 (11) ("Have you heard from him lately?").

Total sample

Sentence no.	Foreignness			Intelligibility difficulty		
	Mean	SD	Mode	Mean	SD	Mode
11	1.13	.49	1	1.04	.19	1
25	1.02	.14	1	1.01	.10	1
36	1.03	.17	1	1.00	0	1
49	1.02	.14	1	1.00	0	1
65	1.07	.42	1	1.00	0	1

The results very clearly show that these five sentences were perceived very differently from all the other sentences, both where foreign impression and intelligibility difficulty are concerned. The means, the modes, and the standard deviations show that nearly all the informants regarded these five sentences as native-like and very easy to understand. These sentences were thus recognized as perfectly normal English sentences, which is a good indication of the reliability of the informants whose answers were included in the statistical analysis.

Sentence 11 has the highest means for both questions, which may indicate that some informants in their search for errors regarded the word has as superfluous or incorrect, perhaps because they thought that the sentence referred to a person who was dead. The results of the control form corroborate these assumptions. As no information was given as to whether or not the person referred to was still alive, this is understandable. The slightly higher means for this sentence should therefore be attributed to the fact that

no such information was given rather than to any objections to the
form of the sentence when it refers to a person who is alive. It
may be, however, that the contracted form He's seemed more natural
to some informants than He has.

It should be remembered that informants who did not indicate the
lowest value for both questions for at least four of the five A-
control sentences had all their answers excluded from the
statistical analysis of the 75 test sentences, as these informants
obviously were not attentive enough or were unreliable in some
other way when they answered the questions in their questionnaires
(cf. 1.2.1 above). However, there were not very many informants
like that, for which reason the means for these five sentences
would have been only slightly higher had the answers from these
informants also been included in the statistical analysis.

Age differences

Sentence no.		Teen-agers		Adults		Pensioners		Significance T-A A-P T-P		
		Mean	SD	Mean	SD	Mean	SD			
F	11	1.21	.67	1.09	.37	1.05	.23	-	-	-
	25	1.05	.21	1.00	0	1.00	0	-	-	-
	36	1.02	.15	1.05	.22	1.00	0	-	-	-
	49	1.00	0	1.02	.15	1.06	.24	-	-	-
	65	1.05	.21	1.02	.15	1.22	.94	-	-	-
ID	11	1.07	.26	1.02	.15	1.00	0	-	-	-
	25	1.02	.15	1.00	0	1.00	0	-	-	-
	36	1.00	0	1.00	0	1.00	0	-	-	-
	49	1.00	0	1.00	0	1.00	0	-	-	-
	65	1.00	0	1.00	0	1.00	0	-	-	-

There are no statistically significant differences between the
means of the various age groups for any of the five A-control
sentences, which is a further indication of the good standard of
reliability of the informants whose answers were included in the
statistical analysis.

Sex differences

Sentence no.		Females		Males		Significance
		Mean	SD	Mean	SD	
F	11	1.10	.43	1.17	.59	-
	25	1.01	.12	1.02	.16	-
	36	1.03	.18	1.03	.16	-
	49	1.00	0	1.05	.22	-
	65	1.09	.52	1.02	.15	-
ID	11	1.03	.17	1.05	.22	-
	25	1.00	0	1.02	.16	-
	36	1.00	0	1.00	0	-
	49	1.00	0	1.00	0	-
	65	1.00	0	1.00	0	-

There are no statistically significant differences between the means of the female and the male informants for any of the five A-control sentences, which, in this case, is still another indication of the good standard of reliability of the informants whose answers were included in the statistical analysis.

18. AVERAGE OF THE MEANS

The averages of the means of the answers to the questions on the foreignness and intelligibility difficulty of all the test sentences in the questionnaires were calculated both inclusive of and exclusive of the five A-control sentences (abbreviated Inc A-C and Exc A-C respectively in the tables below).

Total sample

Sentence no.	Foreignness Average		Intelligibility difficulty Average	
	Mean	SD	Mean	SD
Inc A-C 1-75	3.33	1.40	1.87	1.10
Exc A-C 1-75	3.49	1.30	1.93	1.12

The average means indicate that the 'average test sentence' made a foreign impression on the informants but was found to be fairly easy to understand.

Age differences

							Significance		
Sentence no.	Teen-agers Average		Adults Average		Pensioners Average		T-A	A-P	T-P
F	Mean	SD	Mean	SD	Mean	SD			
Inc A-C 1-75	3.22	1.35	3.33	1.35	3.37	1.65	-	-	-
Exc A-C 1-75	3.48	1.24	3.49	1.25	3.53	1.57	-	-	-
ID									
Inc A-C 1-75	2.13	1.13	1.73	1.03	1.61	1.14	I	G	I
Exc A-C 1-75	2.21	1.13	1.78	1.05	1.65	1.17	I	G	I

The most important differences between the average means of the age groups are found between the average means of the teen-agers and either of the other two age groups for the question on intelligibility difficulty. These differences are statistically highly significant and indicate that the teen-agers found the 'average test sentence' considerably more difficult to understand than the other two age groups did. Whether this is a result of a more frank attitude to this question on the part of the teen-agers compared with the other two age groups can only be speculated upon. It is possible that the adults and the pensioners for various reasons, one of which may be social prestige, did not as readily want to admit to finding some of the sentences difficult to understand or that they underestimated their problems in this respect. If so, this may or may not have been done deliberately. However, these differences may also be a result of the greater experience of non-native English a person is likely to get as he grows older. It seems reasonable to assume that the more experience a person has of non-native English, the easier he will find it to understand such English. The results of the examination of social variables below corroborate this assumption (cf. 19.2 and 19.4).

Even the slight difference between the average means of the adults and the pensioners is statistically highly significant both when the average means are based on all the 75 test sentences and when based only on the 70 test sentences that were not A-control sentences.

Sex differences

Sentence no.	Females Average		Males Average		Significance
F	Mean	SD	Mean	SD	
Inc A-C 1-75	3.31	1.43	3.37	1.34	-
Exc A-C 1-75	3.47	1.34	3.53	1.23	A
ID					
Inc A-C 1-75	1.85	1.13	1.90	1.06	A
Exc A-C 1-75	1.91	1.15	1.97	1.07	A

There are hardly any differences between the average means or between the average standard deviations of the two sexes. The female and the male informants thus seem to have had virtually the same opinions as regards the foreignness and the intelligibility of the 'average test sentence'. However, when the statistical significance tests are based on as many as 70 or 75 test sentences, both the t test and the GLM test reveal that the slight differences between the average means of the female and the male informants are significant on the A level. However, in the case of the average means for foreignness based also on the five A-control sentences, the error probability (p) of the difference is just slightly too high (.0657) for statistical significance. It was also shown above that there were four instances where statistically significant differences were found between the means of the female and the male informants for individual test sentences. In the table above, the average means are slightly higher for the male informants than for the female informants, which indicates that the male informants found the 'average test sentence' slightly more foreign and difficult to understand than the female informants did. The opposite is the case for the average standard deviations, which may indicate that the female informants, looked at as a group, were slightly more uncertain about their answers compared with the group of male informants.

The correlation coefficients between the answers to the questions on foreignness and intelligibility difficulty for the total sample vary from -.01353 (for sentence 25, p = .8905) to .84440 (for sentence 11, p = .0001). The average correlation coefficient is .29576. Only one sentence has a negative correlation coefficient between the means of the two questions (sentence 25), whereas all the other correlation coefficients are positive, indicating that the means of the questions on foreignness and intelligibility are directly rather than inversely related for most of the test sentences. For three of the test sentences, all A-control sentences, the correlation coefficient is 0 (viz. for sentences 36, p = 1; 49, p = 1; and 65, p = 1), indicating that each variable has no linear predictive ability of the other and that the means of the two questions are independent. All the five

sentences with exceptional correlation coefficients mentioned
above were A-control sentences. Apart from sentence 11, the
correlation coefficient was higher than .50 only for three
sentences (viz. .51155 for sentence 20, p = .0001; .51306 for
sentence 43, p = .0001; and .52047 for sentence 63, p = .0001),
indicating a relatively strong direct relationship between the
answers to the two questions.

19. SOCIAL VARIABLES

19. 1 Education

The informants were asked to indicate their educational background by ticking the appropriate box/boxes for (A) completed education (primary school, secondary school, university, and other type of school) and for (B) ongoing education (secondary school, university, and other type of school) (cf. appendix 3). The informants who ticked the box for secondary school under (A) were also asked to indicate the number of years they attended secondary school. It turns out, however, that this question was of little value, as many informants also included here the number of years they attended primary school and many others left this question unanswered. No account has therefore been taken of these answers in the statistical analysis.

The informants who ticked the box for university under (A) were also asked to tick a box which indicated whether or not they had actually graduated.

In order to form a large enough group of informants representing people with a relatively advanced educational background, it was decided that the informants who had graduated from a university should be grouped together with the informants with a university training but no degree and with those informants who were currently attending university courses. No teen-agers belong to this group, representing people with a more advanced education.

Out of the 113 informants who completed questionnaire 1, 27 informants or 23.9 per cent in this way fell into the group representing people with a more advanced educational background (education = HIGH). The rest, 86 informants or 76.1 per cent thus represent people with a less advanced educational background (education = LOW). The average age of the former group is 48 and of the latter group 36. One reason for this difference is that there are no teen-agers in the former group (cf. the table below).

Out of the 113 informants who completed questionnaire 1, 71 informants or 62.8 per cent were female and 42 informants or 37.2 per cent were male. In the group of informants with a more advanced education, 51 per cent are female and 49 per cent male, which means that the male informants are overrepresented in this group. This probably reflects reality fairly well, as there still are more men than women who have an advanced education. This should nevertheless be borne in mind when comparisons are made between the answers of the two sex groups above (cf. the tables titled sex differences).

Education group	No.	Per cent	Average age	Females No.	Per cent	Males No.	Per cent
HIGH	27	23.9	48	14	19.7	13	31.0
LOW	86	76.1	36	57	80.3	29	69.0
TOTAL	113	100.0	39	71	100.0	42	100.0

19.1.1 Comparison of answers given by informants with and without an academic training.

Only statistically significant differences will be dealt with (cf. 1.2.3).

The informants with the more advanced education found many of the test sentences easier to understand than did the other informants. There are 24 such statistically significant differences between the means of the two education groups and there is no statistically significant difference where the reverse is true. This seems to indicate that a more advanced education often facilitates the comprehension of foreign and erroneous English sentences, as the degree of intelligibility difficulty attributed to the test sentences is considerably lower among the informants with the more advanced education than among the informants with the less advanced education.

This result is consistent with the finding that most of the test sentences were judged to be easier to understand by the older informants, as there are no informants with an advanced education in the group of teen-agers.

There are no statistically significant differences between the means of the two education groups where the question on foreign impression is concerned.

Intelligibility difficulty

Sentence no.	HIGH Mean	SD	LOW Mean	SD	Sign.	Error type	Sentence quoted
4	1.42	.58	1.92	1.00	D	CONCORD	I don't know much people in this town.
6	1.25	1.25	1.67	1.67	C	ADV/ADJ	This soup tastes well!
7	1.80	1.00	2.33	1.20	A	OM.DO-PPH	Became he a dentist?
11	1.00	0	1.05	.22	A	A-CONTROL	He has lived in London all his life.
13	1.67	.70	2.12	1.05	B	INS.RELPRO	I don't know what improvements that are being planned.
20	1.15	.37	1.41	.69	B	WORD ORDER	He told me to not worry.
21	1.56	.77	1.99	1.24	A	VOC	The car was badly injured in the accident.
22	1.31	.55	1.67	.80	B	CONCORD	My brother have worked for this company for many years.
23	1.42	.64	1.85	1.01	B	NUMB	He had to pay five hundreds of pounds.
26	1.46	.58	1.84	.93	B	WR.INDPRO	I haven't heard something from him for a long time.
27	2.04	1.10	2.79	1.30	B	OM.PREP	This room smells food, doesn't it?
30	1.38	.75	1.98	1.06	C	ADV/ADJ	This cake smells well!
40	1.31	.62	1.73	.90	B	OM.INDART	My sister is nurse.
45	1.31	.68	1.92	1.17	E	GENITIVE	This is my brother's-in-law cap.
50	1.60	.96	2.40	1.16	E	INS.PREP	Smell on these flowers!
51	1.23	.51	1.80	.94	H	INS.INDART	What an awful weather!
52	1.19	.40	1.44	.67	B	SIMPVF/ING	I look forward to hear from you.
53	1.58	.99	2.16	1.12	B	PRE/ATTADJ	He is a very alone man.
62	1.00	0	1.24	.49	I	WR.INDART	It took me a hour to get there.
67	1.30	.78	1.74	1.03	A	DBL-NEG	I didn't buy nothing at the supermarket.

69	1.15	.36	1.59	.72	I	CONCORD	There is one chair too much.
73	1.54	.71	1.94	1.03	A	WORD ORDER	When I five years ago visited London, I didn't realize how big it was.
74	1.37	.49	2.01	1.17	I	ING/SIMPVF	He is meaning this book, not that one.
75	1.15	.36	1.59	.85	G	VOC	You do good coffee!

19.2 Contact with foreigners

The informants were asked to indicate how often they talk to foreigners, by ticking the appropriate box for (A) 'at least once a week', (B) 'at least once a month', (C) 'at least once a year', and (D) 'never'.

The question asked was 'How often do you talk to foreigners?', and all the informants were informed that what was referred to by this question was conversation in English and not in any other languages and that foreigners referred to non-native users of English (cf. 1.4).

The following table shows how many of the 113 informants that completed questionnaire 1 ticked the various boxes.

Contact group	No.	Per cent	Average age	Females No.	Per cent	Males No.	Per cent
A	46	40.7	45	25	35.2	21	50.0
B	19	16.8	41	15	21.1	4	9.5
C	39	34.5	24	24	33.8	15	35.7
D	8	7.1	68	7	9.9	1	2.4
MISSING ANSWER	1	.9	--	0	0	1	2.4
TOTAL	113	100.0	39	71	100.0	42	100.0

Of the informants in group A, 54 per cent are female and 46 per cent are male. In group B, 79 per cent are female and 21 per cent male. In group C 62 per cent are female and 38 per cent male. In group D 87 per cent are female and 13 per cent male. Bearing in mind that 62.8 per cent of the informants that completed questionnaire 1 were female, this means that group A is dominated by males, groups B and D are dominated by females and group C is fairly evenly balanced with regard to sex.

In order to form large and fairly evenly balanced groups, the informants who ticked either box A or B were grouped together to form group OFTEN, and the informants who ticked either box C or D were grouped together to form group SELDOM. The result is illustrated by the following table.

Contact group	No.	Per cent	Average age	Females		Males	
				No.	Per cent	No.	Per cent
OFTEN	65	57.5	44	40	56.3	25	59.5
SELDOM	47	41.6	32	31	43.7	16	38.1
MISSING ANSWER	1	.9	--	0	0	1	2.4
TOTAL	113	100.0	39	71	100.0	42	100.0

Of the informants in group OFTEN, 62 per cent are female and 38 per cent male, which means that this group is fairly evenly balanced with regard to sex. In group SELDOM 66 per cent are female and 34 per cent male, which means that this group is slightly dominated by females (cf. above and 19.1).

19.2.1 <u>Comparison</u> <u>of</u> <u>answers</u> <u>given</u> <u>by</u> <u>informants</u> <u>with</u> <u>different</u> <u>degrees</u> <u>of</u> <u>contact</u> <u>with</u> <u>foreigners</u>.

Only statistically significant differences will be dealt with (cf. 1.2.3).

The informants who often talk to foreigners (in English) found many of the sentences easier to understand than the other informants did. There are 34 such statistically significant differences between the means of the two groups and there is no statistically significant difference where the reverse is true. This seems to indicate that frequent contacts with foreigners facilitates comprehension of non-native and erroneous English sentences, as the degree of intelligibility difficulty attributed to the sentences is considerably lower among the informants who often talk to foreigners than among the informants who seldom talk to foreigners.

This result was expected and is consistent with the finding that the test sentences were judged to be easier to understand by the older informants, as experience of non-native English is likely to become more common with increasing age. Which of these two factors, age and contact with foreigners, is the more important in facilitating comprehension of non-native English is open to discussion, but, rather obviously, increasing age is often a prerequisite for greater experience of a great variety of things, including non-native English. What matters here is not just how often the informants talk to foreigners but also how long they have done so. Someone who has just begun to have very frequent contacts with foreigners cannot be expected to find non-native English as easy to understand as someone who has had very frequent contacts with foreigners for many years. Generally speaking, teen-agers cannot be expected to have had the same amount of experience of non-native English as adults and pensioners, who may have come in frequent contact with non-native English in their working lives, etc. This is probably the reason for the higher degree of intelligibility difficulty attributed to the sentences by the teen-agers than by either of the other age groups. It should also be pointed out here that, of the three age groups, the pensioners often had the least contact with foreigners, but this seems largely to be compensated by the fact that many of the pensioners had a long previous experience of non-native English.

It seems clear that contact with foreigners and thus experience of non-native English is a very important factor in facilitating comprehension of non-native English and may, in fact, be one of the reasons for the fact that most of the test sentences were judged to be easier to understand with increasing age.

As for the question on foreignness, the results are much less consistent over the various test sentences. There are three statistically significant differences between the means of the two contact groups where the informants who often talk to foreigners found the sentences more foreign than did the informants who seldom talk to foreigners, and three statistically significant differences where the reverse is true.

Foreignness

Sentence no.	Contact with foreigners						
	OFTEN		SELDOM				
	Mean	SD	Mean	SD	Sign.	Error type	Sentence quoted
14	3.31	1.46	2.67	1.13	B	UNC	She has very limited knowledges of German.
28	3.25	1.45	3.84	1.31	A	VOC	Who learnt you Spanish?
38	3.73	1.29	3.14	1.30	B	IRREG-VERB	They fighted bravely in the war.
47	2.19	1.32	1.69	.98	A	CONCORD	We have a great deal of problems.
53	3.52	1.32	3.98	.81	A	PRE/ATTADJ	He is a very alone man.
63	1.79	.97	2.33	1.16	B	ADJ^NOUN	He has a blue car and I have a red.

Intelligibility difficulty

Sentence no.	OFTEN Mean	SD	SELDOM Mean	SD	Sign.	Error type	Sentence quoted
8	1.18	.43	1.43	.62	B	WR.INDPRO	None of my two brothers knew about my plans.
9	1.63	.89	2.09	.86	C	WR.PREP	I met him in the stairs.
10	1.08	.27	1.36	.65	C	OM.DEFART	I am staying at Sheraton hotel for three days.
12	1.77	.89	2.36	1.01	E	VOC	I always tried to make my best at school
13	1.73	.84	2.36	1.06	F	INS.RELPRO	I don't know what improvements that are being planned.
16	1.73	.94	2.16	.89	B	TENSE	I didn't saw him today.
18	1.62	.94	2.09	.91	B	CONCORD	Here are the money I owe you.
19	1.92	1.05	2.73	1.35	F	IDIOM-PHR	I shouted to him to look up for the car when I saw that it was going to hit him
22	1.39	.61	1.84	.88	D	CONCORD	My brother have worked for this company for many years.
26	1.57	.88	1.93	.75	A	WR.INDPRO	I haven't heard something from him for long time.
27	2.27	1.26	3.09	1.19	E	OM.PREP	This room smells food, doesn't it?
29	1.97	1.04	2.45	.90	B	TENSE	Things have went too far.
30	1.65	1.06	2.11	.92	B	ADV/ADJ	This cake smells well!
31	1.34	.54	1.80	.93	C	INS.INDART	It is a hard work to write a book.
33	1.80	1.01	2.40	1.08	D	TO-INF/B	They made me to do it.
34	3.21	1.38	3.88	1.16	B	OM.DO-PPH	He thinks not that they know what to do
37	1.37	.68	1.93	.84	G	WR.PREP	She is married with a German.
38	1.40	.71	1.74	.89	A	IRREG-VERB	They fighted bravely in the war.
40	1.46	.86	1.88	.80	B	OM.INDART	My sister is nurse.
43	2.38	1.28	2.98	1.15	B	VOC	Yesterday's accident depended on the bad weather.
45	1.55	.97	2.09	1.22	B	GENITIVE	This is my brother's-in-law cap.
46	2.75	1.36	3.41	1.24	B	PPRO/RFPRO	She was standing alone, beside her with rage.
51	1.45	.78	1.98	.95	D	INS.INDART	What an awful weather!
53	1.76	1.06	2.33	1.04	C	PRE/ATTADJ	He is a very alone man.
54	1.41	.79	1.93	1.12	C	INS.PREP	Have you ever seen the river of Ganges?
59	2.51	1.35	3.30	1.27	D	TO-INF/ING	Many cities have stopped to expand.
61	1.38	.63	1.69	.70	B	TENSE	The firm is established in 1970.

62	1.10	.30	1.32	.56	B	WR.INDART	It took me a hour to get there.
63	1.17	.52	1.45	.70	A	ADJ^NOUN	He has a blue car and I have a red.
67	1.44	.89	1.93	1.08	B	DBL-NEG	I didn't buy nothing at the supermarket.
70	1.81	.96	2.28	.98	B	COMP.ADV	He drives badlier than his brother.
71	1.22	.55	1.52	.88	A	OM.PREP	We have just come back from the island Rhodes.
73	1.62	.79	2.16	1.14	C	WORD ORDER	When I five years ago visited London, I didn't realize how big it was.
75	1.32	.67	1.71	.87	C	VOC	You do good coffee!

19.3 Knowledge of other languages

The informants were asked to indicate what languages they speak, apart from English. Of the languages indicated, the most common were French and German. The following table shows what languages were indicated by the informants who completed questionnaire 1.

Knowledge of	No.	Per cent	Average age	Females No.	Per cent	Males No.	Per cent
French	74	65.5	33	44	62.0	30	71.4
German	11	9.7	26	10	14.1	1	2.4
Spanish	4	3.5	50	4	5.6	0	0
Italian	1	.9	--	1	1.4	0	0
Russian	1	.9	--	0	0	0	2.4
Swedish	1	.9	--	0	0	1	2.4
None	31	27.4	47	21	29.6	10	23.8
MISSING ANSWER	8	7.1	56	6	8.5	2	4.8

In the table above, the total number of informants exceeds the true number and the total percentage does not equal 100, as several informants belong to more than one 'knowledge group', i.e. can speak more than one language apart from English.

In order to form fairly large and reasonably balanced groups, it was decided that the informants who speak at least one language apart from English should be grouped together to form group YES, and that the informants who indicated that they speak no other language than English should be grouped together with the informants who had missing answers to this question to form group NO. It seems reasonable to assume that most of the informants who did not answer this question in fact could not speak any other language than English. The number of informants in each of these two groups can be seen from the following table.

<u>Ability</u> <u>to</u> <u>speak</u> <u>at</u> <u>least</u> <u>one</u> <u>language</u> <u>apart</u> <u>from</u> <u>English.</u>

Group	No.	Per cent	Average age	Females No.	Per cent	Males No.	Per cent
YES	74	65.5	33	44	62.0	30	71.4
NO	39	34.5	49	27	38.0	12	28.6
TOTAL	113	100.0	39	71	100.0	42	100.0

It can be seen from the two tables above that all the informants who indicated that they could speak another language or other languages apart from English indicated that they could speak French. Of the informants in group YES, 59 per cent are female and 41 per cent male. Bearing in mind that 62.8 per cent of the informants who completed questionnaire 1 were female, this means that group YES is slightly dominated by males. Group NO, on the other hand, is slightly dominated by females, as 69 per cent in this group are female and 31 per cent male. Of the informants questioned, proportionally slightly more men than women thus indicated that they were able to speak at least one language apart from English.

19.3.1 Comparison of answers given by informants with and without the ability to speak at least one language apart from English.

Only statistically significant differences will be dealt with (cf. 1.2.3).

The informants who speak at least one language apart from English found some test sentences more foreign than the other informants did. There are 11 such statistically significant differences between the means of the two groups and there is no statistically significant difference where the reverse is true. This seems to imply that a knowledge of another language than English sometimes makes it easier to identify a non-native English sentence as foreign.

As for the question on intelligibility difficulty, the informants who speak at least one language apart from English found some test sentences more difficult to understand than the other informants did. There are four such statistically significant differences between the means of the two groups and there is no statistically significant difference where the reverse is true. This result seems more difficult to explain. In the case of sentence 5, the large difference between the means may, however, be a result of greater awareness on the part of the informants in group YES that this sentence was ambiguous, and therefore difficult to understand. Such awareness is probably more common among people who have a more profound knowledge of languages, and among people who have a knowledge of one or more other languages than their own native language.

Foreignness

Ability to speak other language/s/

Sentence no.	YES Mean	SD	NO Mean	SD	Sign.	Error type	Sentence quoted
6	3.69	1.08	3.19	1.39	A	ADV/ADJ	This soup tastes well!
7	4.54	.71	3.92	1.08	E	OM.DO-PPH	Became he a dentist?
12	3.86	.99	3.41	1.12	A	VOC	I always tried to make my best at school

14	3.32	1.25	2.57	1.44	C	UNC	She has very limited knowledges of German.
16	4.07	.99	3.57	1.30	A	TENSE	I didn't saw him today.
18	4.06	.94	3.66	1.07	A	CONCORD	Here are the money I owe you.
22	3.63	1.22	2.89	1.26	D	CONCORD	My brother have worked for this company for many years.
27	4.44	.93	3.89	.99	D	OM.PREP	This room smells food, doesn't it?
29	4.19	1.02	3.75	1.02	A	TENSE	Things have went too far.
44	4.23	.98	3.76	1.26	A	WR.ADVERB	He works very hardly.
68	4.26	.86	3.76	1.04	C	INS.PREP	She was here for two years ago.

Intelligibility difficulty

Ability to speak other language/s/

| Sentence | YES | | NO | | | | |
no.	Mean	SD	Mean	SD	Sign.	Error type	Sentence quoted
5	3.00	1.33	2.08	1.25	F	INS.PREP	I was here for two years ago.
13	2.16	1.00	1.76	.95	A	INS.RELPRO	I don't know what improvements that are being planned.
24	2.66	1.24	2.11	1.17	A	SUBJECT	It was little else to do.
58	2.17	1.04	1.73	.93	A	RFPRO/PPRO	She had her radio beside herself.

19.4 Former period's residence abroad

The informants were asked to indicate what other country or countries (apart from the United Kingdom) they had lived in and, if so, for how long. Their answers were then coded differently depending upon whether or not the country indicated was an English-speaking country (i.e. a country where English is the official language or one of the official languages). In this way a comparison was made possible between the answers of informants who had lived in another English-speaking country and the answers of informants who had lived in a non-English speaking country.

As the length of the residence abroad is also of importance, it was first decided that the answers of informants who had indicated a residential period of less than a year in another country were to be excluded from the statistical comparisons. Due to limited coding space, however, only the length of residence in a non-English-speaking country was coded, for which reason fair comparisons of the answers of different groups can be made only if all the informants who have lived in a non-English-speaking country are included, with no consideration of the length of the residence.

Of the 113 informants who completed questionnaire 1, 15 informants indicated that they had lived in a non-English speaking country, 11 of whom had done so for one year or more. It was assumed that the informants who left the question on residence abroad unanswered had not lived abroad. These informants were therefore grouped together with the informants who answered that they had not lived abroad to form group D in the table below. Out of the 5 informants who had lived both in a non-English-speaking country and in another English-speaking country 4 had lived for one year or more in the former type of country. The following table shows the distribution of informants over the various 'residence groups'.

Former period's residence abroad

	Group	No.	Per cent	Average age	Females No.	Females Per cent	Males No.	Males Per cent
	A	15	13.3	41	7	9.9	8	19.1
YES	B	5	4.4	41	3	4.2	2	4.8
	C	16	14.2	47	13	18.3	3	7.1
		----	------	----	----	------	---	------
		36	31.9	43	23	32.4	13	31.0
NO	D	77	68.1	37	48	67.6	29	69.0
		----	------	----	----	------	----	------
	YES+NO	113	100.0	39	71	100.0	42	100.0

A = in non-English-speaking country only

B = in non-English-speaking country and other English-speaking country than the United Kingdom

C = in other English-speaking country than the U K only

D = in no other country than the United Kingdom

It can be seen from the table above that a total of 36 informants, or 31.9 per cent of the informants who completed questionnaire 1, had lived in another country apart from the United Kingdom, whereas more than twice as many had never lived abroad.

19.4.1 Comparison of answers given by informants with different experiences of living abroad.

Only statistically significant differences will be dealt with (cf. 1.2.3).

19.4.1.1 Comparison of groups YES and NO.

The informants who belong to group YES, i.e. those who had lived abroad, found many of the test sentences easier to understand than did the informants who belong to group NO, i.e. those who had not lived abroad. There are 35 such statistically significant differences between the means of the two groups and there is no statistically significant difference where the reverse is true. This indicates that residence abroad facilitates comprehension of non-native and erroneous English sentences, as the degree of intelligibility difficulty attributed to these sentences is considerably lower among the informants who had lived abroad than among the informants who had not done so.

This result was expected and seems consistent with the finding that most of the test sentences were judged to be easier to understand by the older informants, as a period of residence abroad will probably become somewhat more likely with increasing age. This assumption is borne out by the fact that the average age of the informants in group YES is higher than the average age of the informants in group NO.

As for the question on foreignness, the results are more contradictory. Two of the 75 test sentences made a stronger foreign impression on the informants in group YES, whereas the opposite is the case for two other sentences (see table below).

Foreignness

Former residence abroad

Sentence no.	YES Mean	SD	NO Mean	SD	Sign.	Error type	Sentence quoted
13	2.83	1.38	3.35	1.18	A	INS.RELPRO	I don't know what improvements that are being planned.
20	1.81	1.06	2.54	1.39	C	WORD ORDER	He told me to not worry.
46	4.46	.70	4.05	1.04	B	PPRO/RFPRO	She was standing alone, beside her with rage.
71	3.14	1.26	2.40	1.25	C	OM.PREP	We have just come back from the island Rhodes.

Intelligibility difficulty

Former residence abroad

Sentence no.	YES Mean	SD	NO Mean	SD	Sign.	Error type	Sentence quoted
1	1.32	.59	1.88	.91	G	INS.INDART	What a dreadful weather!
4	1.43	.65	1.97	1.01	F	CONCORD	I don't know much people in this town.
6	1.21	.48	1.74	.97	G	ADV/ADJ	This soup tastes well!
7	1.68	.88	2.45	1.21	G	OM.DO-PPH	Became he a dentist?
9	1.50	.83	1.96	.90	B	WR.PREP	I met him in the stairs.
10	1.06	.23	1.32	.71	D	OM.DEFART	I am staying at Sheraton hotel for three days.

12	1.68	.81	2.21	1.04	C	VOC	I always tried to make my best at school
13	1.53	.62	2.23	1.06	I	INS.RELPRO	I don't know what improvements that are planned.
14	1.29	.46	1.68	.80	E	UNC	She has very limited knowledges of German.
15	1.11	.40	1.33	.53	A	ADJ/ADV	He speaks French quite good.
16	1.62	.89	2.04	.93	A	TENSE	I didn't saw him today.
20	1.09	.29	1.47	.72	H	WORD ORDER	He told me to not worry.
22	1.26	.51	1.73	.82	G	CONCORD	My brother have worked for this company for many years.
26	1.50	.71	1.86	.92	A	WR.INDPRO	I haven't heard something from him for a long time.
27	2.12	1.25	2.86	1.25	C	OM.PREP	This room smells food, doesn't it?
30	1.47	.61	2.00	1.13	E	ADV/ADJ	This cake smells well!
31	1.24	.43	1.67	.84	F	INS.INDART	It is a hard work to write a book.
32	1.79	.89	2.25	1.14	A	WR.PREP	I met him in the steps.
33	1.68	.88	2.27	1.17	C	TO-INF/B	They made me to do it.
37	1.27	.52	1.75	.85	F	WR.PREP	She is married with a German.
38	1.24	.44	1.67	.89	E	IRREG-VERB	They fighted bravely in the war.
43	2.20	1.21	2.86	1.25	B	VOC	Yesterday's accident depended on the bad weather.
48	1.09	.28	1.59	.87	I	WR.INDART	He is an useful member of the team.
50	1.74	.99	2.43	1.17	D	INS.PREP	Smell on these flowers!
51	1.30	.59	1.82	.95	F	INS.INDART	What an awful weather!
52	1.18	.39	1.48	.69	D	SIMPVF/ING	I look forward to hear from you.
53	1.71	1.06	2.16	1.12	A	PRE/ATTADJ	He is a very alone man.
55	1.85	1.26	2.39	1.26	A	AUX	He needs not come.
57	1.74	.85	2.23	1.04	B	SUBJECT	There's a long time since I saw her.
59	2.49	1.40	3.04	1.34	A	TO-INF/ING	Many cities have stopped to expand.
60	1.80	1.08	2.30	1.21	A	INS.PREP	I am sure of that he will come.
61	1.26	.61	1.64	.67	C	TENSE	The firm is established in 1970.
62	1.09	.28	1.24	.49	A	WR.INDART	It took me a hour to get there.
64	1.21	.48	1.47	.78	A	IRREG-PLUR	The house was full of mouses.
66	1.26	.51	1.62	.86	C	COMP.ADJ	This is the goodest cake I have ever tasted.

19.4.1.2 Comparison of groups A and C

A comparison of group A (those informants who had lived in one or more non-English-speaking countries) with group C (those informants who had lived in one or more English-speaking countries apart from the United Kingdom) reveals that there are hardly any statistically significant differences at all between the means of these two groups. Thus, the informants in these two groups apparently had very similar opinions about the intelligibility and the foreignness of the test sentences.

Only the means for four of the 75 test sentences differ significantly, according to the statistical tests carried out (cf. 1.2.3). Rather surprisingly, group A found two sentences more difficult to understand and two sentences more foreign than did group C. This is shown by the tables below.

Foreignness

Former residence abroad

Sentence no.	A Mean	SD	C Mean	SD	Sign.	Error type	Sentence quoted
34	4.80	.41	4.13	1.02	B	OM.DO-PPH	He thinks not that they know what to do.
70	4.20	.86	3.31	1.45	A	COMP.ADV	He drives badlier than his brother.

Intelligibility difficulty

Former residence abroad

Sentence no.	A Mean	SD	C Mean	SD	Sign.	Error type	Sentence quoted
42	3.23	1.48	1.93	1.21	B	OM.PREP	I was operated last week.
47	1.40	.63	1	0	A	CONCORD	We have a great deal of problems.

The difference between the means of the two groups for the question on the intelligibility difficulty of sentence 42 is quite remarkable, as it is very great. Apparently the informants who had lived in a non-English speaking country found the four sentences above worse from a communicative point of view than did the informants who had lived in another English-speaking country than the United Kingdom.

19.5 Occupation

The informants were asked to indicate what their present occupations were. Their answers were then coded differently according to which of the following ten categories their occupations belonged to: 1. manual worker, 2. non-manual employee, 3. teacher, 4. pupil/student, 5. housewife/mother, 6. retired/pensioner, 7. secretary/clerk/typist, 8. manager, 9. other, 0. unemployed/none. These ten categories were chosen as they were expected to cover most occupations and situations in the labour-market. This expectation was borne out by the answers given to this question, as very few informants fitted into category 9 (other).

The classification of occupations to match these ten categories was accomplished largely on the basis of the socio-economic classification system Socioekonomisk indelning SEI (Socio-Economic Classification), published by Statistiska Centralbyrån (the Swedish Central Bureau of Statistics) (1982), with a number of aggregations and minor alterations to make it more applicable to the British labour force.

Out of the 113 informants that completed questionnaire 1, the number of informants in each category turned out to be as listed in the following table.

Occupation group	No.	Per cent	Average age	Females No.	Per cent	Males No.	Per cent
1	2	1.8	35	0	0	2	4.8
2	16	14.2	44	8	11.3	8	19.0
3	13	11.5	38	5	7.0	8	19.0
4	45	39.6	16	27	38.0	18	42.9
5	7	6.2	46	7	9.9	0	0
6	22	19.5	77	19	26.8	3	7.1
7	2	1.8	46	2	2.8	0	0
8	2	1.8	30	1	1.4	1	2.4
9	0	0	--	0	0	0	0
0	1	.9	--	1	1.4	0	0
MISSING ANSWER	3	2.7	64	1	1.4	2	4.8
TOTAL	113	100.0	39	71	100.0	42	100.0

As can be seen from the table above, the number of informants in the various occupation groups vary considerably. The reason for this is that some occupation groups were not as readily available for this research or were unwilling to participate. This was particularly noticeable with occupation group 1 (manual workers), many members of which were quite often unwilling to take part in the experiments, for reasons of fear, suspicion, or lack of immediate remuneration for their participation. Unlike some previous investigations of a similar type, the informants were not paid to take part in the investigations, as this study was not externally financed. In order to try to overcome this problem, a lottery was organized in connection with some of the test sessions, in order to tempt people who were unwilling to participate. Each participant was given a ticket with the same number that was found on his or her questionnaire. After the test session, a number was drawn and the winner was given £10. Even though this method helped to persuade a number of people to take part in the three investigations (cf. 1.1), it did not help to persuade a large enough number of people from occupation group 1 to participate. Either the prize was too small for what was asked

of them or it did not help some of the informants overcome their
fear   of   participating,   even though the   informants   were
specifically told that their answers would be anonymous,   as they
were not supposed to write their names or any other means of
identification on their questionnaires (cf. 1.4). It is to be
hoped that, in one way or another, future studies of a similar
type will investigate the opinions of a larger number of people
from occupation group 1, as a great many employees are found in
this occupation group.

The   informants in occupation group 4 are largely the   same   as
those in the age group of teen-agers, and the informants in
occupation group 6 are the same as those in the age-group of
pensioners (cf. 1.3), for which reasons these occupation groups
will not be dealt with here.

Due to the very few informants in occupation groups 1,   5,   7, 8,
9, and 0, the answers of these groups cannot very well be used for
comparisons with those of other occupation groups. This means
that only the answers of occupation groups 2 and 3 remain to be
compared with one another, and this is done below.

19.5.1 <u>Comparison of answers given by non-manual employees and
teachers.</u>

Only statistically significant differences will be dealt with
(cf. 1.2.3).

The group of non-manual employees and the group of teachers
hardly differed in their opinions about the intelligibility and
the foreignness of the test sentences. Only for three of the 75
test sentences are statistically significant differences to be
found between the means of these two occupation groups. These
differences indicate that two sentences made a stronger foreign
impression on the non-manual employees than on the teachers and
that one sentence was judged to be more difficult to understand by
the former group than by the latter. There are no statistically
significant differences where the reverse is true.

Foreignness

Occupation

Sentence no.	NON-MANUAL EMPLOYEES		TEACHERS		Sign.	Error type	Sentence quoted
	Mean	SD	Mean	SD			
62	2.63	1.26	1.69	.75	A	WR.INDART	It took me a hour to get there.
75	3.31	1.20	2.38	1.12	A	VOC	You do good coffee!

Intelligibility difficulty

Occupation

Sentence no.	NON-MANUAL EMPLOYEES		TEACHERS		Sign.	Error type	Sentence quoted
	Mean	SD	Mean	SD			
67	1.81	1.17	1.15	.38	A	DBL-NEG	I didn't buy nothing at the supermarket.

20. COMMENTS ON RANK LISTS OF ERROR TYPES
(cf. Appendix 2)

Indices in brackets refer to the combined rank list of error types (Appendix 2.1.3).

For a more detailed discussion of the test sentences used to exemplify the various error types, please refer to the corresponding sections earlier in this study.

The error types will be discussed in order of descending gravity, according to the combined rank list of error types.

20.1 Pronominal errors

20.1.1 PPRO/RFPRO (Error gravity index: 7.22)

(Personal pronoun for reflexive pronoun)

The use of a personal pronoun instead of a reflexive pronoun caused by far the most serious intelligibility difficulty and the second strongest foreign impression of all the 38 error types included in the investigations. However, it should be remembered that the sentence used to exemplify this error type was a special one, albeit the phrase involved is a fairly common one, with the intended meaning 'at the end of one's self control'. If a different sentence had been used to test reactions to this error type, it would more likely be ambiguous (for instance: She looked at her in the mirror). Such a sentence would probably have resulted in less criticism from the informants, as it would be more readily interpretable and as the interpretation where there is no co-reference with the subject presupposes that the sentence is grammatical. The sentence used may, on the other hand, seem contradictory and a reflexive pronoun is usually considered obligatory in sentences where the phrase meaning 'at the end of one's self control' is used. It is probably for these reasons that the error gravity index turned out to be as high as it did.

Particular attention should therefore be paid in the teaching of English to the importance of using a reflexive pronoun wherever there is a case of co-reference with the subject (except in prepositional adverbial phrases expressing spatial relationship) and to the fact that misunderstandings may result if this is not done.

20.1.2 RFPRO/PPRO (Error gravity index: 5.62)

(Reflexive pronoun for personal pronoun)

Compared to the previous and opposite error type, this error type was much less critized by the informants, both where its effect on the intelligibility difficulty and the foreignness of the test sentence were concerned. It therefore seems less serious to use a reflexive pronoun for a personal pronoun than vice versa. This is understandable, as there is considerable vacillation in the use of objective personal pronouns versus reflexive pronouns even among native users of English. This is, however, not the case with the phrase in the sentence used to test reactions to the previous error type.

20.1.3 INS.RELPRO (Error gravity index: 5.19)

(Insertion of relative pronoun)

Insertion of a relative pronoun (that) in an indirect interrogative clause caused the same amount of intelligibility difficulty as the previous error type, but less foreign impression. The combined effect is that this error type, unlike the two previous ones, is found in the lower half of the combined rank list.

20.1.4 WR.INDPRO (Error gravity index: 4.13)

(Incorrect choice of indefinite pronouns)

The least serious of the pronominal error types turned out to be incorrect choice of indefinite pronouns. Two sentences were used to test reactions to this error type, the more serious of which employed something for anything in a negative clause and the least serious of which none for neither with reference to two people. Some informants did not think that the latter choice was incorrect and some also declared that they themselves often use none with reference to two people or objects.

20.1.5 Conclusions

The four pronominal error types are fairly evenly spread over the rank lists. The first two types are found in the upper half of the combined rank list and the other two in the lower half. The former error types may therefore be regarded as more serious than the latter ones. However, it is clear from the error indices above that the difference between the error gravity of the RFPRO/PPRO and INS.RELPRO error types is rather small, whereas the error gravity indices of the two extreme error types differ considerably from those of the other two error types.

The teaching of the correct use of some and any is often paid a great deal of attention by teachers of English. As regards the use of any instead of some in negative clauses, the correct choice between these two indefinite pronouns seems less important from a purely communicative point of view than the correct use of the other pronouns dealt with above, the one exception being the use of neither instead of none with reference to two people, or objects, which seems to be of such minor importance from a communicative point of view that it ought to be assigned a very low degree of priority in the teaching of English to foreigners where communicative efficiency is the goal. It seems that the use

of neither may be essential only when it is in no other way clear
from the context that two people, or objects, are referred to.

The average error gravity index for the pronominal error types is
5.54. In comparison, if an average error gravity index is struck
for all the 38 error types tested, it turns out to be 5.38. The
average error gravity index for the pronominal error types is thus
slightly higher.

20.2 Errors in the use of verbs

20.2.1 OM.DO-PPH (error gravity index: 6.97)

(Omission of the periphrastic auxiliary do)

Omission of the periphrastic auxiliary do   made by far the
strongest foreign impression on the informants of all the 38
error types included in the investigations and was the fifth most
serious where intelligibility difficulty is concerned. Three
different sentences were used to test reactions to this error
type, two of which were interrogative sentences and one a negated
sentence.

The results showed that when this error type occurs in a sentence
negated by not it is even more serious than when made in an
interrogative sentence. In the former case the sentence was found
to be difficult to understand, in fact the most difficult to
understand of all the 75 test sentences, and it also made a
stronger foreign impression on the informants than any of the
other 74 test sentences. The results of the control form show that
some informants found this error type to be an OPAQUE error when
made in a negated sentence, that is, it made the sentence defy
interpretation altogether. Particular attention should therefore
be paid to the use of the periphrastic auxiliary do in sentences
negated by not.

The two interrogative sentences were polar questions. Though these were judged somewhat more leniently than the negated sentence, particularly as regards intelligibility, they still represent very serious errors.

As this error type may, in practice, affect an infinite number of sentences, it may be said to be even more serious than the PPRO/RFPRO error type previously discussed, according to the principle of generality (cf. 1.8).

20.2.2 AUX (error gravity index: 6.79)

(Improper use of modal auxiliaries)

Improper use of the modal auxiliaries can and need, the latter of which can also be used as a main verb, was also judged to be one of the most serious error types, viz. the third most serious in the combined rank list. However, the improper use of can was considered a great deal worse than the improper use of need in the sentences tested.

Interference from Swedish often leads to the wrong choice between can and the main verb know, leading to the error committed in test sentence 39. For Swedish users of English it is therefore particularly important to pay attention to the correct use of the modal auxiliary can. The high frequency of can in English makes this even more imperative.

20.2.3 TO-INF/ING (error gravity index: 6.69)

(Use of the <u>to</u>-infinitive instead of the -<u>ing</u> participle
after a verb which takes only the participle construction as
object)

Use of the <u>to</u>-infinitive as object instead of the -<u>ing</u> participle
caused the second most serious intelligibility difficulty and the
eighth strongest foreign impression of all the 38 error types.

This result agrees fairly well with the reactions Johansson
(1978:70) found to his group of 'miscellaneous grammatical
errors', among which a similar type of error was found
(exemplified by <u>worth to be read</u> for <u>worth reading</u>). The sentence
used here, however, could probably be considered worse than
Johansson's example, because of the awkward interpretation it may
give rise to (cf. 8.5.3).

Generally speaking, knowledge of which verbs require the -<u>ing</u>
participle as object thus seems to be important.

20.2.4 TO-INF/B (error gravity index: 5.80)

(<u>to</u>-infinitive for bare infinitive)

Use of the <u>to</u>-infinitive for the bare infinitive was found to be
the fourth most serious error type involving verbs. The ranks show
that this error type is in the upper halves of the rank lists.
However, the error gravity index for this error type is
considerably lower than for the preceding error type. The result
nevertheless indicates that it is important to learn which verbs
should be followed by (an object and) a bare infinitive. Failure
to learn this may result in production of ambiguous sentences (cf.
8.6).

20.2.5 TENSE (error gravity index: 5.58)

(Incorrect tense)

Incorrect choice of tenses was tested by means of four different sentences. The worst of these sentences from a communicative point of view was an example of the use of the preterite form of the verb (go) for the required past participle in the present perfect tense.

Clearly, it is important to learn when and how to use the various tenses, as errors in this respect can give rise to a strong foreign impression of the sentence in which the error occurs. On the other hand, this error type does not seem to cause any great amount of intelligibility difficulty. Nevertheless, it is found in the upper half of the combined rank list of error types.

These results agree with Johansson's finding that this type of morphological error is in the upper half of the 'irritability scale' (Johansson 1978:70).

20.2.6 ING/SIMPVF (error gravity index: 5.47)

(Use of the -ing participle with stative verb)

Use of the -ing participle instead of the base form of a usually stative verb (mean) made a fairly strong foreign impression on the informants but did not cause much intelligibility difficulty. This error type is found in the upper halves of the rank lists and thus deserves to be regarded as more serious than most of the other 37 error types.

As many non-native users of English tend to exaggerate the use of the -ing participle and the progressive aspect, it seems particularly important that it is made clear to them which verbs are usually stative and thus cannot normally be used in the progressive.

20.2.7 IRREG-VERB (error gravity index: 5.03)

(Irregular verb used as regular verb)

An irregular verb used with a regular conjugation was tested in one sentence, which made a rather strong foreign impression on the informants. However, this error seems to have caused little intelligibility difficulty. From a mere intelligibility point of view it cannot therefore be said to be particularly important to learn the correct forms of irregular verbs, at least not as far as the verb fight is concerned. However, if additional aspects of communicative efficiency are taken into consideration, such as foreignness, this error type is more serious. Nevertheless, this error type is found in the lower halves of the rank lists.

20.2.8 SIMPVF/ING (error gravity index: 4.84)

(Use of simple verb form after a preposition)

Compared to the opposite case, the use of the base form of a verb (simple verb form) instead of the -ing participle did not cause nearly as much criticism from the informants. The two sentences used to test this error type do, however, differ considerably as to the reactions of the informants but they were both examples of the use of a preposition without a following -ing participle form of the verb.

Judging from the results obtained, if a verb is to follow the preposition, it is clearly more important to use the -ing participle form of the verb after the phrase be used to than after the phrase look forward to, as failure to do so rather easily may give rise to misinterpretations in the former case but not in the latter.

20.2.9 Conclusions

Six of the eight error types involving the use of verbs were found in the upper half of the combined rank list of error types. The average error gravity index for the error types involving the use of verbs is 5.90, which is somewhat higher than the average error gravity index for all the 38 error types tested (5.38). Generally speaking, it thus seems that knowledge of how to make proper use of verbs is important from a communicative point of view.

This result agrees with Johansson's findings (1978). He found that errors in the use of verbs, subsumed under the notion of morphological and miscellaneous errors, were in the upper half of the 'irritability scale'.

20.3 Adjectival errors

20.3.1 ADJ-PHR (error gravity index: 6.76)

(Improper use of adjective phrase)

Use of own in attributive position, preceded by the indefinite article (an), made the third strongest foreign impression on the informants, gave rise to the fourth most serious intelligibility difficulty of all the 38 error types, and turned out to be the most serious error type involving adjectives represented in the questionnaires.

Swedish users of English should therefore pay particular attention to constructions with own, as they tend to make errors in such constructions, as a result of interference from Swedish.

20.3.2 PRE/ATTADJ (error gravity index: 5.73)

(Predicative adjective used in attributive position)

Use of a predicative adjective (<u>alone</u>) in attributive position turned out to be the second most serious error type involving adjectives. It therefore seems comparatively important to learn which adjectives are used only in predicative position.

20.3.3 COMP.ADJ (error gravity index: 5.08)

(Improper comparison)

Incorrect comparison of adjectives was tested by means of a sentence with the adjective <u>good</u>, affixed to which was the regular superlative inflectional suffix (-<u>est</u>).

This error type was considered a great deal less serious than incorrect comparison of adverbs (cf. 20.4.2) and is found in the lower half of the combined rank list of error types. It may therefore be said to be less serious than most of the other 37 error types tested, particularly where intelligibility difficulty is concerned.

20.3.4 ADJ^NOUN (error gravity index: 4.35)

(Use of adjective as head of a noun phrase without generic reference)

Use of an adjective as the head of a noun phrase without generic reference may be considered a minor error type, compared to most of the other error types tested, particularly if the adjective is preceded by the indefinite article and the real noun-phrase head has been previously mentioned. This error type is found a long way down in the rank lists of error types and in the lowest fourth of the combined rank list.

20.3.5 ADJ/ADV (error gravity index: 3.79)

(Adjective used as adverb)

Use of an adjective instead of the corresponding adverb was found to be considerably less serious than the opposite error (cf. 20.4.3). It was also found to be the least serious of all the error types involving adjectives and close to the bottom of the rank lists.

As this type of usage is fairly frequent in American English and sometimes also in British English, perhaps it should not be regarded as an error. At any rate, there does not seem to be much point in enforcing the use of adverbs with reference to verbs at the cost of other error types, which are more serious from a communicative point of view. Also, indications were found that the use of adjectives in such contexts is perhaps becoming more common (cf. 5.5).

20.3.6 Conclusions

The five adjectival error types are fairly evenly spread over the rank lists. Only two of the five error types involving adjectives are found in the upper halves of the rank lists and the remaining three are found in the lower halves. Many errors in the use of adjectives thus seem to be less serious than, for example, errors in the use of adverbs (cf. 20.4). The average error gravity index for the adjectival error types is 5.14, as compared to 5.38 for all the 38 error types tested. The error gravity indices show that some adjectival error types deserve to be regarded as serious from a communicative point of view, particularly the incorrect use of own, and the use of a predicative adjective in attributive position.

20.4 Adverbial errors

20.4.1 WR.ADVERB (error gravity index: 6.54)

(Incorrect choice of adverbs)

Use of the wrong adverb made the fifth strongest foreign impression on the informants and caused the sixth most serious intelligibility difficulty of all the 38 error types. Only one sentence was used to test this error type, which may have bearing on the result. As the sentence used (cf. 7.3) may give rise to two very different interpretations and thus cause uncertainty as to what is really meant, it may very well be that this sentence was considered to be more serious than would otherwise have been the case. Consequently, this error type may have been assigned a more prominent place in the rank lists.

Nevertheless, it can be said that the error of using hardly for hard seems to be a serious one. Attention should therefore be paid to the importance of using the right adverb and to what might be the result if this is not done.

20.4.2 COMP.ADV (error gravity index: 5.94)

(Improper comparison of adverbs)

Incorrect comparison of adverbs was tested by means of a sentence where the regular comparative inflectional suffix (-er) was affixed to the adverb badly (and the y was replaced by an i) as a substitute for the correct irregular comparative form (worse).

This error type was considered to be a great deal more serious than incorrect comparison of adjectives (cf. 20.3.3), and is found in the upper third of the rank lists. The importance of correct comparison of at least this particular adverb thus seems clear, particularly as regards conformity.

20.4.3 ADV/ADJ (error gravity index: 5.30)

(Adverb used as adjective)

Use of an adverb instead of the corresponding adjective was tested by means of two sentences where the adverb <u>well</u> was used as a complement, after the verb <u>smell</u> in one case and after the verb <u>taste</u> in another.

This error type was found to be a great deal more serious than the opposite error, viz. the use of an adjective instead of an adverb (cf. 20.3.5). However, it is found in the lower halves of the rank lists, with the exception of the rank list for foreignness, and it was found to be the least serious error type involving adverbs.

20.4.4 Conclusions

Two of the three adverbial error types are found in the upper halves of the rank lists of error types. Errors in the use of adverbs thus seem to be more serious from a communicative point of view than, for example, errors in the use of adjectives (cf. 20.3). The average error gravity index for the adverbial error types is 5.93 whereas the average error gravity index for the adjectival error types is 5.14. In comparison, the average error gravity index for all the 38 error types tested is 5.38. This means that two of the three adverbial error types have an error gravity index which is above the total average, whereas only two of the five adjectival errors have an error gravity index which is above the total average. These figures might, of course, have been different if other test sentences had been used to exemplify the various error types and if the classification of error types had been carried out in a different way, for which reason they should be taken as a very rough indication only.

20.5 IDIOM-PHR (error gravity index: 6.27)

(Improper use of certain idiomatic phrases)

Incorrect use of idiomatic phrases almost defies classification as an error type altogether because of the wide variety of such phrases in the language and their relative frequencies. For reasons of limited space, only two examples of the incorrect use of idiomatic phrases could be included in the questionnaires. These were judged very differently as regards their foreignness, but surprisingly similarly as regards their intelligibility.

The most serious violation of an idiomatic phrase turned out to be the phrase what is the clock, please? (for what is the time, please?), which, according to the answers given by the informants, made a very strong foreign impression on them, in fact the strongest foreign impression of all the 75 test sentences. However, it was found to give rise to only some intelligibility difficulty.

The less serious violation of an idiomatic phrase turned out to be the phrase look up for (for look out for), which was judged to be about as difficult to understand as the preceding idiomatic phrase, but was not perceived as making such an extreme foreign impression.

Improper use of the two idiomatic phrases tested gave rise to so much criticism that this error type is found among the seven worst error types in the rank lists. The only conclusion that can be drawn from this is that the two idiomatic phrases tested ought to be treated as important in the teaching of English to foreigners. In particular, it seems important to learn the correct usage for asking about time, and probably also for answering such questions and talking about time in general.

20.6 <u>Prepositional</u> <u>errors</u>

20.6.1 INS.PREP (error gravity index: 6.11)

(Insertion of preposition)

Reactions to improper insertion of a preposition were tested by means of five different sentences, two of which were B-control sentences.

The results show that the two B-control sentences, which tested reactions to insertion of the preposition <u>for</u> in sentences with <u>ago</u> were found to be a great deal more serious both from the foreignness and the intelligibility points of view than any of the other three examples of this error type. This is a particularly important consideration for all those who, like Swedish users of English, tend to make this type of error, perhaps as a result of interference from their mother tongue.

Generally speaking, out of all the 38 error types tested, this error type is one of the most serious, both from the foreignness and the intelligibility points of view, as well as the most serious error type having to do with prepositions. One of the reasons for this seems to be that insertion of a preposition can make a sentence ambiguous. This is the case for the two most serious of the five examples of this error type. The only case where the error of inserting a preposition was not judged to be very serious was the insertion of the appostive indicator (<u>of</u>) between <u>river</u> and the proper noun. This example was considerably more favourably met with than any of the other examples of this error type.

20.6.2 OM.PREP (Error gravity index: 5.93)

(Omission of preposition)

Omission of a preposition was tested by means of three different sentences and was found to be the second most serious error type having to do with prepositions, and more serious than most of the other 37 error types tested. The examples of this error type that were judged to be the most serious might give rise to ambiguity.

20.6.3 WR.PREP (Error gravity index: 5.43)

(Incorrect choice of prepositions)

Incorrect choice of prepositions was tested by means of three different sentences and was found to be the least serious of the error types having to do with prepositions. Compared to the other 37 error types tested it may be said to be of medium gravity, as it is found in the middle of the rank lists of error types and its error gravity index is very close to the average error gravity index for all the 38 error types tested (5.38).

One of the sentences used to test this error type was an example of incorrect choice of prepositions in a context where the preposition did not have a full lexical meaning. The results show that this error did not cause any great amount of intelligibility difficulty. This is consistent with Olsson's assumption (1977:52) that incorrect choice of prepositions in such contexts may be considered to constitute a small deviance from well-formed utterances. However, the sentence referred to (no. 37, cf. 10.1) made a fairly strong foreign impression on the informants, for which reason Olsson's assumption should not be generalized to apply outside the field of intelligibility. If foreignness is also considered, this error does, in fact, constitute more than a small deviance from well-formedness.

20.6.4 Conclusions

The three error types concerning prepositions are found fairly high up in the rank lists of error types. The least serious of them is found in the middle of the rank lists. They may therefore be said to be more serious than most of the other error types tested. This result is consistent with Johansson's finding that prepositional errors were close to the top of the 'irritability scale' (Johansson 1978:70), even though his investigation of prepositional errors was limited to incorrect choice of prepositions only. The average error gravity index for the three prepositional error types tested is 5.82, that is, somewhat higher than the average error gravity index for all the 38 error types (5.38).

20.7 SUBJECT (Error gravity index: 6.05)

(Improper use of subjects)

Incorrect choice between the prop subject it and the existential subject there was tested by means of two different sentences, one of which tested the use of it for there and the other one the opposite case. From the intelligibility point of view, the use of it instead of there was found to be more serious than the opposite case. This is important to consider, because this error seems to be made more often than the other error by many non-native users of English. There was no statistically significant difference between the means of the two sentences as regards foreignness.

This error type is found in the upper third of the rank lists and should therefore be regarded as more serious than most of the other error types tested.

20.8 <u>Article</u> <u>errors</u>

20.8.1 INS.DEFART (Error gravity index: 5.57)

(Insertion of the definite article)

Insertion of the definite article was exemplified by a sentence
with <u>most</u> in the sense 'more than half of' or 'nearly all',
before which the article was placed.

This error type was found to be the most serious of all the error
types involving articles. Even so, it only barely made its way
into the upper half of the combined rank list, and its error
gravity index is only slightly higher than the average error
gravity index for all the 38 error types (5.38). It may therefore
be said that one of the most important things to learn about
articles is when the definite article should not be used, such as
before <u>most</u>, when this word is used with the sense referred to
above. This is particularly important in view of the fact that
many non-native users of English tend to over-use the definite
article.

20.8.2 INS.INDART (error gravity index: 5.17)

(Insertion of the indefinite article)

Insertion of the indefinite article was tested by means of three
different sentences   where the article was inserted before an
adjective premodifying a following non-count noun.

This error type is found in the lower halves of the rank lists
and its error gravity index is lower than the average error
gravity index for all the 38 error types (5.38). Thus, it cannot
be said to be one of the more serious error types, compared to the
other 37 error types tested. Nevertheless, it was found to be the
second most serious error type involving articles.

20.8.3 OM.INDART (error gravity index: 5.16)

(Omission of the indefinite article)

Omission of the indefinite article was tested by means of a sentence where the article had been omitted after a copula followed by a complement designating a profession. The gravity of this error type was practically the same as for the preceding and opposite error type (cf. 20.8.2).

20.8.4 WR.INDART (error gravity index: 3.76)

(Incorrect form of the indefinite article)

Use of the wrong form of the indefinite article was exemplified by two sentences, in one of which a was used for an before a noun normally beginning with a vowel sound, whereas the other sentence tested the opposite case before a noun normally beginning with a consonant sound. The latter of these sentences was found to be the more serious example of this error type. However, neither of these sentences made a particularly strong foreign impression on the informants and both were judged to be easy to understand.

Generally speaking, this error type may be said to be a minor one, if not unimportant, as it is found almost at the bottom of the rank lists of error types, and its error gravity index is very low, compared to most of the other error types tested.

20.8.5 OM.DEFART (error gravity index: 3.36)

(Omission of the definite article)

Omission of the definite article was exemplified by a sentence with the name of a well-known hotel, before which the article was omitted. The proper noun was immediately followed by the common noun (hotel).

This error type did not only turn out to be the least serious of all the error types having to do with articles, it was also found to be the least serious of all the 38 error types tested, both from the foreignness and the intelligibility points of view. This may have to do with the indications found, that there may be a linguistic change in progress in this respect, perhaps eventually leading to a more general tendency to omit the definite article before the names of hotels, at least when the common noun is also used.

The results clearly show that this error type caused practically no intelligibility difficulty at all and only caused the sentence to make a slight foreign impression on the informants. This error type may therefore be regarded as a minor one. There are clearly more important things for learners and teachers of English to bother with than the use of the definite article with the names of hotels.

20.8.6 Conclusions

Four of the five error types having to do with articles are found in the lower halves of the rank lists, and two are at the very bottom of the lists. The most serious of the error types is found only about half way down the rank lists. None of the test sentences exemplifying these error types made a very strong foreign impression and they were all fairly easy or very easy to understand. The average error gravity index for these five error types is 4.60, which is considerably lower than the average error gravity index for the total 38 error types tested (5.38).

These results indicate that article errors generally may be considered to be minor errors. This agrees with Johansson's observation that article errors were at the bottom of the 'irritability scale'. He commented that his findings 'could perhaps be taken to indicate that articles play a minor role in understanding' (Johansson 1978:69).

Similar results have been obtained by Bradley (1970:87-93), even though he seems to be stretching the point a bit when he claims that the deletion of articles makes texts easier to understand.

Earlier assumptions and observations regarding articles have thus been borne out by this investigation.

20.9 NUMB (error gravity index: 5.52)

(Improper use of quantitative noun)

The use of the s-plural of the quantitative noun hundred premodified by a numeral and followed by an of-construction is found in the upper third of the rank list of error types for foreignness and just below the middle of the rank list of error types for intelligibility difficulty. It is found just above the middle of the combined rank list of error types. The error gravity index indicates that the combined effect of this error type is slightly more serious than the average combined effect of the 38 error types tested (5.38).

20.10 VOC (error gravity index: 5.49)

(Vocabulary errors)

Five sentences were used to test reactions to incorrect choice of words. In each of the five sentences the incorrect choice was made between two different verbs. As this error type consists in the choice between two lexical items and not in the choice of the actual forms of these verbs, it has been classified as a vocabulary error type and not as a verb error type.

This error type is found on either side of the middle of the two
rank lists of error types, viz. in the upper half of the rank list
for intelligibility difficulty and in the lower half of the rank
list for foreignness. In the combined list of error types it is
found just above the middle. The standard deviation from the
average mean is, however, greater in the rank list for
intelligibility difficulty (.43) than in the rank list for
foreignness (.24), which means that the various sentences used to
test this error type were perceived to be more different in their
relative intelligibility difficulty than in their relative
foreignness. There was, in other words, more agreement among the
informants as to the degree of foreignness of these sentences than
as to the degree of their intelligibility difficulty. There is a
lower correlation between the mean degrees of foreignness and the
mean degrees of intelligibility difficulty than is the case with
the sentences used to test concord errors (cf. 20.12), which can
be seen from the histogram below.

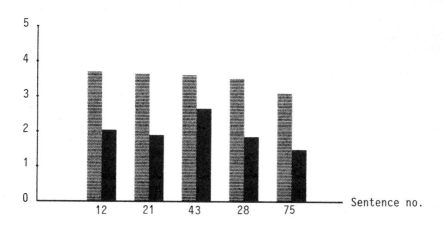

Histogram showing the correlation between the mean degrees of
foreignness and the mean degrees of intelligibility difficulty of
the five test sentences exemplifying vocabulary errors.
Correlation coefficient: .66609.

Generally speaking, the combined effect of this error type may be said to be of medium gravity, compared to the other 37 error types, as this error type is found just above the middle of the combined rank list and its error gravity index is close to the average error gravity index for all the 38 error types tested (5.38).

Johansson found that his informants answered in such a way that lexical errors were assigned a higher degree of irritation than were grammatical errors. However, a closer examination of the lexical errors he used reveals that some of them seem rather far-fetched (e.g. rapebones for ribs, and homage for headquarters) and in some cases more constructed than natural. Johansson's lexical errors also came from a wider variety of parts of speech (nouns, verbs, and adjectives) and in some cases were of a more complex type, such as the substitution of a single-word verb for a prepositional verb, and the substitution of a non-count noun for a count noun. He also substituted fictitious words for real ones, and in one case a word from one part of speech for a word from another part of speech.

This means that the lexical errors used by Johansson were less likely to be TRANSPARENT ERRORS, that is, errors which do not defy interpretation, than the errors used in this investigation. This is probably the reason why the lexical error type was assigned such a high degree of error gravity in Johansson's study. It also points to the importance of distinguishing between transparent errors and OPAQUE ERRORS, the latter defying interpretation altogether.

Even though lexical errors may seriously impair communication in certain cases, the principle of generality (cf. 1.8) ought to be considered as well. Thus, lexical errors cannot be treated as being on the same level as morphological or syntactical errors, apart from certain functional words. 'Taking a functional, pedagogical, approach we may say that infringements of general rules are more serious than lexical errors because the former are part of the process of learning skills at all stages, whereas the

latter have no "generality" and chiefly involve recall' (Petti
1979:10).

20.11 Improper use of nouns

20.11.1 GENITIVE (error gravity index: 4.94)

(Improper use of the group genitive)

Incorrect use of the group genitive was tested by means of a
sentence where the s-inflection was affixed to the head noun
rather than to the final part of the postmodification of the noun
phrase.

This turned out to be the most serious of all the error types
involving nouns. Nevertheless, it is found in the lower halves of
the rank lists. It should be noted, however, that it is
considerably higher up in the rank list for intelligibility
difficulty than in the rank list for foreignness, which means that
it was more of a medium error type in the former case, even though
it apparently did not cause any great amount of intelligibility
difficulty. Generally speaking, this error type may be said to be
less serious than most of the other error types tested. Its error
gravity index is also considerably lower than the average error
gravity index for all the 38 error types tested (5.38).

20.11.2 IRREG-PLUR (error gravity index: 4.81)

(Regular plural inflection for irregular plural form)

Use of the regular plural s-suffix instead of the irregular
mutation plural turned out to be the next most serious error type
involving nouns. Compared to the other 37 error types, this is one
of the least serious as regards intelligibility difficulty.

20.11.3 UNC   (error gravity index: 4.62)

(Non-count noun used as count noun)

Use of a non-count noun in the same way as a count noun was
tested by means of a sentence where the regular plural -s̲ suffix
was affixed to a non-count noun. Found in the lowest fourth of the
rank lists, this is one of the least serious of all the 38 error
types tested, both from the foreignness and the intelligibility
points of view.

20.11.4 <u>Conclusions</u>

The three error types involving the use of nouns were all found
well down in the lower halves of the rank lists and may therefore
be said to be less serious than most of the other error types
tested. It should be remembered, however, that none of these three
error types tested lexical errors, but rather the use of these
lexical items from a grammatical point of view. The average error
gravity index for the three error types involving nouns is 4.79,
as compared to 5.38 for all the 38 error types tested.

Johansson's examples of the improper use of nouns were subsumed
under the notion of morphological errors in the report on one of
his experiments and consisted merely in the repeated use of the
wrong plural form of the noun <u>shelf</u> (viz. <u>shelfs</u> for <u>shelves</u>).
This morphological error type was found to be the least serious
but one of his seven error types in that experiment. As slightly
different items were tested in Johansson's experiment compared to
this investigation, his result as regards reactions to incorrect
use of nouns cannot really be compared to the results obtained
here, even though the results of the two studies agree in
assigning a low degree of error gravity to improper use of nouns.

20.12 CONCORD (error gravity index: 4.79)

(Incongruity)

Five sentences were used to test reactions to the use of
incongruous elements within the same sentence. Out of these five
sentences, two were examples of incongruity between subject and
verb, two between quantifier and object, and one between
quantifier and subject.

This error type is found in the lowest third of the rank lists.
The standard deviation from the average mean, however, is much
larger in the rank list for foreignness (.74) than in the rank
list for intelligibility difficulty (.23), which means that the
various sentences used to test this error type were perceived more
differently as regards their relative foreignness than as regards
their relative intelligibility difficulty. In other words, there
was more agreement among the informants as to the degree of
intelligibility difficulty of these sentences than as to the
degree of their foreignness. However, there is a somewhat higher
correlation between the mean values for foreignness and the mean
values for intelligibility difficulty than was the case with the
sentences used to test vocabulary errors (cf. 20.10), which is
shown by the histogram below.

Mean

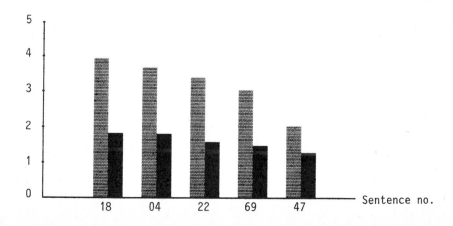

■ = foreignness ■ = intelligibility difficulty

Histogram showing the relatively high correlation between the mean degrees of foreignness and the mean degrees of intelligibility difficulty of the five test sentences exemplifying incongruity. As one value falls, either the other value also falls or stays (just about) the same. Correlation coefficient: .96319.

Generally speaking, this error type may be said to be of medium or minor gravity, compared to the other 37 error types tested, as it is found far down in the rank lists, and as the error gravity index is well below the average error gravity index for all the 38 error types tested (5.38). However, owing to the large number of test sentences that may be affected by this error type, its importance, particularly for conformity and acceptability, must not be underestimated. The principle of generality (cf. 1.8) therefore ought to be considered as well.

This result is consistent with that reported by Johansson (1978), who, in one of his experiments, found that the mean rating of concord errors placed them just below the middle of his rank list[24]. Even though Johansson's rank list consisted of only six error types and the group of concord errors was ranked number 3 (compared to this study Johansson used the reversed ranking system and ranked the most serious error type 6 and the least serious error type 1), it still shows that concord errors were not found to be among the most serious error types in his experiment. A similar result is reported in one of Johansson's earlier studies (1975).

20.13 WORD ORDER (error gravity index: 4.53)

(Improper word order)

Two sentences were used to test reactions to word-order errors. The relative gravity of this error type was nearly the same, as far as rank number is concerned, in the rank lists for foreignness and intelligibility difficulty, far down in the lower halves of the lists. This error type may thus be said to be of less gravity than most of the other error types tested. Its error gravity index is also well below the average error gravity index of the 38 error types tested (5.38).

The two sentences used to exemplify this error type were, however, judged very differently. The most serious one exemplified the placing of an adverbial clause of time between a pronominal subject and the verb in a subordinate clause and the least serious one exemplified the use of the split infinitive. The former sentence is found in the middle of the rank lists for the test sentences, whereas the latter sentence is found near the bottom of those lists.

This result runs counter to that obtained by Johansson (1978), who found that word-order errors were more serious, or just above the middle of his rank lists. However, Johansson did not investigate nearly as many different error types as have been investigated here, and in the case of word-order errors he used five sentences rather than two, none of which was an example of the use of what has here been found to be a less serious word-order error, viz. the split infinitive. Johansson's investigation of reactions to word-order errors is therefore not really comparable to the investigation of word-order errors made here. However, if the sentence exemplifying the use of the split infinitive is excluded from the comparison, the two investigations will be more readily comparable and the results more consistent.

20.14 DBL-NEG (error gravity index: 4.19)

(Multiple negation)

One sentence was used to test reactions to multiple negation, a phenomenon which, as was pointed out in chapter 14, is also very common in the English of many native speakers of the language. The sentence used was an example of double negation, that is, the use of two negatives with the meaning of that of a single negative. This error type is found in the lowest fifth of the combined rank list and may therefore be said to be a minor error compared to most of the other 37 error types tested. Its error gravity index is much lower than the average error gravity index for all the 38 error types tested (5.38). However, it is found considerably higher up in the rank list for intelligibility difficulty than in the rank list for foreignness.

Compared to the other error types, this error type was thus considered to be more of a medium error in the former case and a minor one in the latter. Nevertheless, the mean for foreignness is still higher than the mean for intelligibility difficulty.

Even though the reactions to the test sentence exemplifying multiple negation were rather mild, which probably has to do with the fact that this type of construction is very common in the English of many native speakers of the language, it is, of course, best to avoid multiple negation. Indeed it is wise never to make a statement negative if it could be made positive. In that way the reader or listener is spared the trouble of sorting the negatives out.

NOTES

1. It is important to make clear that within the range of language norms used by native speakers of English one would talk of SUBSTANDARD, DIALECT (cf. note 8), etc., rather than of errors. The term ERROR usually refers to a usage which differs from English norms of all dialects, and is thus, with the exception of misspellings, mainly used about the language of foreigners.

2. 'In fact, if we look closely at the number of informants representing a given cell, about whom a sociolinguistic generalization is made, more often than not, no more than a few informants are involved. For example, in both the Detroit dialect survey (cf. Wolfram 1969) and Macaulay's (1973) study of Glasgow, two speakers are representative of a particular cell, so that Macaulay's conclusions about "working class Glasgow women", for example, are based on the data from two women. Similarly, when the informants in Labov's (1966) study of New York City and Trudgill's (1974) study of Norwich are distributed among the parameters of age, sex, social class, etc. fewer than four informants are often involved.' (Romaine, 1982:109-110).

Le Page (1975) has also commented on the smallness of most sociolinguistic samples. He suggests that five informants should represent each cell, although there is no evidence to suggest that this number would provide more reasonable or representative results. 'Intuitively, this seems likely; but any such claim would have to be made on the basis of more sophisticated statistical operations than sociolinguists typically indulge in. An increase in sample size will not eliminate or reduce any bias already present in the selection procedure' (Romaine, 1982:110). Labov made the comment that 'linguistic behavior is far more general and compelling than many social attitudes or survey responses' (1966: 180). 'Since it is to be expected that the size of a sample is dependent on the expected homogeneity of the behavior to be observed, it has been assumed that reliable samples might be obtained by using much smaller numbers of informants in sociolinguistic research than in sociological surveys' (Romaine, 1982:108-109).

The reason for using a comparatively large number of informants here is that these investigations may be said to be both sociological and socio-linguistic in nature, as both attitudes to the English of foreigners and the linguistic behaviour of the test subjects is investigated (cf. 1.8).

3. Stratified is used here in the sense that each age group of informants makes up a predetermined proportion of the entire corpus (cf. 1.3). Random sampling is used here in the sense that each of the institutions referred to (in 1.2.2), located in the research area (cf. 1.2.2) had an equal chance of being chosen, independently of the other choices that were being made.

The method of random sampling as a means of selecting informants has been adopted from the social sciences and has sometimes been considered one of the methodological advances in sociolinguistics. It has been used for large-scale urban dialect studies, e.g. Labov in New York City, Macaulay in Glasgow, Trudgill in Norwich, and Wolfram in Detroit, to mention only a few. The Brown and Lancaster corpora constitute other examples of the use of random sampling in linguistics. The essential principle underlying the theory of random sampling is that the method of sampling is independent of the characteristic which is being sampled. Cf., however, Romaine for some critical comments on the value of random sampling in sociolinguistic studies (1982:107ff).

4. Cf., for instance, the following example and comment in Romaine (1982:108): 'Labov presented data to assess to what extent losses from the original sample affected the representativeness of his sample in comparison with the Lower East Side and the city as a whole (as does Trudgill for his sample in relation to Norwich as a whole), but there is no indication of what differences are likely to be significant. This problem could have been approached with more statistical sophistication, as is normally the case in social surveys where claims are made about randomness and representativeness of samples with respect to larger populations; but neither Labov nor Trudgill has done this.'
Cf. also note 2, second paragraph, above.

5. Analysis of variance is a statistical technique that is used to study the variability of experimental data. It can be used to see if certain factors contribute to that variability.

6. Linear regression is a statistical procedure used when you want to study relationships between variables. It can be used to learn if one variable can be expressed in terms of another and to predict one variable's values from another's values.

7. Correlation measures the closeness of a linear relationship between two variables. It is used to measure the strength of the relationship between two variables. If one variable x can be expressed exactly as a linear function of another variable y, then the correlation is 1 or -1, depending on whether the two variables are directly related or inversely related. A correlation of 0 between two variables means that each variable has no linear predictive ability for the other. If the values are normally distributed (cf. 1.2.4), then a correlation of 0 means that the variables are independent. The full name for this statistic is the Pearson product-moment correlation.

8.   The term DIALECT here refers to varieties of English distinguished from one another by differences of grammar and vocabulary, in accordance with the use of this term in Hughes-Trudgill (1979:8), and Trudgill-Hannah (1982:1).

9.   RP means received pronunciation. 'Received' here is to be understood in its nineteenth-century sense of 'accepted in the best society'. It is 'essentially the accent of those educated at public schools.--- It is largely through these schools that the accent is perpetuated. For RP, unlike prestige accents in other countries, is not the accent of any region (except historically: its origins were in the speech of London and the surrounding area). It is quite impossible to say from his pronunciation where an RP speaker comes from)' (Hughes-Trudgill 1979:3).

10.   The term ACCENT here refers to varieties of pronunciation, in accordance with the use of this term in Hughes-Trudgill (1979:8), and Trudgill-Hannah (1982:1).

11.   Cf. the following comment in Crystal (1971:137): 'Techniques of testing the acceptability or otherwise of language patterns are nowadays quite sophisticated--- I can give an idea of the kind of problem present by instancing some of the range of factors which need to be controlled in any investigation. First, a number of informants need to be selected. Exactly how many will vary, depending on my feelings as to how much variability I am likely to find in the results, and depending also, of course, on practical considerations of time and people available. They all have to be native speakers of the language, they have to be as unpreconceived as possible about linguistics ("linguistically naïve", as it is usually put), and they should come from as nearly homogeneous a background as possible (regional and educational variables being the most important). '

12.   By an OVERT ERROR is meant a readily identifiable error, like the breaking of a grammatical rule, the mispronunciation or misspelling of a certain word, etc., whereas a COVERT ERROR refers to a poverty of expression in the second language, i.e. 'exaggerated concentration on high-frequency forms and a propensity for circumlocution of difficult forms' (Weinreich 1953: 53, quoted by Johansson 1978:2).

13.   'An acceptable utterance is one that has been, or might be, produced by a native speaker in some appropriate context and is, or would be, accepted by other native speakers as belonging to the language in question' (Lyons 1968:137).

14.   Cf. the following example of another such phrase in Quirk et al, A Grammar of Contemporary English:

'He winced inside himself' (Quirk et al, 1972:212).

In that case, however, a reflexive pronoun is not considered obligatory, unlike the phrase which was tested in sentence 46.

15. The Oxford English Dictionary, volume 5 (1970).

16. ibid.

17.   POLAR QUESTION is an alternative and perhaps more convenient term for yes-no-question, found, for example, in Strang (1970: 84).

18. A Supplement to the Oxford English Dictionary, volume 1 (1972)

19. This term refers to the separation of to from the infinitive.

20.   Cf. the following comment in Quirk et al, A Grammar of Contemporary English:

'It must be acknowledged, however, that in some cases the "split infinitive" is the only tolerable ordering, or at least that avoiding the "split infinitive" is only possible at the cost of clumsiness or ambiguity. Examples for which there is no satisfactory alternative ordering to the "split infinitive" are:

I have tried to consciously stop worrying about it.

Part of your job, as a teacher, is to really understand your pupils' personal problems.' (Quirk et al 1972:725).

21.   'It is safe to say that constructions of the type I didn't have no dinner are employed by a majority of English speakers. --- It is, like most non-standard grammatical forms, most typical of working-class speech, and for that reason tends to have low prestige' (Hughes-Trudgill, 1979:14).

22.   Cf. the following example and comment in Quirk et al, A Grammar of Contemporary English:

'No one ever said nothing (Standard English No one ever said anything). The explanation of this construction is that substandard English chooses a negative word wherever Standard

English would choose a non-assertive word after a negative.'
(Quirk et al, 1972:379).

23. 'It is thus possible to have three or more negatives in most
non-standard English dialects, e.g. She couldn't get none nowhere'
(Hughes-Trudgill, 1979:13).

24. The mean rating for concord errors in Johansson's study was
3.28, which would correspond to 4.876 in the rating system used in
this study, according to the conversion tables below (ratings have
been rounded off to two decimals only). The results of the two
studies are thus almost identical as far as concord errors are
concerned. Cf. the conversion tables below.

Conversion table between Hultfors's and Johansson's rating system
for error gravity.

	Hultfors	Johansson
Highest degree of error gravity	10.0	1.00
	9.5	1.22
	9.0	1.44
	8.5	1.67
	8.0	1.89
	7.5	2.11
	7.0	2.33
	6.5	2.56
	6.0	2.78
	5.5	3.00
	5.0	3.22
	4.5	3.44
	4.0	3.67
	3.5	3.89
	3.0	4.11
	2.5	4.33
	2.0	4.56
Lowest degree of error gravity	1.5	4.78
	1.0	5.00

	Johansson	Hultfors
Highest degree of error gravity	1.0	10.00
	1.5	8.88
	2.0	7.75
	2.5	6.63
	3.0	5.50
	3.5	4.38
	4.0	3.25
Lowest degree of error gravity	4.5	2.13
	5.0	1.00

BIBLIOGRAPHY

Bansal, R K. 1965/1966. The Intelligibility of Indian English: Measurements of the Intelligibility of Connected Speech and Sentence and Word Material, Presented to Listeners of Different Nationalities. PhD dissertation. University College, London.

--- 1969. The Intelligibility of Indian English. Monograph 4. Central Institute of English. Hyderabad.

Bradley, M. 1970. 'Effects on Reading Tests of Deletions of Selected Grammatical Categories.' Nineteenth Yearbook of the National Reading Conference.87-93. Milwaukee, Wisconsin.

Chambers, Jack K and Peter Trudgill. 1980. Dialectology. Cambridge: Cambridge University Press.

Corder, Stephen Pit. 1973. Introducing Applied Linguistics. Harmondsworth: Penguin.

Crystal, David. 1971. Linguistics. Harmondsworth: Penguin.

Engh, Bertil. 1971. 'En toleransundersökning: tyska elever tolkar svenska elevers språkfel.' Pedagogisk-psykologiska problem. No. 137. Malmö: Malmö School of Education.

French, Frederick George. 1949. Common Errors in English; Their Cause, Prevention and Cure. London: Oxford University Press.

Hatch, Evelyn, and Hossein Farhady. 1982. Research Design and Statistics for Applied Linguistics. Newbury Applied Linguistics. Rowley, Mass.: Newbury House Publishers, Inc.

Hudson, Richard Anthony. 1980. Sociolinguistics. Cambridge: Cambridge University Press.

Hughes, Arthur and Peter Trudgill. 1979. English Accents and Dialects: an introduction to social and regional varieties of British English. London: Edward Arnold.

Hultfors, Pär. Forthcoming. Reactions to Non-Native English, Part 2: Foreigner Role and Interpretation. Stockholm Studies in English. Stockholm: Almqvist & Wiksell International.

James, C. 1972. 'The Diagnosis and Analysis of Error - Some Insights from Linguistics.' Audio-Visual Language Journal 10.75-79.

Johannesson, Nils-Lennart. 1986. English Language Essays. Investigation Method and Writing Strategies. Stockholm: Stockholm University, English Department.

Johansson, Stig. 1975. Papers in Contrastive Linguistics and Language Testing. Lund Studies in English 50. Lund: Gleerup.

---   1978. Studies of Error Gravity: Native Reactions to Errors Produced by Swedish Learners of English. Gothenburg Studies in English 44. Gothenburg: Acta Universitatis Gothoburgensis.

Labov, William. 1966. The Social Stratification of English in New York City. Washington, DC: Center for Applied Linguistics.

Landén, R and Arne Trankell. 1975. 'Människor som talar svenska med brytning', in Invandrarproblem: Fem uppsatser om invandrar- och minoritetsproblem från IMFO-gruppen vid Stockholms Universitet. 23-71. Stockholm: Pan/Norstedts.

Le Page, Robert Brock. 1975. Projection; focussing; diffusion; steps towards a sociolinguistic theory of language. Paper given to the Linguistics Association of Great Britain Meeting. Nottingham.

Linnarud, Moira. 1986. Lexis in Composition. A Performance Analysis of Swedish Learners' Written English. Lund Studies in English 74. Lund: CWK Gleerup.

Lyons, John. 1968. Introduction to Theoretical Linguistics. Cambridge: Cambridge University Press.

Macaulay, R K S. 1973. Language, Education and Employment in Glasgow. Report to the Social Science Research Council.

Olsson, Margareta. 1972. 'Intelligibility.' The GUME Project, No. 12. Gothenburg: Department of Educational Research, Gothenburg School of Education.

---   1973. 'The Effects of Different Types of Errors in the Communication Situation.' Errata, ed. by Jan Svartvik, 153-160. Lund: Gleerup.

---   1977. Intelligibility. An Evaluation of Some Features of English Produced by Swedish 14-Year-Olds. Gothenburg Studies in English 40. Gothenburg: Acta Universitatis Gothoburgensis.

The Oxford English Dictionary. 1970. London: Oxford University Press.

Petti, Vincent. 1979. Code of Errors. An assessment of errors in English made by Swedish students. Stockholm: Akademilitteratur.

Quirk, Randolph and Jan Svartvik. 1966. Investigating Linguistic Acceptability. The Hague: Mouton.

Quirk, Randolph, Sidney Greenbaum, Geoffrey Leech, and Jan Svartvik. 1972. A Grammar of Contemporary English. London: Longman.

Robinson, P. 1973. 'Testing the Second-Language Competence of Children and Adults.' English Language Teaching 27.190-199.

Romaine, Suzanne. 1982. Socio-Historical Linguistics, its status and methodology. Cambridge: Cambridge University Press.

Socioekonomisk indelning. SEI. 1982. Stockholm: Statistiska Centralbyrån.

Strang, Barbara. 1970. Modern English Structure. London: Edward Arnold.

Svartvik, Jan (ed.). 1973. Errata. Papers in Error Analysis. Lund: Gleerup.

Thagg Fisher, Ulla. 1985. The Sweet Sound of Concord. A Study of Swedish Learners' Concord Problems in English. Lund Studies in English 73. Lund: CWK Gleerup.

Trudgill, Peter. 1974. The Social Differentiation of English in Norwich. Cambridge: Cambridge University Press.

--- (ed.). 1978. Sociolinguistic Patterns in British English. London: Edward Arnold.

Trudgill, Peter, and Jean Hannah. 1982. International English: a guide to varieties of Standard English. London: Edward Arnold.

Wakelin, Martyn Francis. 1972. English Dialects: an introduction. London: Athlone Press.

Weinreich, Uriel. 1953. Languages in Contact - Findings and Problems. Publications of the Linguistic Circle of New York, No 1. New York, N.Y.

Winter, Jenny. 1973. Undersøgelsesmetodik og rapportskrivning. Copenhagen: Munksgaard.

Wolfram, Walter A. 1969. A Sociolinguistic Description of Detroit Negro Speech. Washington, D.C.: Center for Applied Linguistics.

APPENDIX 1

RANK LISTS OF TEST SENTENCES

Which of the test sentences made the strongest foreign impression on the informants and which of them was considered to be the most difficult to understand? In order to answer questions like these, rank lists of the mean values of the gradings, from the highest to the lowest mean value for both the question on foreignness and the question on intelligibility difficulty, were drawn up by means of several additional computations, both for the total sample of informants and for the three age groups, as well as for the two sex groups. The results of these computations are found in the following tables.

It should be noted that mean values have been rounded off to only two decimals in the following rank lists. However, the rank numbers are based on means with up to seven decimals, for which reason sentences with the same means in the rank lists may have been assigned different rank numbers. Sentences with exactly the same means have, however, been assigned the same rank number (tied ranks). Missing values are not included in the basic data on which the means have been calculated. Mean values with only one decimal or integers are exact values.

In the combined tables, the error gravity indices have been arrived at by adding the corresponding means for foreignness and intelligibility difficulty on the basis of the original means consisting of seven decimals. Therefore the sums may not be identical to those which are arrived at if the approximate means in the rank lists are added.

Rank lists of test sentences
Total sample

FOREIGNNESS (F)

Rank no.	(ID)	F	Mean	SD	Mode	Error type	Sentence quoted
1	(1)	34	4.53	.70	5	OM.DO-PPH	He thinks not that they know what to do.
2	(13)	41	4.5	.85	5	IDIOM-PHR	Excuse me, what is the clock, please?
3	(17)	39	4.45	.80	5	AUX	Can you French?
4	(17)	7	4.33	.90	5	OM.DO-PPH	Became he a dentist?
5	(10)	27	4.26	.99	5	OM.PREP	This room smells food, doesn't it?
6	(18)	46	4.19	.96	5	PPRO/RFPRO	She was standing alone,beside her with rage.
7	(18)	72	4.17	.97	5	OM.DO-PPH	Came he to the party yesterday?
8	(8)	2	4.11	.97	4	ADJ-PHR	He has an own company.
9	(4)	68	4.09	.95	4	INS.PREP	She was here for two years ago.
10	(12)	44	4.07	1.10	5	WR.ADVERB	He works very hardly.
11	(5)	42	4.05	1.08	5	OM.PREP	I was operated last week.
12	(19)	29	4.05	1.04	5	TENSE	Things have went too far.
13	(7)	5	4.05	1.05	5	INS.PREP	I was here for two years ago.
14	(38)	18	3.92	1.00	4	CONCORD	Here are the money I owe you.
15	(23)	57	3.91	1.05	4	SUBJECT	There's a long time since I saw her.
16	(25)	70	3.91	1.02	4	COMP.ADV	He drives badlier than his brother.
17	(31)	16	3.90	1.13	5	TENSE	I didn't saw him today.
18	(16)	50	3.89	1.11	4	INS.PREP	Smell on these flowers!
19	(45)	3	3.86	1.08	4	TENSE	I am born in 1945.
20	(20)	60	3.83	1.37	5	INS.PREP	I am sure of that he will come.
21	(15)	59	3.83	1.20	5	TO-INF/ING	Many cities have stopped to expand.
22	(42)	23	3.77	1.17	4	NUMB	He had to pay five hundreds of pounds.
23	(15)	55	3.73	1.13	4	AUX	He needs not come.
24	(22)	33	3.72	1.16	4	TO-INF/B	They made me to do it.
25	(44)	1	3.71	1.09	4	INS.INDART	What a dreadful weather!
26	(46)	51	3.71	1.11	4	INS.INDART	What an awful weather!
27	(27)	53	3.71	1.15	4	PRE/ATTADJ	He is a very alone man.
28	(24)	12	3.70	1.05	4	VOC	I always tried to make my best at school.
29	(21)	32	3.69	1.12	4	WR.PREP	I met him in the steps.
30	(37)	30	3.67	1.20	4	ADV/ADJ	This cake smells well!
31	(40)	4	3.66	1.10	4	CONCORD	I don't know much people in this town.
32	(11)	24	3.65	1.15	4	SUBJECT	It was little else to do.
33	(32)	21	3.64	1.33	5	VOC	The car was badly injured in the accident.
34	(34)	74	3.62	1.10	4	ING/SIMPVF	He is meaning this book, not that one.
35	(30)	43	3.61	1.20	4	VOC	Yesterday's accident depended on the bad.
36	(28)	58	3.61	1.12	4	RFPRO/PPRO	She had her radio beside herself.
37	(36)	73	3.59	1.19	4	WORD ORDER	When I five years ago visited London.....
38	(57)	66	3.58	1.07	4	COMP.ADJ	This is the goodest cake I have ever tasted!
39	(29)	56	3.57	1.04	4	INS.DEFART	The most people would agree with you.
40	(50)	47	3.56	1.13	4	WR.PREP	She is married with a German.
41	(33)	35	3.54	1.22	4	SIMPVF/ING	I am used to get up early in the morning.
42	(48)	40	3.54	1.16	4	OM.INDART	My sister is nurse.
43	(39)	9	3.53	1.16	4	WR.PREP	I met him in the stairs.
44	(52)	6	3.51	1.22	4	ADV/ADJ	This soup tastes well!
45	(35)	28	3.50	1.42	5	VOC	Who learnt you Spanish?
46	(54)	38	3.5	1.31	5	IRREG-VERB	They fighted bravely in the war.
47	(30)	17	3.45	1.29	4	ADJ^NOUN	I took the blind by the arm and led him...
48	(61)	64	3.43	1.19	3	IRREG-PLUR	The house was full of mouses.
49	(51)	22	3.38	1.27	2	CONCORD	My brother have worked for this company...
50	(14)	19	3.38	1.32	4	IDIOM-PHR	I shouted to him to look up for the car...

Rank lists of test sentences
Total sample

FOREIGNNESS (F)   /contd/

Rank no.	(ID)	F	Mean	SD	Mode	Error type	Sentence quoted
51	(56)	61	3.23	1.12	3	TENSE	The firm is established in 1970.
52	(55)	31	3.20	1.41	4	INS.INDART	It is a hard work to write a book.
53	(26)	13	3.18	1.27	4	INS.RELPRO	I don't know what improvements that are bei...
54	(41)	45	3.17	1.34	4	GENITIVE	This is my brother's-in-law cap.
55	(49)	54	3.13	1.29	4	INS.PREP	Have you ever seen the river of Ganges?
56	(59)	75	3.09	1.28	2,4	VOC	You do good coffee!
57	(53)	14	3.06	1.36	4	UNC	She has very limited knowledges of German...
58	(42)	26	3.06	1.21	4	WR.INDPRO	I haven't heard something from him.....
59	(58)	69	3.03	1.20	3	CONCORD	There is one chair too much.
60	(62)	52	2.89	1.28	4	SIMPVF/ING	I look forward to hear from you.
61	(60)	48	2.79	1.23	3	WR.INDART	He is an useful member of the team.
62	(63)	71	2.64	1.30	2	OM.PREP	We have just come back from the island Rhod...
63	(47)	67	2.56	1.28	2	DBL-NEG	I didn't buy nothing at the supermarket.
64	(68)	15	2.53	1.28	2	ADJ/ADV	He speaks French quite good.
65	(64)	20	2.29	1.33	1	WORD ORDER	He told me to not worry.
66	(66)	8	2.19	1.22	1	WR.INDPRO	None of my two brothers knew about my plan...
67	(69)	10	2.13	1.29	1	OM.DEFART	I am staying at Sheraton hotel for three...
68	(70)	62	2.10	1.21	1	WR.INDART	It took me a hour to get there.
69	(65)	63	2.03	1.09	1	ADJ^NOUN	He has a blue car and I have a red.
70	(67)	47	2.02	1.24	1	CONCORD	He has a great deal of problems.
71	(71)	11	1.13	.49	1	A-CONTROL	He has lived in London all his life.
72	(73)	65	1.07	.42	1	A-CONTROL	Have you heard from him lately?
73	(73)	36	1.03	.17	1	A-CONTROL	They were badly shaken by the news.
74	(73)	49	1.02	.14	1	A-CONTROL	Why did he leave so early?
75	(72)	25	1.02	.14	1	A-CONTROL	She prefers walking to cycling.

Rank lists of test sentences
Total sample

INTELLIGIBILITY DIFFICULTY (ID)

Rank no.	Sentence no.	Mean	SD	Mode	ID (F)	Error type	Sentence quoted
1	34	3.50	1.33	5	(1)	OM.DO-PPH	He thinks not that they know what to do.
2	39	3.19	1.28	3	(3)	AUX	Can you French?
3	46	3.04	1.35	2,3	(6)	PPRO/REFPRO	She was standing alone,beside her with rage.
4	68	2.93	1.37	2,4	(9)	INS.PREP	She was here for two years ago.
5	42	2.89	1.33	2,3	(11)	OM.PREP	I was operated last week.
6	59	2.86	1.38	3	(21)	TO-INF/ING	Many cities have stopped to expand.
7	5	2.69	1.37	1	(13)	INS.PREP	I was here for two years ago.
8	2	2.65	1.17	2	(8)	ADJ-PHR	He has an own company.
9	43	2.65	1.27	3	(35)	VOC	Yesterday's accident depended on the bad...
10	27	2.61	1.29	1	(5)	OM.PREP	This room smells food, doesn't it?
11	24	2.47	1.24	1	(32)	SUBJECT	It was little else to do.
12	44	2.47	1.28	1	(10)	WR.ADVERB	He works very hardly.
13	41	2.42	1.28	1	(2)	IDIOM-PHR	Excuse me, what is the clock, please?
14	19	2.25	1.25	1	(50)	IDIOM-PHR	I shouted to him to look up for the car....
15	55	2.22	1.28	1	(55)	AUX	He needs not come.
16	50	2.21	1.16	1	(18)	INS.PREP	Smell on these flowers!
17	7	2.21	1.17	1	(4)	OM.DO-PPH	Became he a dentist?
18	72	2.17	1.17	1	(7)	OM.DO-PPH	Came he to the party yesterday?
19	29	2.17	1.13	2	(12)	TENSE	Things have went too far.
20	60	2.14	1.19	1	(20)	INS.PREP	I am sure of that he will come.
21	32	2.10	1.08	1	(29)	WR.PREP	I met him in the steps.
22	33	2.08	1.11	1	(24)	TO-INF/ING	They made me to do it.
23	57	2.07	1.01	1	(15)	SUBJECT	There's a long time since I saw her.
24	12	2.04	1.00	2	(28)	VOC	I always tried to make my best at school.
25	70	2.03	1.03	1,2	(16)	COMP.ADV	He drives badlier than his brother.
26	13	2.02	1.00	1	(53)	INS.RELPRO	He don't know what improvements that are .....
27	53	2.02	1.12	1	(53)	PRE/ATTADJ	He is a very alone man.
28	58	2.02	1.02	1	(36)	RFPRO/PPRO	She had her radio beside herself.
29	56	2	1.05	1	(36)	INS.DEFART	The most people would agree with you.
30	17	1.91	1.02	1	(47)	ADJ'NOUN	I took the blind by the arm and led him....
31	16	1.91	.94	1	(17)	TENSE	I didn't saw him today.
32	21	1.89	1.15	1	(33)	VOC	The car was badly injured in the accident.
33	35	1.86	1.02	1	(41)	SIMPVF/ING	I am used to get up early in the morning.
34	74	1.85	1.08	1	(34)	ING/SIMPVF	He is meaning this book, not that one.
35	28	1.85	.96	1	(45)	VOC	Who learnt you Spanish?
36	73	1.84	.98	1	(37)	WORD ORDER	When I five years ago visited London...
37	30	1.83	1.02	1	(30)	ADV/ADJ	This cake smells well!
38	18	1.82	.95	1	(18)	CONCORD	Here are the money I owe you.
39	9	1.81	.90	1	(43)	WR.PREP	I met him in the stairs.
40	4	1.80	.94	1	(31)	CONCORD	I don't know much people in this town.
41	45	1.77	1.10	1	(54)	GENITIVE	This is my brother's-in-law cap.
42	23	1.75	.95	1	(22)	NUMB	He had to pay five hundreds of pounds.
43	26	1.75	.87	1	(26)	WR.INDPRO	I haven't heard something from him....
44	1	1.70	.86	1	(25)	INS.INDART	What a dreadful weather!
45	3	1.68	.79	1	(19)	TENSE	I am born in 1945.
46	51	1.66	.89	1	(26)	INS.INDART	What an awful weather!
47	67	1.63	.99	1	(63)	DBL-NEG	I didn't buy nothing at the supermarket.
48	40	1.62	.86	1	(42)	OM.INDART	My sister is nurse.
49	54	1.61	.97	1	(55)	INS.PREP	Have you ever seen the river of Ganges?
50	37	1.6	.79	1	(40)	WR.PREP	She is married with a German.

Rank lists of test sentences
Total sample

INTELLIGIBILITY DIFFICULTY (ID) /contd/

Rank no.	Sentence no.	Mean	SD	Mode	ID (F)	Error type	Sentence quoted
51	22	1.58	.76	1	(49)	CONCORD	My brother have worked for this company..
52	6	1.58	.88	1	(44)	ADV/ADJ	This soup tastes well!
53	14	1.56	.73	1	(57)	UNC	She has very limited knowledges of German.
54	38	1.53	.80	1	(46)	IRREG-VERB	They fighted bravely in the war.
55	31	1.53	.76	1	(52)	INS.INDART	It is a hard work to write a book.
56	61	1.51	.68	1	(51)	TENSE	The firm is established in 1970.
57	66	1.50	.78	1	(38)	COMP.ADJ	This is the goodest cake I have ever tasted
58	69	1.48	.68	1	(59)	CONCORD	There is one chair too much.
59	75	1.48	.78	1	(56)	VOC	You do good coffee!
60	48	1.43	.77	1	(61)	WR.INDART	He is an useful member of the team.
61	64	1.39	.71	1	(48)	IRREG-PLUR	The house was full of mouses.
62	52	1.38	.62	1	(60)	SIMPVF/ING	I look forward to hear from you.
63	71	1.35	.71	1	(62)	OM.PREP	We have just come back from the island Rhod
64	20	1.35	.64	1	(65)	WORD ORDER	He told me to not worry.
65	63	1.31	.66	1	(69)	ADJ'NOUN	He has a blue car and I have a red.
66	8	1.28	.53	1	(66)	WR.INDPRO	None of my two brothers knew about my plans
67	47	1.28	.54	1	(70)	CONCORD	We have a great deal of problems.
68	15	1.26	.50	1	(64)	ADJ/ADV	He speaks French quite good.
69	10	1.23	.61	1	(67)	OM.DEFART	I am staying at Sheraton hotel for three days
70	62	1.19	.44	1	(68)	WR.INDART	It took me a hour to get there.
71	11	1.04	.19	1	(71)	A-CONTROL	He has lived in London all his life.
72	25	1.01	.10	1	(75)	A-CONTROL	She prefers walking to cycling.
73	36	1	0	1	(73)	A-CONTROL	They were badly shaken by the news.
73	49	1	0	1	(74)	A-CONTROL	Why did he leave so early?
73	65	1	0	1	(72)	A-CONTROL	Have you heard from him lately?

Rank lists of test sentences

Total sample

COMBINED TABLE (error gravity with regard to both F and ID)

Rank no.	Error gravity index	Sentence no.	Error type	Sentence quoted
1	8.04	34	OM.DO-PPH	He thinks not that they know what to do.
2	7.64	39	AUX	Can you French?
3	7.22	46	PPRO/RFPRO	She was standing alone, beside her with rage.
4	7.02	68	INS.PREP	She was here for two years ago.
5	6.93	42	OM.PREP	I was operated last week.
6	6.92	41	IDIOM-PHR	Excuse me, what is the clock, please?
7	6.87	27	OM.PREP	This room smells food, doesn't it?
8	6.76	2	ADJ-PHR	He has an own company.
9	6.74	5	INS.PREP	I was here for two years ago.
10	6.69	59	TO-INF/ING	Many cities have stopped to expand.
11	6.54	44	WR.ADVERB	He works very hardly.
12	6.53	7	OM.DO-PPH	Became he a dentist?
13	6.34	72	VOC	Came he to the party yesterday?
14	6.26	43	OM.DO-PPH	Yesterday's accident depended on the bad weather.
15	6.21	29	TENSE	Things have went too far.
16	6.12	24	SUBJECT	It is little else to do.
17	6.10	50	INS.PREP	Smell on these flowers!
18	5.98	57	SUBJECT	There's a long time since I saw her.
19	5.97	60	INS.PREP	I am sure of that he will come.
20	5.95	55	AUX	He needs not come.
21	5.94	70	COMP.ADV	He drives badlier than his brother.
22	5.80	16	TENSE	I didn't saw him today.
23	5.80	33	TO-INF/B	They made me to do it.
24	5.79	32	WR.PREP	I met him in the steps.
25	5.74	12	VOC	I always tried to make my best at school.
26	5.74	18	CONCORD	Here are the money I owe you.
27	5.73	53	PRE/ATTADJ	He is a very alone man.
28	5.62	58	RFPRO/PPRO	She had her radio beside herself.
29	5.62	19	IDIOM-PHR	I shouted to him to look up for the car when I saw...
30	5.57	56	INS.DEFART	The most people would agree with you.
31	5.54	3	TENSE	I am born in 1945.
32	5.52	21	VOC	The car was badly injured in the accident.
33	5.52	23	NUMB	He had to pay five hundreds of pounds.
34	5.50	30	ADV/ADJ	This cake smells well!
35	5.47	74	ING/SIMPVF	He is meaning this book, not that one.
36	5.46	4	CONCORD	I don't know much people in this town.
37	5.43	73	WORD ORDER	When I five years ago visited London...
38	5.41	1	INS.INDART	What a dreadful weather!
39	5.40	35	SIMPVF/ING	I am used to get up early in the morning.
40	5.37	51	INS.INDART	What an awful weather!
41	5.36	17	ADJ^NOUN	I took the blind by the arm and led him...
42	5.36	28	VOC	Who learnt you Spanish?
43	5.34	9	WR.PREP	I met him in the stairs.
44	5.19	13	INS.RELPRO	I don't know what improvements that are...
45	5.16	40	OM.INDART	My sister is nurse.
46	5.16	37	WR.PREP	She is married with a German.
47	5.09	6	ADV/ADJ	This soup tastes well!
48	5.08	66	COMP.ADJ	This is the goodest cake I have ever tasted!
49	5.03	38	IRREG-VERB	They fighted bravely in the war.
50	4.96	22	CONCORD	My brother have worked for this company...

Rank lists of test sentences

Total sample

COMBINED TABLE (error gravity with regard to both F and ID) /contd/

Rank no.	Error gravity index	Sentence no.	Error type	Sentence quoted
51	4.94	45	GENITIVE	This is my brother's-in-law cap.
52	4.81	64	IRREG-PLUR	The house was full of mouses.
53	4.80	26	WR.INDPRO	I haven't heard something from him...
54	4.75	54	INS.PREP	Have you ever seen the river of Ganges?
55	4.74	61	TENSE	The firm is established in 1970.
56	4.73	31	INS.INDART	It is a hard work to write a book.
57	4.62	14	UNC	She has very limited knowledges of German.
58	4.57	75	VOC	You do good coffee!
59	4.51	69	CONCORD	There is one chair too much.
60	4.27	52	SIMPVF/ING	I look forward to hear from you.
61	4.23	48	WR.INDART	He is an useful member of the team.
62	4.19	67	DBL-NEG	I didn't buy nothing at the supermarket.
63	3.99	71	OM.PREP	We have just come back from the island Rhodes.
64	3.79	15	ADJ/ADV	He speaks French quite good.
65	3.64	20	WORD ORDER	He told me to not worry.
66	3.47	8	WR.INDPRO	None of my two brothers knew about my plans.
67	3.36	10	OM.DEFART	I am staying at Sheraton hotel for three days.
68	3.34	63	ADJ^NOUN	He has a blue car and I have a red.
69	3.30	47	CONCORD	We have a great deal of problems.
70	3.29	62	WR.INDART	It took me a hour to get there.
71	2.17	11	A-CONTROL	He has lived in London all his life.
72	2.07	65	A-CONTROL	Have you heard from him lately?
73	2.03	36	A-CONTROL	They were badly shaken by the news.
74	2.03	25	A-CONTROL	She prefers walking to cycling.
75	2.02	49	A-CONTROL	Why did the leave so early?

Rank lists of test sentences

Age groups

Teen-agers

FOREIGNNESS (F)

Rank no.	F (ID)	Sentence no.	Mean	SD	Mode	Error type	Sentence quoted
1	(3)	27	4.63	.62	5	OM.PREP	This room smells food, doesn't it?
2	(1)	34	4.53	.74	5	OM.DO-PPH	He thinks not that they know what to do.
4	(14)	41	4.53	.74	5	IDIOM-PHR	Excuse me, what is the clock, please?
4	(5)	39	4.43	.73	5	AUX	Can you French?
5	(22)	7	4.37	.85	5	OM.DO PPH	Became he a dentist?
6	(5)	42	4.27	.69	4	OM.PREP	I was operated last week.
7	(10)	2	4.26	.69	4	ADJ-PHR	He has an own company.
8	(2)	46	4.25	.89	5	PPRO/RFPRO	She was standing alone, beside her with rage.
9	(9)	5	4.23	.78	4,5	INS.PREP	I was here for two years ago.
11	(16)	29	4.23	.81	4	TENSE	Things have went too far.
11	(15)	72	4.09	.94	4	OM.DO-PPH	Came he to the party yesterday?
12	(12)	50	4.07	.90	4	INS.PREP	Smell on these flowers!
13	(7)	68	4.05	.75	4	INS.PREP	She was here for two years ago.
14	(13)	44	4.02	1.05	4	WR.ADVERB	He works very hardly.
14	(24)	57	4.02	.85	4	SUBJECT	There's a long time since I saw her.
16	(33)	16	4	.88	4	TENSE	I didn't saw him today.
16	(43)	23	4	1.02	4,5	NUMB	He had to pay five hundreds of punds.
18	(36)	18	3.98	.78	4	CONCORD	Here are the money I owe you.
19	(18)	55	3.95	.78	4	AUX	He needs not come.
20	(21)	33	3.93	.89	4	TO-INF/B	They made me to do it.
21	(41)	1	3.91	.68	4	INS.INDART	What a dreadful weather!
21	(49)	3	3.91	.92	4	TENSE	I am born in 1945.
24	(34)	30	3.91	1.15	4,5	ADV/ADJ	This cake smells well!
24	(42)	51	3.86	.95	4	INS.INDART	What an awful weather!
25	(30)	32	3.84	.95	4	WR.PREP	I met him in the steps.
26	(26)	70	3.82	.84	4	COMP.ADV	He drives badlier than his brother.
27	(43)	28	3.81	1.35	5	VOC	Who learnt you Spanish?
28	(23)	12	3.79	.94	4	VOC	I always tried to make my best at school.
29	(31)	35	3.77	1.09	4	SIMPVF/ING	I am used to get up early in the morning.
30	(32)	53	3.75	1.08	3	PRE/ATTADJ	He is a very alone man.
31	(8)	43	3.73	.95	4	VOC	I am sure of that he will come.
32	(18)	60	3.66	1.48	5	INS.PREP	Yesterday's accident depended on the bad ...
33	(48)	6	3.65	1.11	3,4,5	ADV/ADJ	This soup tastes well!
34	(37)	9	3.63	1.09	4	WR.PREP	I met him in the stairs.
36	(4)	59	3.63	1.16	4	TO-INF/ING	Many cities have stopped to expand.
36	(40)	4	3.62	1.01	4	CONCORD	The most people would agree with you.
37	(25)	56	3.61	.89	4	INS.DEFART	I don't know much people in this town.
38	(43)	22	3.60	1.07	4	CONCORD	My brother have worked for this company for...
39	(26)	74	3.59	1.09	4	ING/SIMPVF	He is meaning this book, not that one.
40	(39)	21	3.57	1.33	5	VOC	The car was badly injured in the accident.
41	(46)	40	3.52	1.05	4	OM.INDART	My sister is nurse.
42	(49)	31	3.51	1.32	4	INS.INDART	It is a hard work to write a book.
43	(11)	24	3.49	1.14	4	SUBJECT	It was little else to do.
44	(56)	66	3.45	.82	4	COMP.ADJ	This is the goodest cake I have ever tasted!
45	(29)	17	3.43	1.25	4	ADJ^NOUN	I took the blind by the arm and led him...
46	(38)	58	3.41	1.04	4	WORD ORDER	She had her radio beside herself.
47	(28)	73	3.41	1.21	3,4	RFPRO/PPRO	When I five years ago visited London...
48	(53)	37	3.40	1.03	3,4	WR.PREP	She is married with a German.
49	(35)	45	3.39	1.08	3,4	GENITIVE	This is my brother's-in-law cap.
50	(16)	13	3.33	1.08	4	INS.RELPRO	I don't know what improvements that are being..

Rank lists of test sentences

Age groups

Teen-agers

FOREIGNNESS (F) /contd/

Rank no.	F (ID)	Sentence no.	Mean	SD	Mode	Error type	Sentence quoted
51	(63)	64	3.20	.93	3	IRREG-PLUR	The house was full of mouses.
52	(20)	19	3.07	1.42	3	IDIOM-PHR	I shouted to him to look up for the car...
53	(59)	38	3.07	1.30	4	IRREG-VERB	They fighted bravely in the war.
53	(54)	61	3.07	.97	3	TENSE	The firm is established in 1970.
55	(49)	14	2.95	1.07	2,3	UNC	She has very limited knowledges of German.
56	(57)	75	2.84	1.16	2,3	VOC	You do good coffee!
57	(52)	26	2.84	1.11	3	WR.INDPRO	I haven't heard something from him...
58	(60)	48	2.82	1.23	3	WR.INDART	He is an useful member of the team.
59	(57)	69	2.68	1.01	3	CONCORD	There is one chair too much.
60	(62)	52	2.66	1.26	2	SIMPVF/ING	I look forward to hear from you.
61	(55)	54	2.64	1.26	4	INS.PREP	Have you ever seen the river of Ganges?
62	(47)	67	2.41	1.13	4	DBL-NEG	I didn't buy nothing at the supermarket.
63	(65)	20	2.38	1.36	1	ADJ^NOUN	He told me to not worry.
64	(61)	63	2.20	1.09	1,2	ADJ^NOUN	We have a blue car and I have a red.
65	(64)	71	2.18	1.13	1	OM.PREP	We have just come back from the island Rhodes.
66	(68)	15	2.17	1.06	2	ADJ/ADV	He speaks French quite good.
67	(67)	62	2.12	1.14	1	WR.INDART	It took me a hour to get there.
68	(66)	8	2.05	1.02	2	WR.INDPRO	None of my two brothers knew about my plans.
69	(69)	10	1.72	1.05	1	OM.DEFART	I am staying at Sheraton hotel for three...
70	(70)	47	1.48	.76	1	CONCORD	We have a great deal of problems.
71	(71)	11	1.21	.67	1	A-CONTROL	He has lived in London all his life.
72	(72)	25	1.05	.21	1	A-CONTROL	She prefers walking to cycling.
73	(73)	65	1.05	.21	1	A-CONTROL	Have you heard from him lately?
74	(73)	36	1.02	.15	1	A-CONTROL	They were badly shaken by the news.
75	(73)	49	1	0	1	A-CONTROL	Why did he leave so early?

Rank lists of test sentences

Age groups

Teen-agers

INTELLIGIBILITY DIFFICULTY (ID)

Rank no.	(F)	Sentence no.	Mean	SD	Mode	Error type	Sentence quoted
ID							
1	(2)	34	3.90	1.21	5	OM.DO-PPH	He thinks not that they know what to do.
2	(8)	46	3.52	1.19	3	PPRO/RFPRO	She was standing alone, beside her with rage.
3	(1)	27	3.45	1.11	3	OM.PREP	This room smells food, doesn't it?
4	(34)	59	3.35	1.18	3	TO-INF/ING	Many cities have stopped to expand.
5	(4)	39	3.34	1.18	3	AUX	Can you French?
6	(6)	42	3.34	1.12	3	OM.PREP	I was operated last week.
7	(13)	68	3.30	1.13	4	INS.PREP	She was here for two years ago.
8	(31)	43	3.14	1.09	4	VOC	Yesterday's accident depended on the bad ...
9	(5)	5	3.12	1.18	3	INS.PREP	I was here for two years ago.
10	(7)	2	2.98	1.06	2	ADJ-PHR	He has an own company.
11	(43)	24	2.79	1.21	2	SUBJECT	It was little else to do.
12	(12)	50	2.66	1.01	2	INS.PREP	Smell on these flowers!
13	(14)	44	2.64	1.18	2	WR.ADVERB	He works very hardly.
14	(22)	41	2.63	1.22	3	IDIOM-PHR	Excuse me, what is the clock, please?
15	(11)	72	2.61	1.10	2	OM.DO-PPH	Came he to the party yesterday?
16	(50)	13	2.60	1.05	2	INS.RELPRO	I don't know what improvements that are ...
16	(9)	29	2.60	.83.	1	TENSE	Things have went too far.
18	(32)	55	2.59	1.15	2	AUX	He needs not come.
18	(32)	60	2.59	1.30	1,3	INS.PREP	I am sure of that he will come.
20	(52)	19	2.5	1.31	2	IDIOM-PHR	I shouted to him to look up for the car...
21	(20)	33	2.48	1.04	3	TO-INF/B	They made me to do it.
22	(5)	7	2.44	1.10	2	OM.DO-PPH	Became he a dentist?
23	(28)	12	2.40	.93	2	VOC	I always tried to make my best at school.
24	(14)	57	2.39	.97	2	SUBJECT	There's a long time since I saw her.
25	(37)	56	2.36	1.04	2	INS.DEFART	The most people would agree with you.
26	(26)	70	2.34	.94	2	COMP.ADV	He drives badlier than his brother.
26	(39)	74	2.34	1.16	2	ING/SIMPVF	He is meaning this book, not that one.
28	(73)	73	2.32	1.16	1	WORD ORDER	When I five years ago visited London....
29	(45)	17	2.29	1.13	2	ADJ^NOUN	I took the blind by the arm and led him...
30	(23)	32	2.28	.88	2	WR.PREP	I met him in the steps.
31	(29)	35	2.26	1.03	2	SIMPVF/ING	I am used to get up early in the morning.
32	(30)	53	2.23	1.03	2	TENSE	He is a very alone man.
33	(16)	16	2.21	.78	2	TENSE	I didn't saw him today.
34	(21)	30	2.19	1.10	2	ADV/ADJ	This cake smells well!
35	(45)	45	2.16	1.22	1	GENITIVE	This is my brother's-in-law cap.
36	(18)	18	2.14	.84	2	CONCORD	Here are the money I owe you.
37	(34)	9	2.14	.86	2	WR.PREP	I met him in the stairs.
38	(46)	58	2.11	.89	2	RFPRO/PPRO	She had her radio beside herself.
39	(40)	21	2.10	1.28	1	VOC	The car was badly injured in the accident.
40	(36)	4	2.07	.92	2	CONCORD	I don't know how much people in this town.
41	(21)	1	2.05	.79	2	INS.INDART	What a dreadful weather!
42	(24)	51	2.05	.94	2	INS.INDART	What an awful weather!
43	(38)	22	1.98	.83	2	CONCORD	My brother have worked for this company...
43	(16)	23	1.98	.99	2	NUMB	He had to pay five hundreds of pounds.
43	(27)	28	1.98	.89	2	VOC	Who learnt you Spanish?
46	(41)	40	1.93	.87	2	OM.INDART	My sister is nurse.
47	(62)	67	1.89	1.06	1	DBL-NEG	I didn't buy nothing at the supermarket.
48	(33)	6	1.88	.93	2	ADV/ADJ	This soup tastes well!
48	(21)	3	1.84	.75	2	TENSE	I am born in 1945.
49	(55)	14	1.84	.72	2	UNC	She has very limited knowledges of German.

Rank lists of test sentences

Age groups

Teen-agers

INTELLIGIBILITY DIFFICULTY (ID) /contd/

Rank no.	(F)	Sentence no.	Mean	SD	Mode	Error type	Sentence quoted
ID							
49	(42)	31	1.84	.87	2	INS.INDART	It is a hard work to write a book.
52	(57)	26	1.81	.88	1	WR.INDPRO	I haven't heard something from him.
53	(48)	37	1.79	.77	1	WR.PREP	She is married with a German.
54	(53)	61	1.77	.74	2	TENSE	The firm is established in 1970.
55	(61)	54	1.75	.99	1	INS.PREP	Have you ever seen the river of Ganges?
56	(44)	66	1.64	.61	2	COMP.ADJ	This is the goodest cake I have ever tasted!
57	(59)	69	1.61	.60	2	CONCORD	There is one chair too much.
57	(56)	75	1.61	.69	1	VOC	You do good coffee!
59	(53)	38	1.59	.69	1	IRREG-VERB	They fighted bravely in the war.
60	(58)	48	1.57	.70	1	WR.INDART	He is an useful member of the team.
61	(64)	63	1.52	.70	1	ADJ^NOUN	He has a blue car and I have a red.
62	(60)	52	1.5	.63	1	SIMPVF/ING	I look forward to hear from you.
63	(51)	64	1.45	.50	1	IRREG-PLUR	The house was full of mouses.
64	(65)	71	1.41	.82	1	OM.PREP	We have just come back from the island Rhodes.
65	(63)	20	1.40	.59	1	WORD ORDER	He told me to not worry.
66	(68)	8	1.40	.58	1	WR.INDPRO	None of my two brothers knew about my plans.
67	(67)	62	1.35	.57	1	WR.INDART	It took me a hour to get there.
68	(66)	15	1.26	.54	1	ADJ/ADV	He speaks French quite good.
69	(69)	10	1.26	.49	1	OM.DEFART	I am staying at Sheraton hotel for three days
70	(70)	47	1.23	.52	1	CONCORD	We have a great deal of problems.
71	(71)	11	1.07	.26	1	A-CONTROL	He has lived in London all his life.
72	(72)	25	1.02	.15	1	A-CONTROL	She prefers walking to cycling.
73	(74)	36	1	0	1	A-CONTROL	They were badly shaken by the news.
73	(75)	49	1	0	1	A-CONTROL	Why did he leave so early?
73	(73)	65	1	0	1	A-CONTROL	Have you heard from him lately?

Rank lists of test sentences

Age groups

Teen-agers

COMBINED TABLE (error gravity with regard to both F and ID)

Rank no.	Error gravity index	Sentence no.	Error type	Sentence quoted
1	8.44	34	OM.DO-PH	He thinks not that they know what to do.
2	8.08	27	OM.PREP	This room smells food, doesn't it?
3	7.77	46	PPRO/RFPRO	She was standing alone, beside her with rage.
3	7.77	39	AUX	Can you French?
5	7.61	42	OM.PREP	I was operated last week.
6	7.35	5	INS.PREP	I was here for two years ago.
7	7.34	68	INS.PREP	She was here for two years ago.
8	7.23	2	ADJ-PHR	He has an own company.
9	7.16	41	IDIOM-PHR	Excuse me, what is the clock, please?
10	6.98	59	TO-INF/ING	Many cities have stopped to expand.
11	6.86	43	VOC	Yesterday's accident depended on the bad weather.
12	6.84	29	TENSE	Things have went too far.
13	6.81	7	OM.DO-PH	Became he a dentist?
14	6.73	50	INS.PREP	Smell on these flowers!
15	6.70	72	OM.DO-PH	Came he to the party yesterday?
16	6.66	44	WR.ADVERB	He works very hardly.
17	6.55	55	AUX	He needs not come.
18	6.41	57	SUBJECT	There's a long time since I saw her.
19	6.40	33	TO-INF/B	They made me to do it.
20	6.28	24	SUBJECT	It was little else to do.
21	6.25	60	INS.PREP	I am sure of that he will come.
22	6.21	16	TENSE	I didn't saw him today.
23	6.19	12	VOC	I always tried to make my best at school.
24	6.16	70	COMP.ADV	He drives badlier than his brother.
25	6.12	18	CONCORD	Here are the money I owe you.
26	6.12	32	WR.PREP	I met him in the steps.
27	6.09	30	ADV/ADJ	This cake smells well!
28	6.02	35	SIMPVF/ING	I am used to get up early in the morning.
29	5.98	53	PRE/ATTADJ	He is a very alone man.
29	5.98	56	INS.DEFART	The most people would agree with you.
31	5.98	23	NUMB	He had to pay five hundreds of punds.
32	5.95	1	INS.INDART	What a dreadful weather!
33	5.93	74	ING/SIMPVF	He is meaning this book, not that one.
34	5.93	13	INS.RELPRO	I don't know what improvements that are...
35	5.91	51	INS.INDART	What an awful weather!
36	5.79	28	VOC	Who learnt you Spanish?
37	5.77	9	WR.PREP	I met him in the stairs.
38	5.74	3	TENSE	I am born in 1945.
39	5.73	73	WORD ORDER	When I five years ago visited London...
40	5.71	17	ADJ-NOUN	I took the blind by the arm and led him...
41	5.69	4	CONCORD	I don't know much people in this town.
42	5.67	21	VOC	The car was badly injured in the accident.
43	5.58	22	CONCORD	My brother have worked for this company...
44	5.57	19	IDIOM-PHR	I shouted to him to look up for the car when I saw...
45	5.55	45	GENITIVE	This is my brother's-in-law cap.
46	5.53	6	ADV/ADJ	This soup tastes well!
47	5.52	58	RFPRO/PPRO	She had her radio beside herself.
48	5.45	40	OM.INDART	My sister is nurse.
49	5.35	31	INS.INDART	It is a hard work to write a book.
50	5.19	37	WR.PREP	She is married with a German.

Rank lists of test sentences

Age groups

Teen-agers

COMBINED TABLE (error gravity with regard to both F and ID) /contd/

Rank no.	Error gravity index	Sentence no.	Error type	Sentence quoted
51	5.09	66	COMP.ADJ	This is the goodest cake I have ever tasted!
52	4.84	61	TENSE	The firm is established in 1970.
53	4.79	14	UNC	She has very limited knowledges of German.
54	4.66	38	IRREG-VERB	They fighted bravely in the war.
54	4.66	64	IRREG-PLUR	The house was full of mouses.
56	4.65	26	WR.INDPRO	I haven't heard something from him...
57	4.45	75	VOC	You do good coffee!
58	4.39	48	WR.INDART	He is an useful member of the team.
58	4.39	54	INS.PREP	Have you ever seen the river of Ganges?
60	4.30	67	DBL-NEG	I didn't buy nothing at the supermarket.
60	4.30	69	CONCORD	There is one chair too much.
62	4.16	52	SIMPVF/ING	I look forward to hear from you.
63	3.79	20	WORD ORDER	He told me to not worry.
64	3.73	63	ADJ-NOUN	He has a blue car and I have a red.
65	3.59	71	WR.INDART	It took me a hour to get there.
66	3.47	62	WR.INDPRO	None of my two brothers knew about my plans.
67	3.44	8	ADJ/ADV	He speaks French quite good.
68	3.43	15	OM.PREP	I am staying at Sheraton hotel for three days.
69	2.98	10	OM.DEFART	We have a great deal of problems.
70	2.70	47	CONCORD	He has lived in London all his life.
71	2.28	11	A-CONTROL	She prefers walking to cycling.
72	2.07	25	A-CONTROL	Have you heard from him lately?
73	2.05	65	A-CONTROL	They were badly shaken by the news.
74	2.02	36	A-CONTROL	Why did he leave so early?
75	2	49	A-CONTROL	

Rank lists of test sentences

Age groups
Adults
FOREIGNNESS (F)

Rank no. F	Sentence no.	(ID)	Mean	SD	Mode	Error type	Sentence quoted
1	41	(12)	4.59	.66	5	IDIOM-PHR	Excuse me, what is the clock, please?
2	34	(1)	4.57	.66	5	OM.DO-PPH	He thinks, not that they know what to do.
3	39	(2)	4.5	.70	5	AUX	Can you French?
4	14	(14)	4.27	.97	5	OM.DO-PPH	Became he a dentist?
5	72	(16)	4.26	.90	5	OM.DO-PPH	Came he to the party yesterday?
6	68	(3)	4.21	.86	5	INS.PREP	She was here for two years ago.
7	44	(5)	4.16	1.08	5	WR.ADVERB	She works very hardly.
8	46	(4)	4.09	.92	5	PPRO/REFPRO	She was standing alone, beside her with rage
9	60	(20)	4.09	1.05	4,5	INS.PREP	I am sure of that he will come.
10	5	(8)	4	1.10	4,5	INS.PREP	I was here for two years ago.
11	59	(6)	4	1.18	5	TO-INF/ING	Many cities have stopped to expand.
12	27	(13)	3.98	1.11	5	OM.PREP	This room smells food, doesn't it?
13	42	(6)	3.95	1.11	5	OM.PREP	I was operated last week.
14	2	(10)	3.91	1.12	5	ADJ-PHR	He has an own company.
15	29	(23)	3.84	1.18	5	TENSE	Things have went too far.
16	70	(34)	3.84	1.04	4	COMP.ADV	He drives badlier than his brother.
17	16	(33)	3.80	1.25	4	TENSE	I didn't saw him today.
18	57	(18)	3.80	1.02	4	SUBJECT	There's a long time since I saw her.
19	73	(37)	3.79	.99	4	WORD ORDER	When I five years ago visited London....
20	18	(42)	3.75	1.18	4	TENSE	I am born in 1945.
21	18	(39)	3.73	1.11	4	CONCORD	Here are the money I owe you.
22	24	(11)	3.73	1.11	4	SUBJECT	It was little else to do.
23	50	(39)	3.73	1.15	4	INS.PREP	Smell on these flowers!
24	38	(49)	3.70	1.13	4,5	IRREG-VERB	They fought bravely in the war.
25	21	(27)	3.70	1.12	4	VOC	Yesterday's accident depended on the bad ...
26	43	(21)	3.67	1.21	4	INS.INDART	What an awful weather!
27	51	(59)	3.66	1.16	4	OM.INDART	My sister is nurse.
28	40	(51)	3.64	1.04	4	PRE/ATTADJ	He is a very alone man.
29	53	(23)	3.64	1.14	4	CONCORD	I don't know much people in this town.
30	4	(36)	3.63	1.11	4	VOC	I always tried to make my best at school.
31	12	(20)	3.61	1.04	4	WR.PREP	I met him in the steps.
32	32	(15)	3.61	1.13	4	NUMB	He had to pay five hundreds of pounds.
33	23	(39)	3.60	1.16	4	INS.DEFART	The most people would agree with you.
34	56	(22)	3.60	1.00	4	RFPRO/PPRO	She had her radio beside herself.
35	58	(50)	3.60	1.14	4	COMP.ADJ	This is the goodest cake I have ever tasted!
36	66	(46)	3.60	1.14	4	INS.INDART	What a dreadful weather!
37	1	(44)	3.59	1.23	4	WR.PREP	She is married with a German.
38	37	(58)	3.58	1.14	4	ADJ.NOUN	I took the blind by the arm and led him .....
39	17	(29)	3.57	1.19	4	AUX	He needs not come.
40	55	(59)	3.51	1.18	4	ADV/ADJ	This cake smells well!
41	30	(37)	3.51	1.13	4	TO-INF/B	They made me to do it.
42	33	(27)	3.5	1.27	4	ING/SIMPVF	He is meaning this book, not that one.
43	74	(46)	3.49	1.12	4	INS.PREP	Have you ever seen the river of Ganges?
44	54	(52)	3.48	1.02	4	SIMPVF/ING	I am used to get up early in the morning.
45	36	(35)	3.43	1.13	4	IRREG-PLUR	The house was full of mouses.
46	64	(69)	3.42	1.26	4	WR.PREP	I met him in the stairs.
47	9	(34)	3.34	1.20	4	UNC	She has very limited knowledges of German.
48	14	(43)	3.34	1.43	4	IDIOM-PHR	I shouted to him to look up for the car....
49	19	(23)	3.32	1.09	4	ADV/ADJ	This soup tastes well!
50	6	(55)	3.30	1.24	4		

Rank lists of test sentences

Age groups
Adults
FOREIGNNESS (F) /contd/

Rank no. F	Sentence no.	(ID)	Mean	SD	Mode	Error type	Sentence quoted
51	69	(53)	3.23	1.11	4	CONCORD	There is one chair too much.
52	22	(55)	3.23	1.29	4	CONCORD	My brother have worked for this company..
52	52	(57)	3.23	1.05	4	SIMPVF/ING	I look forward to hear from you.
54	61	(53)	3.21	1.09	4	TENSE	The firm is established in 1970.
55	26	(35)	3.14	1.09	4	WR.INDPRO	I haven't heard something from him...
56	45	(44)	3.09	1.39	4	GENITIVE	This is my brother's-in-law cap.
57	28	(29)	3.09	1.33	2	VOC	Who learnt you Spanish?
57	31	(58)	3.09	1.31	4	INS.INDART	It is a hard work to write a book.
59	13	(32)	3.07	1.25	4	INS.RELPRO	I don't know what improvements that are ...
60	71	(63)	3	1.13	4	OM.PREP	We have just come back from the island Rhod
60	75	(66)	3	1.20	2	VOC	You do good coffee!
62	15	(60)	2.65	1.21	2	ADJ/ADV	He speaks French quite good.
63	10	(64)	2.58	1.30	2	OM.DEFART	I am staying at Sheraton hotel for three....
64	48	(68)	2.56	1.18	2	WR.INDART	He is an useful member of the team.
65	67	(48)	2.47	1.22	2	DBL-NEG	I didn't buy nothing at the supermarket.
66	47	(60)	2.40	1.29	1	CONCORD	We have a great deal of problems.
67	8	(65)	2.36	1.28	1	WR.INDPRO	None of my two brothers knew about my plans
68	20	(62)	2.26	1.20	1	WORD ORDER	He told me to not worry.
69	62	(70)	2.14	1.19	1	WR.INDART	It took me a hour to get there.
70	63	(71)	2.02	1.05	1	ADJ.NOUN	He has a blue car and I have a red.
71	11	(71)	1.09	.37	1	A-CONTROL	He has lived in London all his life.
72	36	(72)	1.05	.22	1	A-CONTROL	They were badly shaken by the news.
73	49	(72)	1.02	.15	1	A-CONTROL	Why did he leave so early?
73	65	(72)	1.02	.15	1	A-CONTROL	Have you heard from him lately?
75	25	(72)	1	0	1	A-CONTROL	She prefers walking to cycling.

Rank lists of test sentences

Age groups

Adults

INTELLIGIBILITY DIFFICULTY (ID) /contd/

Rank.no.	ID (F)	Sentence no.	Mean	SD	Mode	Error type	Sentence quoted
51	(28)	40	1.42	.70	1	OM.INDART	My sister is nurse.
52	(44)	54	1.41	.76	1	INS.PREP	Have you ever seen the river of Ganges?
53	(54)	61	1.40	.54	1	TENSE	The firm is established in 1970.
53	(51)	69	1.40	.63	1	CONCORD	There is one chair too much.
55	(50)	6	1.40	.73	1	ADV/ADJ	This soup tastes well!
55	(52)	22	1.40	.66	1	CONCORD	My brother have worked for this company..
57	(52)	52	1.37	.66	1	SIMPVF/ING	I look forward to hear from you.
58	(57)	31	1.35	.61	1	INS.INDART	It is a hard work to write a book.
59	(27)	51	1.33	.61	1	INS.INDART	What an awful weather!
60	(62)	15	1.32	.52	1	ADJ/ADV	He speaks French quite good.
60	(66)	47	1.32	.56	1	CONCORD	We have a great deal of problems.
62	(68)	20	1.31	.52	1	WORD ORDER	He told me to not worry.
63	(60)	71	1.30	.64	1	OM.PREP	We have just come back from the island Rhodes
64	(63)	10	1.30	.79	1	OM.DEFART	I am staying at Sheraton hotel for three days
65	(67)	8	1.28	.55	1	WR.INDPRO	None of my two brothers knew about my plans
66	(60)	75	1.26	.45	1	VOC	You do good coffee!
67	(70)	63	1.25	.72	1	ADJ'NOUN	He has a blue car and I have a red.
68	(64)	48	1.23	.53	1	WR.INDART	He is an useful member of the team.
69	(46)	64	1.19	.39	1	IRREG-PLUR	The house was full of mouses.
70	(69)	62	1.10	.30	1	WR.INDART	It took me a hour to get there.
71	(71)	11	1.02	.15	1	A-CONTROL	He has lived in London all his life.
72	(75)	25	1	0		A-CONTROL	She prefers walking to cycling.
72	(72)	36	1	0		A-CONTROL	They were badly shaken by the news.
72	(73)	49	1	0		A-CONTROL	Why did he leave so early?
72	(73)	65	1	0		A-CONTROL	Have you heard from him lately?

Rank lists of test sentences

Age groups

Adults

INTELLIGIBILITY DIFFICULTY (ID)

Rank.no.	ID (F)	Sentence no.	Mean	SD	Mode	Error type	Sentence quoted
1	(2)	34	3.51	1.24	4	OM.DO-PPH	He thinks not that they know what to do.
2	(3)	39	3.16	1.36	3	AUX	Can you French?
3	(6)	68	2.88	1.45	4	INS.PREP	She was here for two years ago.
4	(8)	46	2.77	1.27	2	PPRO/RFPRO	She was standing alone, beside her with rage.
5	(7)	44	2.71	1.33	2	WR.ADVERB	He works very hardly.
6	(13)	42	2.69	1.37	2	OM.PREP	I was operated last week.
6	(10)	59	2.69	1.33	1,2,3	TO-INF/ING	Many cities have stopped to expand.
8	(10)	5	2.65	1.43	1	INS.PREP	I was here for two years ago.
9	(26)	43	2.56	1.28	2	VOC	Yesterday's accident depended on the bad ...
10	(14)	2	2.48	1.06	3	ADJ-PHR	He has an own company.
11	(21)	24	2.38	1.23	1	SUBJECT	It was little else to do.
12	(1)	41	2.37	1.25	1	IDIOM-PHR	Excuse me, what is the clock, please?
13	(12)	27	2.10	1.07	1	OM.PREP	This room smells food, doesn't it?
14	(4)	7	2.09	1.19	1	OM.DO-PPH	Became he a dentist?
15	(31)	32	2.02	1.17	1	WR.PREP	I met him in the steps.
15	(40)	55	2	1.33	1	AUX	He needs not come.
16	(5)	72	1.95	1.05	1	OM.DO-PPH	Came he to the party yesterday?
18	(17)	57	1.95	.92	1	SUBJECT	There's a long time since I saw her.
19	(21)	50	1.93	1.18	1,2	INS.PREP	Smell on these flowers!
20	(31)	12	1.90	.96	1	VOC	I always tried to make my best at school.
20	(9)	60	1.90	.96	1	INS.PREP	I am sure of that he will come.
22	(33)	58	1.88	.99	1	RFPRO/PPRO	She had her radio beside herself.
23	(49)	19	1.86	.89	1	IDIOM-PHR	I shouted to him to look up for the car...
23	(15)	29	1.86	.80	2	TENSE	Things have went too far.
23	(28)	53	-1.86	1.15	1	PRE/ATTADJ	He is a very alone man.
23	(33)	56	1.86	.94	1	INS.DEFART	The car was badly injured in the accident.
27	(25)	21	1.79	1.01	1	VOC	The most people would agree with you.
27	(42)	33	1.79	1.04	1	TO-INF/B	They made me to do it.
29	(39)	17	1.77	.81	1	ADJ'NOUN	I took the blind by the arm and led him across..
29	(57)	28	1.77	.95	1	VOC	Who learnt you Spanish?
31	(16)	70	1.74	.90	1	COMP.ADV	He drives badlier than his brother.
32	(59)	13	1.74	.80	1	INS.RELPRO	I don't know what improvements that are...
33	(17)	16	1.72	.85	1	TENSE	I didn't saw him today.
34	(45)	35	1.70	.91	1	SIMPVF/ING	I am used to get up early in the morning.
35	(55)	26	1.67	.79	1	WR.INDPRO	I haven't heard something from him...
36	(30)	4	1.64	.89	1	CONCORD	This cake smells well!
37	(41)	30	1.60	.88	1	ADV/ADJ	I don't know much people in this town.
37	(19)	73	1.60	.69	1	WORD ORDER	When I five years ago visited London...
39	(21)	18	1.60	.69	1	CONCORD	Here are the money I owe you,
39	(33)	23	1.60	.86	1	NUMB	He had to pay five hundreds of pounds.
41	(47)	9	1.56	.73	1	WR.PREP	I met him in the stairs.
42	(20)	3	1.53	.70	1	TENSE	I am born in 1945.
43	(47)	14	1.51	.70	1	UNC	She has very limited knowledges of German.
44	(38)	37	1.49	.70	1	WR.PREP	She is married with a German.
44	(56)	45	1.49	.77	1	GENITIVE	This is my brother's-in-law cap.
46	(37)	1	1.48	.71	1	INS.INDART	What a dreadful weather!
46	(43)	74	1.48	.67	1	ING/SIMPVF	He is meaning this book, not that one.
48	(65)	67	1.47	.88	1	DBL-NEG	I didn't buy nothing at the supermarket.
49	(24)	38	1.45	.80	1	IRREG-VERB	They fighted bravely in the war.
50	(33)	66	1.44	.83	1	COMP.ADJ	This is the goodest cake I have ever tasted!

Rank lists of test sentences

Age groups

Adults

COMBINED TABLE (error gravity with regard to both F and ID)

Rank no.	Error gravity index	Sentence no.	Error type	Sentence quoted
1	8.08	34	OM.DO-PPH	He thinks not that they know what to do.
2	7.66	39	AUX	Can you French?
3	7.09	68	INS.PREP	She was here for two years ago.
4	6.96	41	IDIOM-PHR	Excuse me, what is the clock, please?
5	6.87	44	WR.ADVERB	He works very hardly.
6	6.86	46	PPRO/REPRO	She was standing alone, beside her with rage.
7	6.69	59	TO-INF/ING	Many cities have stopped to expand.
8	6.65	5	INS.PREP	I was here for two years ago.
9	6.64	42	OM.PREP	I was operated last week.
10	6.39	2	ADJ-PHR	He has an own company.
11	6.37	7	OM.DO-PPH	Became he a dentist?
12	6.26	72	OM.DO-PPH	Came he to the party yesterday?
13	6.23	43	VOC	Yesterday's accident depended on the bad weather.
14	6.11	24	SUBJECT	It was little else to do.
15	6.07	27	OM.PREP	This room smells food, doesn't it?
16	6.00	60	INS.PREP	I am sure of that he will come.
17	5.75	57	SUBJECT	There's a long time since I saw her.
18	5.70	29	TENSE	Things have went too far.
19	5.66	50	INS.PREP	Smell on these flowers!
20	5.64	32	WR.PREP	He met him in the steps.
21	5.58	70	COMP.ADV	He drives badlier than his brother.
22	5.52	12	VOC	I always tried to make my best at school.
23	5.52	16	TENSE	I didn't saw him today.
24	5.51	55	AUX	He needs not come.
25	5.50	53	PRE/ATTADJ	He is a very alone man.
26	5.49	21	VOC	The car was badly injured in the accident.
27	5.49	58	REPRO/PPRO	She had her radio beside herself.
28	5.47	56	INS.DEFART	The most people would agree with you.
29	5.40	73	WORD ORDER	When I five years ago visited London....
30	5.34	17	ADJ'NOUN	I took the blind by the arm and led him....
31	5.32	18	CONCORD	Here are the money I owe you.
32	5.29	33	TO-INF/B	They made me to do it.
33	5.28	3	TENSE	I am born in 1945.
34	5.26	4	CONCORD	I don't know much people in this town.
35	5.20	23	NUMB	He had to pay five hundreds of pounds.
36	5.18	19	IDIOM-PHR	I shouted to him to look up for the car when I saw...
37	5.16	38	IRREG-VERB	They fighted bravely in the war.
38	5.13	35	SIMPVF/ING	I am used to get up early in the morning.
39	5.10	30	ADV/ADJ	This cake smells well!
40	5.07	37	WR.PREP	She is married with a German.
41	5.07	1	INS.INDART	My sister is nurse.
42	5.05	40	OM.INDART	What a dreadful weather!
43	5.05	66	COMP.ADJ	This is the goodest cake I have ever tasted!
44	4.99	51	INS.INDART	What an awful weather!
45	4.96	74	ING/SIMPVF	He is meaning this book, not that one.
46	4.90	9	WR.PREP	I met him in the stairs.
47	4.89	54	INS.PREP	Have you ever seen the river of Ganges?
48	4.86	28	VOC	Who learnt you Spanish?
49	4.85	14	UNC	She has very limited knowledges of German.
50	4.81	13	INS.RELPRO	I don't know what improvements that are...

Rank lists of test sentences

Age groups

Adults

COMBINED TABLE (error gravity with regard to both F and ID) /contd/

Rank no.	Error gravity index	Sentence no.	Error type	Sentence quoted
51	4.80	26	WR.INDPRO	I haven't heard something from him...
52	4.70	6	ADV/ADJ	This soup tastes well!
53	4.64	69	CONCORD	There is one chair too much.
54	4.62	22	CONCORD	My brother have worked for this company...
55	4.62	61	TENSE	The firm is established in 1970.
56	4.60	64	IRREG-PLUR	The house was full of mouses.
57	4.60	52	SIMPVF/ING	I look forward to hear from you.
58	4.58	45	GENITIVE	This is my brother's-in-law cap.
59	4.44	31	INS.INDART	It is a hard work to write a book.
60	4.30	71	OM.PREP	We have just come back from the island Rhodes.
61	4.26	75	VOC	You do good coffee!
62	3.97	15	ADJ/ADV	He speaks French quite good.
63	3.93	67	DBL-NEG	I didn't buy nothing at the supermarket.
64	3.88	10	OM.DEFART	I am staying at Sheraton hotel for three days.
65	3.79	48	WR.INDART	He is an useful member of the team.
66	3.72	47	CONCORD	We have a great deal of problems.
67	3.64	8	WR.INDPRO	None of my two brothers knew about my plans.
68	3.57	20	WORD ORDER	He told me to not worry.
69	3.27	63	ADJ'NOUN	He has a blue car and I have a red.
70	3.23	62	WR.INDART	It took me a hour to get there.
71	2.12	11	A-CONTROL	He has lived in London all his life.
72	2.05	36	A-CONTROL	They were badly shaken by the news.
73	2.02	49	A-CONTROL	Why did he leave so early?
74	2.02	65	A-CONTROL	Have you heard from him lately?
75	2	25	A-CONTROL	She prefers walking to cycling.

Rank lists of test sentences

Age groups

Pensioners

FOREIGNNESS (F)

Rank no.	Sentence no.	(ID)	Mean	SD	Mode*	Error type	Sentence quoted
1	34	(4)	4.47	.77	5	OM.DO-PPH	He thinks not that they know what to do.
2	39	(1)	4.35	1.22	5	AUX	Can you French?
3	7	(11)	4.35	.93	5	OM.DO-PPH	Became he a dentist?
4	70	(20)	4.26	1.33	5	COMP.ADV	He drives badlier than his brother.
5	41	(10)	4.24	1.44	5	IDIOM-PHR	Excuse me, what is the clock, please?
6	46	(47)	4.22	1.22	5	PPRO/RFPRO	She was standing alone, beside her with rage.
7	72	(47)	4.21	1.27	5	OM.DO-PPH	Came he to the party yesterday?
8	18	(32)	4.2	1.20	5	CONCORD	Here are the money I owe you.
9	2	(5)	4.19	1.12	5	ADJ-PHR	He has an own company.
10	19	(2)	4.15	1.39	5	IDIOM-PHR	I shouted to him to look up for the car when...
11	27	(17)	4.11	1.20	5	OM.PREP	This room smells food, doesn't it?
12	38	(41)	4.06	1.57	5	IRREG-VERB	They fighted bravely in the war.
13	29	(14)	4.06	1.16	5	TENSE	They have went too far.
14	3	(29)	4	1.25	5	TENSE	I am born in 1945.
14	32	(32)	4	1.37	5	WR.ADVERB	He works very hardily.
16	9	(9)	3.95	1.35	5	RFPRO/PPRO	She had her radio beside herself.
16	6	(6)	3.95	1.51	5	INS.PREP	She was here for two years ago.
18	74	(34)	3.94	1.20	5	ING/SIMPVF	He is meaning this book, not that one.
19	49	(49)	3.94	1.39	5	WR.PREP	She is married with a German.
20	57	(30)	3.89	1.52	5	SUBJECT	There's a long time since I saw her.
21	18	(18)	3.89	1.32	5	TO-INF/B	They made me to do it.
21	59	(8)	3.89	1.41	5	TO-INF/ING	Many cities have stopped to expand.
23	16	(36)	3.84	1.38	5	TENSE	I didn't saw him today.
23	64	(30)	3.84	1.54	5	IRREG-PLUR	The house was full of mouses.
25	75	(35)	3.83	1.50	5	VOC	You do good coffee!
26	24	(24)	3.82	1.55	5	OM.PREP	Who learnt you Spanish?
27	42	(22)	3.81	1.64	5	VOC	I was operated last week.
27	50	(50)	3.81	1.52	5	INS.PREP	Smell on these flowers!
29	66	(51)	3.79	1.47	5	COMP.ADJ	This is the goodest cake I have ever tasted!
30	34	(34)	3.75	1.37	5	CONCORD	I don't know much people in this town.
30	5	(14)	3.75	1.45	5	INS.PREP	I was here for two years ago.
30	24	(11)	3.75	1.33	5	SUBJECT	It was little else to do.
33	53	(11)	3.73	1.49	.5	PRE/ATTADJ	He is a very alone man.
34	25	(25)	3.72	1.32	5	WR.PREP	I met him in the stairs.
35	27	(27)	3.68	1.70	5	VOC	The car was badly injured in the accident.
36	41	(41)	3.67	1.41	5	VOC	I always tried to make my best at school.
36	54	(21)	3.67	1.54	.5	INS.PREP	Have you ever seen the river of Ganges?
38	62	(62)	3.65	1.50	5	TENSE	The firm is established in 1970.
39	23	(37)	3.63	1.54	5	NUMB	He had to pay five hundreds of pounds.
40	19	(55)	3.63	1.71	5	AUX	He needs not come.
41	6	(59)	3.61	1.46	5	ADV/ADJ	This soup tastes well!
42	73	(73)	3.58	1.57	5	WORD ORDER	When I five years ago visited London....
43	60	(37)	3.56	1.76	5	INS.PREP	I am sure of that he will come.
44	30	(40)	3.53	1.50	5	ADV/ADJ	This cake smells well!
45	1	(44)	3.52	1.47	5	INS.INDART	What a dreadful weather!
46	32	(14)	3.44	1.54	5	WR.PREP	I met him in the steps.
47	51	(48)	3.44	1.59	5	INS.INDART	What an awful weather!
48	17	(46)	3.35	1.69	5	ADJ'NOUN	I took the blind by the arm and led him...
48	69	(48)	3.35	1.69	5	CONCORD	There is one chair too much.
50	56	(45)	3.33	1.54	.	INS.DEFART	The most people would agree with you.

Rank lists of test sentences

Age groups

Pensioners

FOREIGNNESS (F) /contd/

Rank no.	Sentence no.	(ID)	Mean	SD	Mode*	Error type	Sentence quoted
51	26	(23)	3.32	1.67	5	WR.INDPRO	I haven't heard something from him...
52	40	(54)	3.25	1.73	.,5	OM.INDART	My sister is nurse.
53	35	(57)	3.24	1.75	5	SIMPVF/ING	I am used to get up early in the morning.
53	48	(43)	3.24	1.35	.3	WR.INDART	He is an useful member of the team.
55	43	(25)	3.16	1.68	5	VOC	Yesterday's accident depended on the bad...
56	22	(64)	3.11	1.68	5	CONCORD	My brother have worked for this company..
57	67	(50)	3.11	1.66	1,5	DBL-NEG	I didn't buy nothing at the supermarket.
58	15	(64)	3.05	1.68	1,5	ADJ/ADV	He speaks French quite good.
59	13	(54)	2.89	1.68	1	INS.RELPRO	I don't know what improvements that are...
60	45	(37)	2.81	1.76	.1	GENITIVE	This is my brother's-in-law cap.
61	31	(59)	2.79	1.72	1	INS.INDART	It is a hard work to write a book.
62	71	(61)	2.76	1.79	1	OM.PREP	We have just come back from the island Rhodes
63	14	(69)	2.67	1.78	1	UNC	She has very limited knowledges of German.
64	47	(54)	2.35	1.62	1	CONCORD	We have a great deal of problems.
65	52	(63)	2.33	1.68	1	SIMPVF/ING	I look forward to hear from you.
66	20	(52)	2.22	1.59	1	WR.INDPRO	None of my two brothers knew about my plans.
67	8	(67)	2.11	1.53	1	WORD ORDER	It took me a hour to get there.
68	62	(68)	2.06	1.51	1	WR.INDART	
69	10	(66)	1.95	1.51	1	OM.DEFART	I am staying at Sheraton hotel for three days.
70	63	(69)	1.65	1.17	1	ADJ'NOUN	He has a blue car and I have a red.
71	65	(69)	1.22	.94	1	A-CONTROL	Have you heard from him lately?
72	11	(69)	1.06	.24	1	A-CONTROL	Why did he leave so early?
73	13	(69)	1.05	.23	1	A-CONTROL	He has lived in London all his life.
74	25	(69)	1	0	1	A-CONTROL	She prefers walking to cycling.
74	36	(69)	1	0	1	A-CONTROL	They were badly shaken by the news.

* Periods indicate that the mode is the missing value.

Rank lists of test sentences

Age groups

Pensioners

INTELLIGIBILITY DIFFICULTY (ID)

Rank no.	Sentence no.	Mean	SD	Mode*	Error type	Sentence quoted
	ID (F)					
1	(2) 39	3	1.32	.	AUX	Can you French?
2	(10) 19	2.67	1.61	1	IDIOM-PHR	I shouted to him to look up for the car when...
3	(6) 46	2.67	1.64	1	PPRO/REPRO	She was standing alone, beside her with rage.
4	(1) 34	2.65	1.54	.1	OM.DO-PPH	He thinks not that they know what to do.
5	(9) 2	2.42	1.50	1	ADJ-PHR	He has an own company.
6	(16) 68	2.32	1.49	1	INS.PREP	She was here for two years ago.
7	(27) 42	2.24	1.48	1	OM.PREP	I was operated last week.
8	(21) 59	2.22	1.59	1	TO-INF/ING	Many cities have stopped to expand.
9	(16) 58	2.11	1.37	1	RFPRO/PPRO	She had her radio beside herself.
10	(5) 41	2.06	1.57	1	IDIOM-PHR	Excuse me, what is the clock, please?
11	(3) 1	2	1.33	1	OM.DO-PPH	Became he a dentist?
11	(30) 24	2	1.24	1	SUBJECT	It was little to do.
11	(33) 53	2	1.27	1	PRE/ATTADJ	He is a very alone man.
14	(30) 5	1.94	1.39	1	INS.PREP	I was here for two years ago.
14	(13) 29	1.94	1.30	1	TENSE	Things have went too far.
14	(46) 32	1.94	1.35	1	WR.PREP	I met him in the steps.
17	(11) 27	1.94	1.20	1	OM.PREP	This room smells food, doesn't it?
18	(21) 33	1.94	1.29	1	TO-INF/B	They made me to do it.
19	(40) 55	1.88	1.36	1	AUX	He needs not come.
20	(4) 70	1.83	1.34	1	COMP.ADV	He drives badlier than his brother.
21	(36) 54	1.82	1.33	1	INS.PREP	Have you ever seen the river of Ganges?
22	(27) 50	1.81	1.22	1	INS.PREP	Smell on these flowers!
23	(51) 26	1.79	1.08	1	WR.INDPRO	I haven't heard something from him...
24	(26) 28	1.78	1.17	1	VOC	Who learnt you Spanish?
25	(34) 9	*1.72	1.18	1	WR.PREP	I met him in the stairs.
25	(55) 43	1.72	1.18	1	VOC	Yesterday's accident depended on the bad...
28	(35) 21	1.71	1.21	1	TENSE	I didn't saw him today.
28	(23) 16	1.68	1.29	1	TENSE	I am born in 1945.
29	(14) 3	1.65	1.04	1	SUBJECT	There's a long time since I saw her.
30	(20) 57	1.63	1.12	1	IRREG-PLUR	The house was full of mouses.
30	(25) 64	1.63	1.30	1	CONCORD	Here are the money I owe you.
32	(8) 18	1.61	1.20	1	WR.ADVERB	He works very hardly.
32	(14) 44	1.61	1.14	1	CONCORD	I don't know much people in this town.
34	(30) 4	1.6	1.05	1	ING/SIMPVF	He is meaning this book, not that one.
34	(18) 74	1.6	1.27	1	VOC	You do good coffee!
34	(23) 75	1.6	1.27	1	NUMB	He had to pay five hundreds of pounds.
37	(39) 23	1.58	1.07	1	GENITIVE	This is my brother's-in-law cap.
37	(60) 45	1.58	1.30	1	INS.PREP	I am sure of that he will come.
40	(43) 60	1.58	1.04	1	ADV/ADJ	This cake smells well!
40	(44) 30	1.56	1.04	1	VOC	I always tried to make my best at school.
41	(36) 12	1.53	1.07	1	IRREG-VERB	They fighted bravely in the war.
41	(12) 38	1.53	1.07	1	WR.INDART	He is an useful member of the team.
43	(53) 48	1.53	1.26	1	INS.DEFART	The most people would agree with you.
45	(45) 1	1.47	1.12	1	ADJ-NOUN	What a dreadful weather!
45	(50) 56	1.47	1.07	1	INS.INDART	I took the blind by the arm and led him...
46	(48) 17	1.45	1.00	1	OM.DO-PPH	Came he to the party yesterday?
47	(72) 72	1.44	1.04	1	INS.INDART	What an awful weather!
48	(47) 51	1.44	1.03	1	WR.PREP	She is married with a German.
49	(19) 37	1.41	1.00	1	DBL-NEG	I didn't buy nothing at the supermarket.
50	(57) 67	1.39	1.04			

Rank lists of test sentences

Age groups

Pensioners

INTELLIGIBILITY DIFFICULTY (ID) /contd/

Rank no.	Sentence no.	Mean	SD	Mode*	Error type	Sentence quoted
	ID (F)					
51	(29) 66	1.37	1.01	1	COMP.ADJ	This is the goodest cake I have ever tasted!
52	(66) 20	1.35	1.00	1	WORD ORDER	He told me to not worry.
53	(48) 69	1.32	.95	1	CONCORD	There is one chair too much.
54	(59) 13	1.29	.47	1	INS.RELPRO	I don't know what improvements that are being.
54	(52) 40	1.29	.99	1	OM.INDART	My sister is nurse.
54	(64) 47	1.29	.59	1	CONCORD	We have a great deal of problems.
57	(53) 35	1.28	.96	1	SIMPVF/ING	I am used to get up early in the morning.
57	(12) 73	1.28	.57	1	WORD ORDER	When I five years ago visited London ...
59	(41) 6	1.24	.97	1	ADV/ADJ	This soup tastes well!
59	(61) 31	1.24	.56	1	INS.INDART	It is a hard work to write a book.
61	(62) 71	1.21	.54	1	OM.PREP	We have just come back from the island Rhodes.
62	(38) 61	1.15	.49	1	TENSE	The firm is established in 1970.
63	(65) 52	1.12	.49	1	SIMPVF/ING	I look forward to hear from you.
64	(58) 15	1.11	.32	1	ADJ/ADV	He speaks French quite good.
64	(56) 22	1.11	.32	1	CONCORD	My brother have worked for this company ...
66	(69) 10	1.06	.24	1	OM.DEFART	I am staying at Sheraton hotel for three days.
67	(67) 8	1.06	.24	1	WR.INDPRO	None of my two brothers knew about my plans.
68	(68) 62	1.05	.23	1	WR.INDART	It took me a hour to get there.
69	(73) 11	1	0	1	A-CONTROL	He has lived in London all his life.
69	(63) 14	1	0	1	UNC	She has very limited knowledges of German.
69	(74) 25	1	0	1	A-CONTROL	She prefers walking to cycling.
69	(74) 36	1	0	1	A-CONTROL	They were badly shaken by the news.
69	(72) 49	1	0	1	A-CONTROL	Why did he leave so early?
69	(70) 63	1	0	1	ADJ-NOUN	He has a blue car and I have a red.
69	(71) 65	1	0	1	A-CONTROL	Have you heard from him lately?

* Periods indicate that the mode is the missing value.

Rank lists of test sentences

Age groups

Pensioners

COMBINED TABLE (error gravity with regard to both F and ID)

Rank no.	Error gravity index	Sentence no.	Error type	Sentence quoted
1	7.35	39	AUX	Can you French?
2	7.12	34	OM.DO-PPH	He thinks not that they know what to do.
3	6.89	46	PPRO/RFPRO	She was standing alone, beside her with rage.
4	6.82	19	IDIOM-PHR	I shouted to him to look up for the car when I saw...
5	6.61	2	ADJ-PHR	He has an own company.
6	6.35	7	OM.DO-PPH	Became me, what is the clock, please?
7	6.30	41	IDIOM-PHR	Excuse me, what is the clock, please?
8	6.26	68	INS.PREP	She was here for two years ago.
9	6.11	59	TO-INF/ING	Many cities have stopped to expand.
10	6.10	70	COMP.ADV	He drives badlier than his brother.
11	6.05	58	RFPRO/PPRO	She had her radio beside herself.
12	6.05	42	OM.PREP	I was operated last week.
13	6.05	27	OM.PREP	This room smells food, doesn't it?
14	6	29	TENSE	Things have went too far.
15	5.83	33	TO-INF/B	They made me to do it.
16	5.81	18	CONCORD	Here are the money I owe you.
17	5.75	24	SUBJECT	It was little else to do.
18	5.73	53	PRE/ATTADJ	He is a very alone man.
19	5.69	5	INS.PREP	I was here for two years ago.
20	5.65	72	OM.DO-PPH	Came he to the party yesterday?
21	5.65	3	TENSE	I am born in 1945.
22	5.63	50	INS.PREP	Smell on these flowers!
23	5.61	44	WR.ADVERB	He works very hardly.
24	5.60	28	VOC	Who learnt you Spanish?
25	5.59	38	IRREG-VERB	They fighted bravely in the war.
26	5.54	74	ING/SIMPVF	He is meaning this book, not that one.
27	5.53	16	TENSE	I didn't saw him today.
27	5.53	57	SUBJECT	There's a long time since I saw her.
29	5.5	55	AUX	He needs not come.
30	5.49	54	INS.PREP	Have you ever seen the river of Ganges?
31	5.46	64	IRREG-PLUR	The house was full of mouses.
32	5.44	9	WR.PREP	I met him in the steps.
33	5.44	75	VOC	You do good coffee!
34	5.39	21	VOC	I met him in the stairs.
35	5.39	32	WR.PREP	She is married with a German.
36	5.35	4	CONCORD	I don't know much people in this town.
37	5.35	37	WR.PREP	She is married with a German.
38	5.21	23	NUMB	He had to pay five hundreds of pounds.
39	5.20	12	VOC	I always tried to make my best at school.
40	5.16	66	COMP.ADJ	This is the goodest cake I have ever tasted!
41	5.13	60	INS.PREP	I am sure of that he will come.
42	5.11	26	WR.INDPRO	I haven't heard something from him...
43	5.08	30	ADV/ADJ	This cake smells well!
44	5.00	1	INS.INDART	What a dreadful weather!
45	4.88	43	VOC	Yesterday's accident depended on the bad weather.
46	4.88	51	INS.INDART	What an awful weather!
47	4.86	73	WORD ORDER	When I five years ago visited London...
48	4.85	6	ADV/ADJ	This soup tastes well!
49	4.80	56	INS.DEFART	The most people would agree with you.
50	4.80	17	ADJ'NOUN	I took the blind by the arm and led him...

Rank lists of test sentences

Age groups

Pensioners

COMBINED TABLE (error gravity with regard to both F and ID) /contd/

Rank no.	Error gravity index	Sentence no.	Error type	Sentence quoted
51	4.80	61	TENSE	The firm is established in 1970.
52	4.76	48	WR.INDART	He is an useful member of the team.
53	4.67	69	CONCORD	There is one chair too much.
54	4.54	40	OM.INDART	My sister is nurse.
55	4.51	35	SIMPVF/ING	I am used to get up early in the morning.
56	4.49	67	DBL-NEG	I didn't buy nothing at the supermarket.
57	4.39	45	GENITIVE	This is my brother's-in-law cap.
58	4.22	22	CONCORD	My brother have worked for this company...
59	4.18	13	INS.RELPRO	I don't know what improvements that are...
60	4.16	15	ADJ/ADV	He speaks French quite good.
61	4.02	31	INS.INDART	It is a hard work to write a book.
62	3.98	71	OM.PREP	We have just come back from the island Rhodes.
63	3.67	14	UNC	She has very limited knowledges of German.
64	3.65	47	CONCORD	We have a great deal of problems.
65	3.58	20	WORD ORDER	He told me to not worry.
66	3.45	52	SIMPVF/ING	I look forward to hear from you.
67	3.17	8	WR.INDPRO	None of my two brothers knew about my plans.
68	3.11	62	WR.INDART	It took me a hour to get there.
69	3.01	10	OM.DEFART	I am staying at Sheraton hotel for three days.
70	2.65	63	ADJ'NOUN	He has a blue car and I have a red.
71	2.22	65	A-CONTROL	Have you heard from him lately?
72	2.06	49	A-CONTROL	Why did he leave so early?
73	2.05	11	A-CONTROL	He has lived in London all his life.
74	2	25	A-CONTROL	She prefers walking to cycling.
74	2	36	A-CONTROL	They were badly shaken by the news.

Rank lists of test sentences

Sex groups

Females

FOREIGNESS (F)

Rank no. F	(ID)	Sentence no.	Mean	SD	Mode	Error type	Sentence quoted
1	(14)	41	4.53	.90	5	IDIOM-PHR	Excuse me, what is the clock, please?
2	(1)	34	4.49	.68	5	OM.DO-PPH	He thinks not that they know what to do.
3	(2)	39	4.45	.86	5	AUX	Can you French?
4	(16)	7	4.32	.90	5	OM.DO-PPH	Became he a dentist?
5	(3)	46	4.29	.96	5	PPRO/REFPRO	She was standing alone, beside her with rage.
6	(7)	27	4.28	1.08	5	OM.PREP	This room smells food, doesn't it?
7	(20)	72	4.16	1.07	5	OM.DO-PPH	Came he to the party yesterday?
8	(6)	42	4.09	1.16	5	OM.PREP	I was operated last week.
9	(15)	29	4.09	1.07	5	TENSE	Things has went too far.
10	(5)	2	4.09	1.05	5	ADJ-PHR	He has an own company.
11	(9)	68	4.04	1.02	5	INS.PREP	She was here for two years ago.
12	(12)	44	3.99	1.20	5	WR.ADVERB	He works very hardly.
13	(10)	5	3.94	1.14	5	INS.PREP	I was here for two years ago.
14	(25)	70	3.93	1.11	4,5	COMP.ADV	He drives badlier than his brother.
15	(18)	50	3.92	1.10	5	INS.PREP	Smell on these flowers!
16	(27)	57	3.91	1.13	4	SUBJECT	There's a long time since I saw her.
17	(4)	59	3.86	1.23	5	TO-INF/ING	Many cities have stopped to expand.
18	(31)	18	3.86	1.02	4	CONCORD	Here are the money I owe you.
19	(43)	3	3.85	1.14	4	TENSE	I didn't saw him today.
20	(30)	16	3.82	2.15	4	TENSE	I am born in 1945.
21	(16)	60	3.79	1.39	5	INS.PREP	I am sure of that he will come.
22	(28)	12	3.67	1.09	4	VOC	I always tried to make my best at school.
23	(40)	23	3.66	1.25	5	NUMB	I had to pay five hundreds of pounds.
24	(19)	58	3.66	1.12	4	REFPRO/PPRO	She had her radio beside herself.
25	(11)	24	3.65	1.17	4	SUBJECT	It was little else to do.
26	(47)	51	3.64	1.18	3,4	INS.INDART	What an awful weather!
27	(35)	4	3.63	1.12	4	CONCORD	I don't know much people in this town.
28	(22)	55	3.63	1.12	4	AUX	He needs not come.
29	(20)	33	3.63	1.18	4	TO-INF/B	They made me to do it.
29	(46)	73	3.63	1.18	4	WORD ORDER	When I five years ago visited London...
31	(8)	43	3.61	1.31	5	VOC	Yesterday's accident depended on the bad...
32	(45)	1	3.6	1.12	4	INS.INDART	What a dreadful weather!
33	(49)	6	3.59	1.24	4,5	ADV/ADJ	This soup tastes well!
33	(32)	30	3.59	1.26	4	ADV/ADJ	This cake smells well!
35	(53)	38	3.58	1.32	4	IRREG-VERB	They fighted bravely in the war.
35	(24)	53	3.58	1.30	4	PRE/ATTADJ	He is a very alone man.
37	(29)	56	3.58	1.08	4	INS.DEFART	The most people would agree with you.
38	(32)	28	3.58	1.46	5	VOC	Who learnt you Spanish?
39	(34)	21	3.55	1.37	5	VOC	The car was badly injured in the accident.
40	(37)	74	3.54	1.15	4	ING/SIMPVF	He is meaning this book, not that one.
41	(23)	32	3.54	1.22	4	WR.PREP	I met him in the steps.
41	(56)	66	3.54	1.11	4	COMP.ADJ	This is the goodest cake I have ever tasted!
43	(36)	9	3.52	2.15	4	WR.PREP	I met him in the stairs.
44	(52)	40	3.46	1.21	4	OM.INDART	My sister is nurse.
45	(44)	35	3.44	1.31	4	SIMPVF/ING	I am used to get up early in the morning.
46	(51)	37	3.44	1.19	4	WR.PREP	She is married with a German.
47	(13)	19	3.43	1.37	5	IDIOM-PHR	I shouted to him to look up for the car...
48	(60)	64	3.42	1.29	3	IRREG-PLUR	The house was full of mouses.
49	(59)	61	3.25	1.10	4	TENSE	The firm is established in 1970.
50	(38)	17	3.24	1.38	4	ADJ-NOUN	I took the blind by the arm and led him...

Rank lists of test sentences

Sex groups

Females

FOREIGNESS (F) /contd/

Rank no. F	(ID)	Sentence no.	Mean	SD	Mode	Error type	Sentence quoted
51	(55)	22	3.22	1.32	4	CONCORD	My brother have worked for this company...
52	(39)	13	3.18	1.37	4	INS.RELPRO	I don't know what improvements that are...
53	(26)	45	3.16	1.36	4	GENITIVE	This is my brother's-in-law cap.
54	(54)	31	3.15	1.45	4	INS.INDART	It is a hard work to write a book.
54	(56)	75	3.15	1.30	4	VOC	You do good coffee!
56	(41)	26	3.09	1.27	3	WR.INDPRO	I haven't heard something from him...
57	(48)	54	3.08	1.36	4	INS.PREP	Have you ever seen the river of Ganges?
58	(49)	14	3	1.40	3	UNC	She has very limited knowledges of German.
59	(58)	69	2.97	1.24	3	CONCORD	There is one chair too much.
60	(60)	48	2.86	1.29	3	WR.INDART	He is an useful member of the team.
61	(62)	52	2.78	1.39	1,3	SIMPVF/ING	I look forward to hear from you.
62	(66)	15	2.72	1.37	2	ADJ/ADV	He speaks French quite good.
63	(42)	67	2.69	1.33	2	DBL-NEG	I didn't buy nothing at the supermarket.
64	(63)	71	2.62	1.33	1	WR.PREP	We have just come back from the island Rhodes.
65	(65)	8	2.28	1.28	1	WR.INDPRO	None of my two brothers knew about my plans.
66	(64)	20	2.17	1.30	1	WORD ORDER	He told me to not worry.
67	(70)	62	2.03	1.18	1	WR.INDART	It took me a hour to get there.
68	(67)	47	1.95	1.20	1	CONCORD	We have a great deal of problems.
68	(68)	63	1.95	1.16	1	ADJ-NOUN	He has a blue car and I have a red.
70	(69)	10	1.93	1.23	1	OM.DEFART	I am staying at Sheraton hotel for three days.
71	(71)	11	1.10	.43	1	A-CONTROL	He has lived in London all his life.
72	(72)	65	1.09	.52	1	A-CONTROL	They were badly shaken by the news.
73	(72)	36	1.03	.18	1	A-CONTROL	She prefers walking to cycling.
74	(72)	25	1.01	.12	1	A-CONTROL	Why did he leave so early?
75	(72)	49	1	0	1	A-CONTROL	

Rank lists of test sentences

Sex groups

Females

INTELLIGIBILITY DIFFICULTY (ID)

Rank no.	ID (F)	Sentence no.	Mean	SD	Mode	Error type	Sentence quoted
1	(2)	34	3.38	1.42	5	OM.DO-PPH	He thinks not that they know what to do.
2	(3)	39	3.16	1.31	3	AUX	Can you French?
3	(5)	46	3.03	1.44	3	PPRO/RFPRO	She was standing alone, beside her with rage.
4	(17)	59	2.97	1.41	3	TO-INF/ING	Many cities have stopped to expand.
5	(11)	68	2.93	1.35	3,4	INS.PREP	She was here for two years ago.
6	(8)	42	2.82	1.36	1,4	OM.PREP	I was operated last week.
7	(6)	27	2.75	1.33	1	OM.PREP	This room smells food, doesn't it?
8	(31)	43	2.73	1.24	2,4	VOC	Yesterday's accident depended on the bad...
9	(10)	2	2.70	1.24	1	ADJ-PHR	He has an own company.
10	(13)	5	2.67	1.48	1	INS.PREP	I was here for two years ago.
11	(25)	24	2.4	1.21	1	SUBJECT	It was little else to do.
12	(12)	44	2.34	1.34	1	WR.ADVERB	He works very hardly.
13	(47)	19	2.32	1.34	1	IDIOM-PHR	I shouted to him to look up for the car when...
14	(1)	41	2.31	1.30	1	IDIOM-PHR	Excuse me, what is the clock, please?
15	(9)	29	2.23	1.08	2	TENSE	Things have went too far.
16	(4)	7	2.15	1.21	1	OM.DO-PPH	Became he a dentist?
16	(21)	60	2.15	1.22	1	INS.PREP	I am sure of that he will come.
18	(15)	50	2.12	1.14	1	INS.PREP	Smell on these flowers!
19	(23)	58	2.12	1.09	1	RFPRO/PPRO	She had her radio beside herself.
20	(29)	33	2.11	1.10	1	TO-INF/B	They made me to do it.
20	(7)	72	2.11	1.16	1	OM.DO-PPH	Came he to the party yesterday?
22	(28)	55	2.08	1.22	1	AUX	He needs not come.
23	(41)	32	2.06	1.01	1	WR.PREP	I met him in the steps.
24	(35)	53	2.06	1.18	1	PRE/ATTADJ	He is a very alone man.
25	(14)	70	2.03	1.13	2	COMP.ADV	He drives badlier than his brother.
26	(52)	13	2	1.05	1	INS.RELPRO	I don't know what improvements that are...
27	(16)	57	1.99	1.04	1	SUBJECT	There's a long time since I saw her.
28	(22)	12	1.98	1.03	1	VOC	I always tried to make my best at school.
29	(37)	56	1.92	1.04	1	INS.DEFART	The most people would agree with you.
30	(20)	16	1.88	.98	1	TENSE	I didn't saw him today.
31	(18)	18	1.88	1.03	1	CONCORD	I met him in the stairs.
32	(38)	28	1.85	1.00	1	VOC	Here are the money I owe you.
32	(33)	30	1.85	1.13	1	ADV/ADJ	Who learnt you Spanish?
34	(39)	21	1.82	1.16	1	VOC	This cake smells well!
35	(27)	4	1.81	.99	1	CONCORD	The car was badly injured in the accident.
36	(43)	9	1.80	.95	1	WR.PREP	I don't know much people in this town.
37	(40)	74	1.79	1.08	1	ING/SIMPVF	I met him in the stairs.
38	(50)	17	1.78	.97	1	ADJ^NOUN	He is meaning this book, not that one.
39	(53)	45	1.78	1.20	1	GENITIVE	I took the blind by the arm and led him...
40	(23)	23	1.77	1.00	1	NUMB	This is my brother's-in-law cap.
41	(56)	26	1.76	.93	1	WR.INDPRO	He had to pay five hundreds of pounds.
42	(63)	67	1.74	1.13	1	DBL-NEG	I haven't heard something from him...
43	(19)	3	1.74	.87	1	TENSE	I didn't buy nothing at the supermarket.
44	(45)	35	1.73	1.02	1	SIMPVF/ING	I am born in 1945.
45	(32)	1	1.67	.93	1	INS.INDART	I am used to get up early in the morning.
46	(29)	73	1.65	.89	1	WORD ORDER	What a dreadful weather!
47	(26)	51	1.63	.85	1	INS.INDART	When I five years ago visited London...
48	(57)	54	1.61	1.06	1	INS.PREP	What an awful weather!
49	(33)	6	1.57	.95	1	ADV/ADJ	Have you ever seen the river of Ganges?
49	(58)	14	1.57	.73	1	UNC	This soup tastes well!

Rank lists of test sentences

Sex groups

Females

INTELLIGIBILITY DIFFICULTY (ID) /contd/

Rank no.	ID (F)	Sentence no.	Mean*	SD	Mode	Error type	Sentence quoted
51	(46)	37	1.55	.85	1	WR.PREP	She is married with a German.
52	(44)	40	1.54	.85	1	OM.INDART	My sister is nurse.
53	(35)	38	1.53	.87	1	IRREG-VERB	They fighted bravely in the war.
54	(54)	31	1.52	.81	1	INS.INDART	It is a hard work to write a book.
55	(51)	22	1.52	.75	1	CONCORD	My brother have worked for this company...
56	(41)	66	1.51	.86	1	COMP.ADJ	This is the goodest cake I have ever tasted
56	(54)	75	1.51	.88	1	VOC	You do good coffee!
58	(59)	69	1.47	.73	1	CONCORD	There is one chair too much.
59	(49)	61	1.46	.70	1	TENSE	The firm is established in 1970.
60	(60)	48	1.40	.85	1	WR.INDART	He is an useful member of the team.
60	(48)	64	1.40	.82	1	IRREG-PLUR	The house was full of mouses.
62	(61)	52	1.35	.67	1	SIMPVF/ING	I look forward to hear from you.
63	(64)	71	1.34	.73	1	OM.PREP	We have just come back from the island Rhodes.
64	(66)	20	1.31	.69	1	WORD ORDER	He told me to not worry.
65	(65)	8	1.30	.58	1	WR.INDPRO	None of my two brothers knew about my plans.
66	(62)	15	1.26	.54	1	ADJ/ADV	He speaks French quite good.
67	(68)	47	1.23	.52	1	CONCORD	We have a great deal of problems.
68	(68)	63	1.19	.50	1	ADJ^NOUN	He has a blue car and I have a red.
69	(70)	10	1.17	.45	1	OM.DEFART	I am staying at Sheraton hotel for three days.
70	(69)	62	1.15	.40	1	WR.INDART	It took me a hour to get there.
71	(71)	11	1.03	.17	1	A-CONTROL	He has lived in London all his life.
72	(74)	25	1	0	1	A-CONTROL	She prefers walking to cycling.
72	(73)	36	1	0	1	A-CONTROL	They were badly shaken by the news.
72	(75)	49	1	0	1	A-CONTROL	Why did he leave so early?
72	(72)	65	1	0	1	A-CONTROL	Have you heard from him lately?

Rank lists of test sentences

Sex groups

Females

COMBINED TABLE (error gravity with regard to both F and ID)

Rank no.	Error gravity index	Sentence no.	Error type	Sentence quoted
1	7.87	34	OM.DO-PPH	He thinks not that they know what to do.
2	7.61	39	AUX	Can you French?
3	7.32	46	PPRO/RFPRO	She was standing alone, beside her with rage.
4	7.03	27	OM.PREP	This room smells food, doesn't it?
5	6.97	68	INS.PREP	She was here for two years ago.
6	6.91	42	OM.PREP	I was operated last week.
7	6.84	41	IDIOM-PHR	Excuse me, what is the clock, please?
8	6.83	59	TO-INF/ING	Many cities have stopped to expand.
9	6.79	2	ADJ-PHR	He has an own company.
10	6.61	5	INS.PREP	I was here for two years ago.
11	6.47	7	OM.DO-PPH	Became he a dentist?
12	6.34	43	VOC	Yesterday's accident depended on the bad weather.
13	6.32	44	WR.ADVERB	He works very hardly.
14	6.32	29	TENSE	Things have went too far.
15	6.27	72	SUBJECT	Came he to the party yesterday?
16	6.05	24	SUBJECT	It was little else to do.
17	6.05	50	INS.PREP	Smell on these flowers!
18	5.96	70	COMP.ADV	He drives badlier than his brother.
19	5.94	60	INS.PREP	I am sure of that he will come.
20	5.90	57	SUBJECT	There's a long time since I saw her.
21	5.78	58	RFPRO/PPRO	She had her radio beside herself.
22	5.75	19	IDIOM-PHR	I shouted to him to look up for the car when I saw...
23	5.74	33	TO-INF/B	They made me to do it.
24	5.73	18	CONCORD	Here are the money I owe you.
25	5.71	55	AUX	He needs not come.
26	5.70	16	TENSE	I didn't saw him today.
27	5.66	12	VOC	I always tried to make my best at school.
28	5.65	53	PRE/ATTADJ	He is a very alone man.
29	5.60	32	WR.PREP	I met him in the steps.
30	5.59	3	TENSE	I am born in 1945.
31	5.50	56	INS.DEFART	The most people would agree with you.
32	5.44	4	CONCORD	I don't know much people in this town.
33	5.44	30	ADV/ADJ	This cake smells well!
34	5.43	23	NUMB	He had to pay five hundreds of punds.
35	5.42	28	VOC	Who learnt you Spanish?
36	5.37	21	ING/SIMPVF	He is meaning this book, not that one.
37	5.33	74	WR.PREP	I met him in the stairs.
38	5.33	9	WR.PREP	When I five years ago visited London...
39	5.28	73	WORD ORDER	When I five years ago visited London...
40	5.27	1	INS.INDART	What an awful weather!
41	5.26	51	INS.INDART	What a dreadful weather!
42	5.18	13	INS.RELPRO	I don't know what improvements that are...
43	5.17	35	SIMPVF/ING	I used to get up early in the morning.
44	5.16	6	ADV/ADJ	This soup tastes well!
45	5.12	38	IRREG-VERB	They fighted bravely in the war.
46	5.04	66	COMP.ADJ	This is the goodest cake I have ever tasted!
47	5.02	17	ADJ^NOUN	I took the blind by the arm and led him...
48	5	40	OM.INDART	My sister is nurse.
49	4.99	37	WR.PREP	She is married with a German.
50	4.93	45	GENITIVE	This is my brother-s-in-law cap.

Rank lists of test sentences

Sex groups

Females

COMBINED TABLE (error gravity with regard to both F and ID) /contd/

Rank no.	Error gravity index	Sentence no.	Error type	Sentence quoted
51	4.85	26	WR.INDPRO	I haven't heard something from him...
52	4.83	64	IRREG-PLUR	The house was full of mouses.
53	4.75	22	CONCORD	My brother have worked for this company...
54	4.71	61	TENSE	The firm is established in 1970.
55	4.69	54	INS.PREP	Have you ever seen the river of Ganges?
56	4.67	31	INS.INDART	It is a hard work to write a book.
57	4.65	75	VOC	You do good coffee!
58	4.57	14	UNC	She has very limited knowledges of German.
59	4.44	69	CONCORD	There is one chair too much.
60	4.43	67	DBL-NEG	I didn't buy nothing at the supermarket.
61	4.26	48	WR.INDART	He is an useful member of the team.
62	4.13	52	SIMPVF/ING	I look forward to hear from you.
63	3.98	15	ADJ/ADV	He speaks French quite good.
64	3.96	71	OM.PREP	We have just come back from the island Rhodes.
65	3.59	8	WR.INDPRO	None of my two brothers knew about my plans.
66	3.48	20	WORD ORDER	He told me to not worry.
67	3.18	47	CONCORD	We have a great deal of problems.
68	3.18	62	WR.INDART	It took me a hour to get there.
69	3.15	63	ADJ^NOUN	He has a blue car and I have a red.
70	3.09	10	OM.DEFART	He has lived in London all his life.
71	2.13	11	A-CONTROL	I am staying at Sheraton hotel for three days.
72	2.09	65	A-CONTROL	Have you heard from him lately?
73	2.03	36	A-CONTROL	They were badly shaken by the news.
74	2.01	25	A-CONTROL	She prefers walking to cycling.
75	2	49	A-CONTROL	Why did he leave so early?

Rank lists of test sentences

Sex groups

Males

FOREIGNESS (F)

Rank no. F	Sentence no. (ID)	Mean	SD	Mode	Error type	Sentence quoted
1	(1) 34	4.61	.74	5	OM.DO-PPH	He thinks not that they know what to do.
2	(9) 41	4.45	.78	5	IDIOM-PHR	Excuse me, what is the clock, please?
3	(2) 39	4.44	.71	5	AUX	Can you French?
4	(16) 7	4.34	.91	5	OM.DO-PPH	Became he a dentist?
5	(6) 5	4.22	.88	5	INS.PREP	I was here for two years ago.
5	(14) 27	4.22	.82	4	OM.PREP	This room smells food. doesn't it?
7	(8) 44	4.21	.90	5	WR.ADVERB	He works very hardly.
8	(17) 72	4.19	.80	4	OM.DO-PPH	Came he to the party yesterday?
9	(5) 68	4.17	.82	4	INS.PREP	She was here for two years ago.
10	(11) 2	4.15	.82	4	ADJ-PHR	He has an own company.
11	(34) 16	4.03	1.10	5	TENSE	I didn't saw him today.
11	(44) 18	4.03	.97	4,5	CONCORD	Here are the money I owe you.
13	(46) 46	4.02	.95	4	PPRO/RFPRO	She was standing alone, beside her with rage.
14	(26) 29	3.98	.99	5	TENSE	Things have went too far.
15	(4) 42	3.98	.95	4	OM.PREP	I was operated last week.
16	(45) 23	3.95	1.02	4	NUMB	He had to pay five hundreds of pounds.
17	(19) 32	3.93	.91	4	WR.PREP	I met him in the steps.
18	(18) 57	3.90	.93	4	SUBJECT	There's a long time since I saw her.
18	(25) 60	3.90	1.36	5	INS.PREP	I am sure of that he will come.
20	(41) 1	3.90	1.02	4	INS.INDART	What a dreadful weather!
20	(33) 70	3.88	.86	4	PRE/ATTADJ	He is a very alone man.
22	(22) 53	3.88	.89	4	COMP.ADV	He drives badlier than his brother.
23	(51) 3	3.88	.98	4	TENSE	I am born in 1945.
23	(13) 55	3.88	.98	4	AUX	He needs not come.
25	(29) 33	3.88	1.14	4	TO-INF/B	They made me to do it.
26	(15) 50	3.83	1.14	4	INS.PREP	Smell on these flowers!
26	(45) 51	3.83	1.07	4	INS.INDART	What an awful weather!
28	(38) 30	3.80	1.08	4	ADV/ADJ	This cake smells well!
29	(21) 17	3.8	1.04	4	TO-INF/ING	Many cities have stopped to expand.
30	(7) 59	3.79	1.18	4	TO-INF/ING	The car was badly injured in the accident.
31	(31) 21	3.78	1.25	5	VOC	I always tried to make my best at school.
32	(23) 12	3.76	.99	4	WR.PREP	She is married with a German.
33	(48) 37	3.75	1.01	4	ING/SIMPVF	He is meaning this book, not that one.
34	(32) 74	3.74	1.04	4	SIMPVF/ING	I am used to get up early in the morning.
35	(26) 35	3.71	1.05	4	CONCORD	I don't know much people in this town.
36	(39) 4	3.7	1.09	4	OM.INDART	My sister is nurse.
37	(41) 40	3.66	1.06	4	COMP.ADJ	This is the goodest cake I have ever tasted!
38	(56) 66	3.64	1.03	4	CONCORD	My brother have worked for this company...
39	(47) 22	3.63	1.16	4	SUBJECT	It was little else to do.
39	(10) 24	3.63	1.11	4	VOC	Yesterday's accident depended on the bad...
41	(12) 43	3.62	1.01	4	INS.DEFART	The most people would agree with you.
42	(23) 56	3.56	.98	4	WR.PREP	I met him in the stairs.
43	(37) 9	3.54	1.21	4	RFPRO/PPRO	She had her radio beside herself.
44	(35) 58	3.52	1.13	4	WORD ORDER	When I five years ago visited London...
44	(20) 73	3.52	1.21	4	IRREG-PLUR	The house was full of mouses.
46	(64) 64	3.43	1.02	3	ADV/ADJ	This soup tastes well!
47	(51) 6	3.39	1.18	4	VOC	Who learnt you Spanish?
48	(28) 28	3.39	1.36	4,5	IRREG-VERB	They fighted bravely in the war.
49	(53) 38	3.37	1.30	4	INS.INDART	It is a hard work to write a book.
50	(53) 31	3.29	1.35	4		

Rank lists of test sentences

Sex groups

Males

FOREIGNESS (F) /contd/

Rank no. F	Sentence no. (ID)	Mean	SD	Mode	Error type	Sentence quoted
51	(21) 19	3.28	1.26	4	IDIOM-PHR	I shouted to him to look up for the car...
52	(49) 54	3.22	1.19	4	INS.PREP	Have you ever seen the river of Ganges?
53	(40) 45	3.19	1.33	4	GENITIVE	This is my brother's-in-law cap.
53	(50) 61	3.19	1.15	4	TENSE	The firm is established in 1970.
55	(28) 13	3.17	1.09	3,4	INS.RELPRO	I don't know what improvements that are...
55	(53) 14	3.17	1.30	3,4	UNC	She has very limited knowledges of German.
57	(56) 69	3.12	1.15	3	CONCORD	There is one chair too much.
58	(61) 52	3.05	1.09	2,4	SIMPVF/ING	I look forward to hear from you.
59	(43) 26	3	1.12	4	WR.INDPRO	I haven't heard something from him...
59	(62) 75	3	1.27	2	VOC	You do good coffeee!
61	(59) 48	2.69	1.14	3	WR.INDART	He is an useful member of the team.
61	(64) 71	2.69	1.26	2	OM.PREP	We have just come back from the island Rhodes.
63	(63) 20	2.5	1.38	1	WORD ORDER	He told me to not worry.
64	(67) 10	2.46	1.32	1	OM.DEFART	I am staying at Sheraton hotel for three days.
65	(60) 67	2.36	1.19	2	DBL-NEG	I didn't buy nothing at the supermarket.
66	(68) 15	2.23	1.05	2	ADJ/ADV	He speaks French quite good.
67	(68) 62	2.22	1.27	1	WR.INDART	It took me a hour to get there.
68	(56) 63	2.14	.98	2	ADJ'NOUN	He has a blue car and I have a red.
69	(64) 47	2.12	1.31	1	CONCORD	We have a great deal of problems.
70	(70) 8	2.02	1.11	1	WR.INDPRO	None of my two brothers knew about my plans.
71	(71) 11	1.17	.59	1	A-CONTROL	He has lived in London all his life.
72	(73) 49	1.05	.22	1	A-CONTROL	Why did he leave so early?
73	(73) 36	1.03	.16	1	A-CONTROL	They were badly shaken by the news.
74	(72) 25	1.02	.16	1	A-CONTROL	She prefers walking to cycling.
75	(73) 65	1.02	.15	1	A-CONTROL	Have you heard from him lately?

Rank lists of test sentences

Sex groups

Males

INTELLIGIBILITY DIFFICULTY (ID)

Rank no.	ID (F)	Sentence no.	Mean	SD	Mode	Error type	Sentence quoted
1	(1)	34	3.7	1.16	4	OM.DO-PPH	He thinks not that they know what to do.
2	(3)	39	3.24	1.24	3	AUX	Can you French?
3	(13)	46	3.05	1.23	2	PPRO/RFPRO	She was standing alone, beside her with rage.
4	(15)	42	3	1.30	2	OM.PREP	I was operated last week.
5	(9)	68	2.93	1.40	2	INS.PREP	She was here for two years ago.
6	(5)	5	2.73	1.18	3	INS.PREP	I was here for two years ago.
7	(30)	59	2.69	1.32	2	TO-INF/ING	Many cities have stopped to expand.
8	(7)	44	2.67	1.18	2	WR.ADVERB	He works very hardly.
9	(2)	41	2.6	1.26	2	IDIOM-PHR	Excuse me, what is the clock, please?
10	(39)	24	2.59	1.28	2	SUBJECT	It was little else to do.
11	(10)	2	2.58	1.03	3	SUBJECT	He has an own company.
12	(41)	43	2.52	1.25	2	VOC	He needs not come.
13	(23)	55	2.45	1.36	2	AUX	This room smells food, doesn't it?
14	(5)	27	2.38	1.21	1	INS.PREP	Smell on these flowers!
15	(26)	50	2.34	1.20	2	OM.DO-PPH	Became he a dentist?
16	(4)	7	2.29	1.12	1	OM.DO-PPH	There's a long time since I saw her.
17	(8)	72	2.26	1.11	1	WR.PREP	I met him in the house.
18	(18)	57	2.21	.95	2	SUBJECT	When I five years ago visited London...
19	(17)	32	2.17	1.20	1	WORD ORDER	I took the blind by the arm and led him...
20	(44)	73	2.14	1.05	1,2	ADJ^NOUN	I shouted to him to look up for the car...
21	(51)	19	2.13	1.07	2	IDIOM-PHR	I always tried to make my best at school.
22	(29)	17	2.13	1.09	1	VOC	I am sure of that he will come.
23	(32)	12	2.12	.95	2	INS.PREP	
24	(42)	56	2.12	1.05	1,2	INS.DEFART	The most people would agree with you.
25	(18)	60	2.12	1.15	1	INS.PREP	
26	(14)	29	2.07	.88	2	TENSE	Things have went too far.
27	(35)	35	2.07	1.01	1	SIMPVF/ING	I am used to get up early in the morning.
28	(55)	13	2.05	.92	1	INS.RELPRO	I don't know what improvements that are...
29	(25)	33	2.03	1.14	1	TO-INF/B	They made me to do it.
30	(22)	70	2.02	1.05	2	COMP.ADV	He drives badlier than his brother.
31	(31)	21	2	1.15	2	VOC	The car was badly injured in the accident.
32	(34)	74	1.95	1.08	1	ING/SIMPVF	He is meaning this book, not that one.
33	(20)	53	1.95	1.02	1	PRE/ATTADJ	He is a very alone man.
34	(11)	16	1.95	.88	2	TENSE	I didn't saw him today.
35	(47)	28	1.85	.91	1	VOC	Who learnt you Spanish?
36	(35)	58	1.85	.88	1	RFPRO/PPRO	She had her radio beside herself.
37	(43)	9	1.83	.83	1	WR.PREP	I met him in the stairs.
38	(28)	30	1.80	.84	1	ADV/ADJ	This cake smells well!
39	(36)	4	1.78	.86	2	CONCORD	I don't know much people in this town.
40	(53)	45	1.76	.93	1	GENITIVE	This is my brother's-in-law cap.
41	(20)	1	1.76	.73	2	INS.INDART	What a dreadful weather!
42	(37)	40	1.76	.86	1	OM.INDART	My sister is nurse.
43	(59)	26	1.73	.78	1	WR.INDPRO	I haven't heard something from him...
44	(11)	18	1.72	.79	1	CONCORD	Here are the money I owe you.
45	(16)	23	1.71	.87	1	NUMB	He had to pay five hundreds of pounds.
46	(26)	51	1.71	.96	1	INS'INDART	What an awful weather!
47	(39)	22	1.68	.79	1	CONCORD	My brother have worked for this company...
48	(33)	37	1.68	.69	1	WR.PREP	She is married with a German.
49	(52)	54	1.61	.80	1	INS.PREP	Have you ever seen the river of Ganges?
50	(53)	61	1.60	.63	1	TENSE	The firm is established in 1970.

Rank lists of test sentences

Sex groups

Males

INTELLIGIBILITY DIFFICULTY (ID) /contd/

Rank no.	ID (F)	Sentence no.	Mean	SD	Mode	Error type	Sentence quoted
51	(23)	3	1.59	.63	1	TENSE	I am born in 1945.
51	(47)	6	1.59	.77	1	ADV/ADJ	This soup tastes well!
53	(55)	14	1.54	.74	1	UNC	She has very limited knowledges of German.
53	(50)	31	1.54	.67	1	INS.INDART	It is a hard work to write a book.
53	(49)	38	1.54	.67	1	IRREG-VERB	They fighted bravely in the war.
56	(68)	63	1.5	.83	1	ADJ^NOUN	He has a blue car and I have a red.
56	(38)	66	1.5	.63	1	COMP.ADJ	This is the goodest cake I have ever tasted!
56	(57)	69	1.5	.59	1	CONCORD	There is one chair too much.
59	(61)	48	1.48	.63	1	WR.INDART	He is an useful member of the team.
59	(48)	67	1.48	.71	1	DBL-NEG	I didn't buy nothing at the supermarket.
60	(65)	52	1.45	.55	1	SIMPVF/ING	I look forward to hear from you.
61	(58)	75	1.44	.59	1	VOC	You do good coffee!
62	(59)	20	1.43	.55	1	WORD ORDER	He told me to not worry.
63	(63)	47	1.4	.58	1	CONCORD	We have a great deal of problems.
64	(69)	64	1.36	.48	1	IRREG-PLUR	The house was full of mouses.
64	(46)	71	1.36	.69	1	OM.PREP	We have just come back from the island Rhodes.
67	(64)	10	1.34	.79	1	OM.DEFART	I am staying at Sheraton hotel for three days.
68	(61)	15	1.25	.44	1	ADJ/ADV	He speaks French quite good.
68	(67)	62	1.25	.49	1	WR.INDART	It took me a hour to get there.
70	(70)	8	1.24	.43	1	WR.INDPRO	None of my two brothers knew about my plans.
71	(71)	11	1.05	.22	1	A-CONTROL	He has lived in London all his life.
72	(74)	25	1.02	.16	1	A-CONTROL	She prefers walking to cycling.
73	(73)	36	1	0	1	A-CONTROL	They were badly shaken by the news.
73	(72)	49	1	0	1	A-CONTROL	Why did he leave so early?
73	(75)	65	1		1	A-CONTROL	Have you heard from him lately?

Rank lists of test sentences

Sex groups

Males

COMBINED TABLE (error gravity with regard to both F and ID)

Rank no.	Error gravity index	Error type	Sentence no.	Sentence quoted
1	8.31	OM.DO-PPH	34	He thinks not that they know what to do.
2	7.68	AUX	39	Can you French?
3	7.10	INS.PREP	68	She was here for two years ago.
4	7.07	PPRO/RFPRO	46	She was standing alone, beside her with rage.
5	7.05	IDIOM-PHR	41	Excuse me, what is the clock, please?
6	6.98	OM.PREP	42	I was operated last week.
7	6.95	INS.PREP	5	I was here for two years ago.
8	6.88	WR.ADVERB	44	He works very hardly.
9	6.72	ADJ-PHR	7	He has an own company.
10	6.63	OM.DO-PPH	2	Became he a dentist?
11	6.60	OM.PREP	27	This room smells food, doesn't it?
12	6.48	TO-INF/ING	59	Many cities have stopped to expand.
13	6.45	OM.PREP	72	Came he back to the party yesterday?
14	6.33	AUX	55	He needs not come.
15	6.22	SUBJECT	24	It was little else to do.
16	6.17	INS.PREP	50	Smell on these flowers!
17	6.14	VOC	43	Yesterday's accident depended on the bad weather.
18	6.12	SUBJECT	57	There's a long time since I saw her.
19	6.10	WR.PREP	32	I met him in the steps.
20	6.05	TENSE	29	Things have went too far.
21	6.02	INS.PREP	60	I am sure of that he will come.
22	5.98	TENSE	16	I didn't saw him today.
23	5.93	ADJ^NOUN	17	I took the blind by the arm and led him...
24	5.90	COMP.ADV	70	He drives badlier than his brother.
25	5.9	TO-INF/B	33	They made me to do it.
26	5.88	VOC	12	I always tried to make my best at school.
27	5.85	PRE/ATTADJ	8	He is a very alone man.
28	5.78	SIMPVF/ING	35	I am used to get up early in the morning.
29	5.78	VOC	21	The car was badly injured in the accident.
30	5.74	CONCORD	18	Here are the money I owe you.
31	5.69	ING/SIMPVF	74	He is meaning this book, not that one.
32	5.68	INS.DEFART	56	The most people would agree with you.
33	5.67	WORD ORDER	73	When I five years ago visited London...
34	5.66	NUMB	23	He had to pay five hundreds of punds?
35	5.66	INS.INDART	1	What a dreadful weather!
36	5.61	ADV/ADJ	30	This cake smells well!
37	5.54	INS.INDART	51	What an awful weather!
38	5.48	CONCORD	1	I don't know much people in this town.
39	5.46	TENSE	4	I am born in 1945.
40	5.43	WR.PREP	37	She is married with a German.
41	5.41	OM.INDART	40	My sister is nurse.
42	5.4	IDIOM-PHR	19	I shouted to him to look up for the car when I saw...
43	5.38	RFPRO/PPRO	58	She had her radio beside herself.
44	5.37	WR.PREP	9	I met him in the stairs.
45	5.32	CONCORD	22	My brother have worked for this company...
46	5.24	VOC	28	Who learnt you Spanish?
47	5.22	INS.RELPRO	13	I don't know what improvements that are...
48	5.14	COMP.ADJ	66	This is the goodest cake I have ever tasted!
49	4.98	ADV/ADJ	6	This soup tastes well!
50	4.95	GENITIVE	45	This is my brother's-in-law cap.

Rank lists of test sentences

Sex groups

Males

COMBINED TABLE (error gravity with regard to both F and ID) /contd/

Rank no.	Error gravity index	Error type	Sentence no.	Sentence quoted
51	4.90	IRREG-VERB	38	They fighted bravely in the war.
52	4.83	INS.PREP	54	Have you ever seen the river of Ganges?
52	4.83	INS.INDART	31	It is a hard work to write a book.
54	4.79	TENSE	61	The firm is established in 1970.
54	4.79	IRREG-PLUR	64	The house was full of mouses.
56	4.73	WR.INDPRO	26	I haven't heard something from him.
57	4.71	UNC	14	She has very limited knowledges of German.
58	4.62	CONCORD	69	There is one chair too much.
59	4.49	SIMPVF/ING	52	I look forward to hear from you.
60	4.43	VOC	75	You do good coffee!
61	4.17	WR.INDART	48	He is an useful member of the team.
62	4.05	OM.PREP	71	We have just come back from the island Rhodes.
63	3.9	WORD ORDER	20	He told me to not worry.
64	3.81	DBL-NEG	67	I didn't buy nothing at the supermarket.
65	3.80	OM.DEFART	10	I am staying at Sheraton hotel for three days.
66	3.64	ADJ^NOUN	63	He has a blue car and I have a red.
67	3.48	CONCORD	47	We have a great deal of problems.
68	3.48	ADJ/ADV	15	He speaks French quite good.
69	3.47	WR.INDART	62	It took me a hour to get there.
70	3.27	WR.INDPRO	8	None of my two brothers knew about my plans.
71	2.22	A-CONTROL	11	He has lived in London all his life.
72	2.05	A-CONTROL	25	She prefers walking to cycling.
73	2.05	A-CONTROL	49	Why did he leave so early?
74	2.03	A-CONTROL	36	They were badly shaken by the news.
75	2.02	A-CONTROL	65	Have you heard from him lately?

APPENDIX 2

RANK LISTS OF ERROR TYPES

If a rank list of the various error types is to be made it is very important to bear in mind that such a rank list may look very different depending upon how one chooses to classify the various errors involved. Other factors influencing the resulting rank lists are which errors are assigned to which class or error type, and which sentences exemplify these error types.

The classification of errors into various error types described above (cf. 1.7.1) was used to compile rank lists of the various error types involved. This was accomplished by means of a series of additional computations, carried out by the computer. For each rank list of test sentences for the total number of informants (foreignness and intelligibility difficulty), the means of the various sentences exemplifying a certain error type were added and the resulting figure was then divided by the number of sentences exemplifying that error type. This was done because the various error types are not always exemplified by the same number of test sentences. The resulting average mean for each error type was then put in a new rank list of the highest to the lowest average mean.

The average means are based on the original means consisting of seven decimals and have been rounded off to only two decimals. In the combined table the error gravity index has been arrived at by adding the corresponding average means for foreignness and intelligibility difficulty on the basis of the original means with seven decimals. The sums of the average means may therefore not be identical with those which are arrived at if the approximate average means in the rank lists are added.

The results of the operations described above are listed in the following tables.

Rank lists of error types

Total sample

FOREIGNNESS (F)

Rank no.	(ID)	Error type	Comments on error type (figures refer to rank no. in column 5)	Rank number/s in table	Average mean*
F	(ID)				
1	(5)	OM.DO-PPH	1: negative sentence	1,4,7	4.34
2	(1)	PRO/REFPRO	4,7: interrogative sentence beside her with rage (emotion)	6	4.19
3	(4)	ADJ-PHR	at own company	8	4.11
4	(3)	AUX	3: can, 23: need	3,23	4.09
5	(6)	WR.ADVERB	hardly for hard	10	4.07
6	(7)	IDIOM-PHR	2: What is the clock?,50: look up for	2,50	3.94
7	(12)	COMP.ADV	badlier	16	3.91
8	(2)	TO-INF/ING	cities have stopped to expand	21	3.83
9	(8)	INS.PREP	9,13:for two years ago, 55:the river of	9,13,18,20,55	3.80
10	(10)	SUBJECT	15: there for it, 32: it for there	15,32	3.78
11	(22)	NUMB	five hundreds of	22	3.77
12	(20)	TENSE	12: have went, 51:IAS+historic present**	12,17,19,51	3.76
13	(11)	TO-INF/B	They made me to do it	24	3.72
14	(14)	PRE/ATTADJ	a very alone man	27	3.71
15	(9)	OM.PREP	5: IAS + smells food,62: the island Rhodes	5,11,62	3.65
16	(18)	ING/SIMPVF	He is meaning	34	3.62
17	(15)	REFPRO/PRO	beside herself (spatial relationship)	36	3.61
18	(23)	ADV/ADJ	30:IAS+smells well, 44:IAS + tastes well	30,44	3.593
19	(19)	WR.PREP	29: in the steps, 43: in the stairs	29,40,43	3.590
20	(34)	COMP.ADJ	goodest	38	3.58
21	(16)	INS.DEFART	the most people	39	3.57
22	(25)	INS.INDART	25,26: before weather, 52: before work	25,26,52	3.541
23	(26)	OM.INDART	My sister is nurse	42	3.537
24	(17)	VOC	28: make for do,56:You do good coffee!	28,33,35,45,56	3.51
25	(32)	IRREG-VERB	fighted	46	3.5
26	(35)	IRREG-PLUR	mouses	48	3.43
27	(27)	SIMPVF/ING	41: be used to get, 60: look forward to hear	41,60	3.21
28	(30)	CONCORD	14:Here are the money, 70:a great deal of + problems	14,31,49,59,70	3.20
29	(13)	INS.RELPRO	what improvements that are being	53	3.18
30	(21)	GENITIVE	my brother's-in-law cap	54	3.17
31	(31)	UNC	knowledges	57	3.06
32	(29)	WORD ORDER	37:PRON + ADV.CLAUSE + VERB,65:to not	37,65	2.94
33	(28)	ADJ^NOUN	47:I took the blind by the arm 69:He has a blue car and I have a red	47,69	2.74

Rank lists of error types

Total sample

FOREIGNNESS (F) /contd/

Rank no.	(ID)	Error type	Comment on error type (figures refer to rank no. in column 5)	Rank number/s in table	Average mean
F	(ID)				
34	(33)	WR.INDPRO	58: something for anything	58,66	2.62
35	(24)	DBL-NEG	66: none for neither I didn't buy nothing	63	2.56
36	(37)	ADJ/ADV	good for well	64	2.53
37	(36)	WR.INDART	61: an useful member, 68: a hour	61,68	2.45
38	(38)	OM.DEFART	Sheraton hotel	67	2.13
39	(39)	(A-CONTROL)	faultless sentences	71,72,73,74,75	1.05

* Average mean is given with more than two decimals only where the first two decimals are the same for error types with differing means.

** IAS = Inanimate subject.

Rank lists of error types
Total sample

INTELLIGIBILITY DIFFICULTY (ID)

Rank no.	(F)	Error type	Comments on error type (figures refer to rank no. in column 5)	Rank number/s in table	Average mean*
ID	(F)				
1	(2)	PPRO/RFPRO	beside her with rage (emotion)	3	3.04
2	(8)	TO-INF/ING	cities have stopped to expand	6	2.86
3	(4)	AUX	2: can, 15: need	2,15	2.70
4	(3)	ADJ-PHR	an own company	8	2.65
5	(1)	OM.DO-PPH	1: negative sentence 17,18: interrogative sentence	1,17,18	2.63
6	(5)	WR.ADVERB	hardly for hard	12	2.47
7	(6)	IDIOM-PHR	13:What is the clock?,14: look up for	13,14	2.33
8	(9)	INS.PREP	4,7:for two years ago,49:the river of	4,7,16,20,49	2.32
9	(15)	OM.PREP	5: I was operated last week,63:Rhodes the island	5,10,63	2.28
10	(10)	SUBJECT	11: It for there, 23: there for it	11,23	2.27
11	(13)	TO-INF/B	They made me to do it	22	2.08
12	(7)	COMP.ADV	badlier	25	2.03
13	(29)	INS.RELPRO	what improvements that are being	26	2.0190
14	(14)	PRE/ATTADJ	a very alone man	27	2.0186
15	(17)	RFPRO/PPRO	beside herself (spatial relationship)	28	2.0185
16	(21)	INS.DEFART	the most people	29	2
17	(24)	VOC	9:depend upon, 59: You do good coffee!	9,24,32,35,59	1.98
18	(16)	ING/SIMPVF	He is meaning	34	1.85
19	(19)	WR.PREP	21: in the steps, 50: married with	21,39,50	1.84
20	(12)	TENSE	19: have went, 56:IAS+historic present**	19,31,45,56	1.82
21	(30)	GENITIVE	my brother's-in-law cap	41	1.77
22	(11)	NUMB	five hundreds of	42	1.75
23	(18)	ADV/ADJ	37:IAS + smells well, 52:IAS + tastes well	37,52	1.70
24	(35)	DBL-NEG	I didn't buy nothing	47	1.629
25	(22)	INS.INDART	44,46: before weather, 55: before work	44,46,55	1.628
26	(23)	OM.INDART	My sister is nurse	48	1.622
27	(27)	SIMPVF/ING	33:be used to get, 62: look forward to hear	33,62	1.621
28	(33)	ADJ^NOUN	30: I took the blind by the arm 65: He has a blue car and I have a red.	30,65	1.61
29	(32)	WORD ORDER	36: PRON+ADV.CLAUSE+VERB, 64: to not	36,64	1.594
30	(28)	CONCORD	38: Here are the money, 67: a great deal of problems	38,40,51,58,67	1.592
31	(31)	UNC	knowledges	53	1.56
32	(25)	IRREG-VERB	fighted	54	1.53
33	(34)	WR.INDPRO	43: something for anything, 66: none for neither	43,66	1.51

Rank lists of error types
Total sample

INTELLIGIBILITY DIFFICULTY (ID) /contd/

Rank no.	(F)	Error type	Comments on error type (figures refer to rank no. in column 5)	Rank number/s in table	Average mean*
ID	(F)				
34	(20)	COMP.ADJ	goodest	57	1.50
35	(26)	IRREG-PLUR	mouses	61	1.39
36	(37)	WR.INDART	60: an useful member, 70: a hour	60,70	1.31
37	(36)	ADJ/ADV	good for well	68	1.26
38	(38)	OM.DEFART	Sheraton hotel	69	1.23
39	(39)	(A-CONTROL)	faultless sentences	71,72,73,73,73	1.01

* Average mean is given with more than two decimals only where the first two decimals are the same for error types with differing average means.

** IAS = Inanimate subject

Rank lists of error types

Total sample

COMBINED TABLE (error gravity with regard to both F and ID)

Rank no.	Error gravity index	Error type
1	7.22	PPRO/RFPRO
2	6.97	OM.DO-PPH
3	6.79	AUX
4	6.76	ADJ-PHR
5	6.69	TO-INF/ING
6	6.54	WR.ADVERB
7	6.27	IDIOM-PHR
8	6.11	INS.PREP
9	6.05	SUBJECT
10	5.94	COMP.ADV
11	5.93	OM.PREP
12	5.80	TO-INF/B
13	5.73	PRE/ATTADJ
14	5.62	RFPRO/PPRO
15	5.58	TENSE
16	5.57	INS.DEFART
17	5.52	NUMB
18	5.49	VOC
19	5.47	ING/SIMPVF
20	5.43	WR.PREP
21	5.30	ADV/ADJ
22	5.19	INS.RELPRO
23	5.17	INS.INDART
24	5.16	OM.INDART
25	5.08	COMP.ADJ
26	5.03	IRREG-VERB
27	4.94	GENITIVE
28	4.84	SIMPVF/ING
29	4.81	IRREG-PLUR
30	4.79	CONCORD
31	4.62	UNC
32	4.53	WORD ORDER
33	4.35	ADJ^NOUN
34	4.19	DBL-NEG
35	4.13	WR.INDPRO
36	3.79	ADJ/ADV
37	3.76	WR.INDART
38	3.36	OM.DEFART
39	2.06	(A-CONTROL)

ENGLISH SPEAKERS' ATTITUDES TO MISTAKES MADE BY FOREIGN USERS OF ENGLISH

page 1
(1A)

The purpose of this questionnaire is to chart the reactions of people with English as their mother tongue to various mistakes made by foreign users of the language. We hope the results will help give teachers of English a better guide to what errors should be considered serious from the point of view of communication.

This questionnaire is strictly anonymous, so please do not write your name on it. However, for the answers to be valid, we need to know some other things about those answering the questionnaire. Would you, therefore, please first answer all the questions below on this page. PLEASE WRITE IN BLOCK LETTERS!

1. YOUR SEX   (tick box)   Male □   Female □

2. YOUR AGE _____

3. YOUR PLACE OF BIRTH _____ , _____ , _____
   (town or village)   (county)   (country)

4. WHERE DID YOU SPEND MOST OF THE FIRST 15 YEARS OF YOUR LIFE?
   _____ , _____ , _____
   (town or village)   (county)   (country)

5. YOUR PLACE OF RESIDENCE TODAY _____ , _____ , _____
   (town or village)   (county)   (country)

6. HOW LONG HAVE YOU LIVED WHERE YOU LIVE NOW?

7. WHAT DIALECT/ACCENT DO YOU SPEAK (IF ANY)?

8. WHAT IS YOUR MOTHER TONGUE?

9. WHAT LANGUAGES DO YOU SPEAK (apart from English)?

10. YOUR OCCUPATION

11. YOUR EDUCATION (tick box if yes)

A. I have completed primary school □
   I have completed secondary school □
   I have completed university a) with a degree □ ⎱ (no. of years)
                                b) without a degree □
   I have completed some other type of school □

B. I am now attending secondary school □
   I am now attending university □
   I am now attending some other type of school □

12. HOW OFTEN DO YOU TALK TO FOREIGNERS?   (tick one box only)
    At least once a week □
    At least once a month □
    At least once a year □
    Never □

13. WHAT OTHER COUNTRY/COUNTRIES (apart from Britain) HAVE YOU LIVED IN (IF ANY)?
    FOR HOW LONG AND WHEN? _____

14. OTHER RELEVANT INFORMATION YOU WOULD LIKE TO GIVE _____

INSTRUCTIONS

Please put a cross in one of the five boxes of each five-graded scale to indicate your opinion of the sentence. If you have any idea of where the foreigner who used the sentence comes from, please indicate this in the empty space provided. If not, just answer the scales.

EXAMPLE:

He has lived in London since a long time.   native-like + □□□▣□ - very foreign

Spain   very easy to □▣□□□ very difficult
         understand   to understand

These answers mean that this sentence is judged to be foreign (but not very foreign), and that it is easy to understand (but not very easy). Here the person answering the questions thought that the foreigner came from Spain.

In other words: The more native-like you think the sentence is, the further left you put your cross. The more foreign you think the sentence is, the further right you put your cross. In the same way you judge how easy or difficult it is to understand.

NOW PLEASE INDICATE WHAT YOU THINK OF THE FOLLOWING SENTENCES:

1. What a dreadful weather!   native-like + □□□□□ - very foreign
                               very easy to □□□□□ very difficult
                               understand   to understand

2. He has an own company.   native-like + □□□□□ - very foreign
                               very easy to □□□□□ very difficult
                               understand   to understand

3. I am born in 1945.   native-like + □□□□□ - very foreign
                               very easy to □□□□□ very difficult
                               understand   to understand

4. I don't know much people in this town.   native-like + □□□□□ - very foreign
                               very easy to □□□□□ very difficult
                               understand   to understand

5. I was here for two years ago.   native-like + □□□□□ - very foreign
                               very easy to □□□□□ very difficult
                               understand   to understand

1A

13. I don't know what improvements that are being planned.

native-like + ☐ ☐ ☐ ☐ ☐ - very foreign

very easy to understand   ☐ ☐ ☐ ☐ ☐   very difficult to understand

14. She has very limited knowledge of German.

native-like + ☐ ☐ ☐ ☐ ☐ - very foreign

very easy to understand   ☐ ☐ ☐ ☐ ☐   very difficult to understand

15. He speaks French quite good.

native-like + ☐ ☐ ☐ ☐ ☐ - very foreign

very easy to understand   ☐ ☐ ☐ ☐ ☐   very difficult to understand

16. I didn't saw him today.

native-like + ☐ ☐ ☐ ☐ ☐ - very foreign

very easy to understand   ☐ ☐ ☐ ☐ ☐   very difficult to understand

17. I took the blind by the arm and led him across the street.

native-like + ☐ ☐ ☐ ☐ ☐ - very foreign

very easy to understand   ☐ ☐ ☐ ☐ ☐   very difficult to understand

18. Here are the money I owe you.

native-like + ☐ ☐ ☐ ☐ ☐ - very foreign

very easy to understand   ☐ ☐ ☐ ☐ ☐   very difficult to understand

19. I shouted to him to look up for the car when I saw that it was going to hit him.

native-like + ☐ ☐ ☐ ☐ ☐ - very foreign

very easy to understand   ☐ ☐ ☐ ☐ ☐   very difficult to understand

6. This soup tastes well!

native-like + ☐ ☐ ☐ ☐ ☐ - very foreign

very easy to understand   ☐ ☐ ☐ ☐ ☐   very difficult to understand

7. Became he a dentist?

native-like + ☐ ☐ ☐ ☐ ☐ - very foreign

very easy to understand   ☐ ☐ ☐ ☐ ☐   very difficult to understand

8. None of my two brothers knew about my plans.

native-like + ☐ ☐ ☐ ☐ ☐ - very foreign

very easy to understand   ☐ ☐ ☐ ☐ ☐   very difficult to understand

9. I met him in the stairs.

native-like + ☐ ☐ ☐ ☐ ☐ - very foreign

very easy to understand   ☐ ☐ ☐ ☐ ☐   very difficult to understand

10. I am staying at Sheraton hotel for three days.

native-like + ☐ ☐ ☐ ☐ ☐ - very foreign

very easy to understand   ☐ ☐ ☐ ☐ ☐   very difficult to understand

11. He has lived in London all his life.

native-like + ☐ ☐ ☐ ☐ ☐ - very foreign

very easy to understand   ☐ ☐ ☐ ☐ ☐   very difficult to understand

12. I always tried to make my best at school.

native-like + ☐ ☐ ☐ ☐ ☐ - very foreign

very easy to understand   ☐ ☐ ☐ ☐ ☐   very difficult to understand

20. He told me to not worry.

native-like + □□□□□ - very foreign

very easy to □□□□□ very difficult
understand to understand

21. The car was badly injured in the accident.

native-like + □□□□□ - very foreign

very easy to □□□□□ very difficult
understand to understand

22. My brother have worked for this company for many years.

native-like + □□□□□ - very foreign

very easy to □□□□□ very difficult
understand to understand

23. He had to pay five hundreds of pounds.

native-like + □□□□□ - very foreign

very easy to □□□□□ very difficult
understand to understand

24. It was little else to do.

native-like + □□□□□ - very foreign

very easy to □□□□□ very difficult
understand to understand

25. She prefers walking to cycling.

native-like + □□□□□ - very foreign

very easy to □□□□□ very difficult
understand to understand

26. I haven't heard something from him for a long time.

native-like + □□□□□ - very foreign

very easy to □□□□□ very difficult
understand to understand

27. This room smells food, doesn't it?

native-like + □□□□□ - very foreign

very easy to □□□□□ very difficult
understand to understand

28. Who learnt you Spanish?

native-like + □□□□□ - very foreign

very easy to □□□□□ very difficult
understand to understand

29. Things have went too far.

native-like + □□□□□ - very foreign

very easy to □□□□□ very difficult
understand to understand

30. This cake smells well!

native-like + □□□□□ - very foreign

very easy to □□□□□ very difficult
understand to understand

31. It is a hard work to write a book.

native-like + □□□□□ - very foreign

very easy to □□□□□ very difficult
understand to understand

32. I met him in the steps.

native-like + □□□□□ - very foreign

very easy to □□□□□ very difficult
understand to understand

33. They made me to do it.

native-like + □□□□□ - very foreign

very easy to □□□□□ very difficult
understand to understand

Page 7 (left column):

34. He thinks not that they know what to do.

native-like + ☐ ☐ ☐ ☐ ☐ - very foreign

very easy to understand ☐ ☐ ☐ ☐ ☐ very difficult to understand

35. I am used to get up early in the morning.

native-like + ☐ ☐ ☐ ☐ ☐ - very foreign

very easy to understand ☐ ☐ ☐ ☐ ☐ very difficult to understand

36. They were badly shaken by the news.

native-like + ☐ ☐ ☐ ☐ ☐ - very foreign

very easy to understand ☐ ☐ ☐ ☐ ☐ very difficult to understand

37. She is married with a German.

native-like + ☐ ☐ ☐ ☐ ☐ - very foreign

very easy to understand ☐ ☐ ☐ ☐ ☐ very difficult to understand

38. They fightd bravely in the war.

native-like + ☐ ☐ ☐ ☐ ☐ - very foreign

very easy to understand ☐ ☐ ☐ ☐ ☐ very difficult to understand

39. Can you French?

native-like + ☐ ☐ ☐ ☐ ☐ - very foreign

very easy to understand ☐ ☐ ☐ ☐ ☐ very difficult to understand

40. My sister is nurse.

native-like + ☐ ☐ ☐ ☐ ☐ - very foreign

very easy to understand ☐ ☐ ☐ ☐ ☐ very difficult to understand

Page 8 (right column):

41. Excuse me, what is the clock, please?

native-like + ☐ ☐ ☐ ☐ ☐ - very foreign

very easy to understand ☐ ☐ ☐ ☐ ☐ very difficult to understand

42. I was operated last week.

native-like + ☐ ☐ ☐ ☐ ☐ - very foreign

very easy to understand ☐ ☐ ☐ ☐ ☐ very difficult to understand

43. Yesterday's accident depended on the bad weather.

native-like + ☐ ☐ ☐ ☐ ☐ - very foreign

very easy to understand ☐ ☐ ☐ ☐ ☐ very difficult to understand

44. He works very hardly.

native-like + ☐ ☐ ☐ ☐ ☐ - very foreign

very easy to understand ☐ ☐ ☐ ☐ ☐ very difficult to understand

45. This is my brother's-in-law cap.

native-like + ☐ ☐ ☐ ☐ ☐ - very foreign

very easy to understand ☐ ☐ ☐ ☐ ☐ very difficult to understand

46. She was standing alone, beside her with rage.

native-like + ☐ ☐ ☐ ☐ ☐ - very foreign

very easy to understand ☐ ☐ ☐ ☐ ☐ very difficult to understand

47. We have a great deal of problems.

native-like + ☐ ☐ ☐ ☐ ☐ - very foreign

very easy to understand ☐ ☐ ☐ ☐ ☐ very difficult to understand

48. He is an useful member of the team.

native-like + □ □ □ □ □ - very foreign

very easy to □ □ □ □ □ very difficult
understand to understand

49. Why did he leave so early?

native-like + □ □ □ □ □ - very foreign

very easy to □ □ □ □ □ very difficult
understand to understand

50. Smell on these flowers!

native-like + □ □ □ □ □ - very foreign

very easy to □ □ □ □ □ very difficult
understand to understand

51. What an awful weather!

native-like + □ □ □ □ □ - very foreign

very easy to □ □ □ □ □ very difficult
understand to understand

52. I look forward to hear from you.

native-like + □ □ □ □ □ - very foreign

very easy to □ □ □ □ □ very difficult
understand to understand

53. He is a very alone man.

native-like + □ □ □ □ □ - very foreign

very easy to □ □ □ □ □ very difficult
understand to understand

54. Have you ever seen the river of Ganges?

native-like + □ □ □ □ □ - very foreign

very easy to □ □ □ □ □ very difficult
understand to understand

55. He needs not come.

native-like + □ □ □ □ □ - very foreign

very easy to □ □ □ □ □ very difficult
understand to understand

56. The most people would agree with you.

native-like + □ □ □ □ □ - very foreign

very easy to □ □ □ □ □ very difficult
understand to understand

57. There's a long time since I saw her.

native-like + □ □ □ □ □ - very foreign

very easy to □ □ □ □ □ very difficult
understand to understand

58. She had her radio beside herself.

native-like + □ □ □ □ □ - very foreign

very easy to □ □ □ □ □ very difficult
understand to understand

59. Many cities have stopped to expand.

native-like + □ □ □ □ □ - very foreign

very easy to □ □ □ □ □ very difficult
understand to understand

60. I am sure of that he will come.

native-like + □ □ □ □ □ - very foreign

very easy to □ □ □ □ □ very difficult
understand to understand

61. The firm is established in 1970.

native-like + □ □ □ □ □ - very foreign

very easy to □ □ □ □ □ very difficult
understand to understand

62. It took me a hour to get there.

native-like + □ □ □ □ □ - very foreign

very easy to understand □ □ □ □ □ very difficult to understand

63. He has a blue car and I have a red.

native-like + □ □ □ □ □ - very foreign

very easy to understand □ □ □ □ □ very difficult to understand

64. The house was full of mouses.

native-like + □ □ □ □ □ - very foreign

very easy to understand □ □ □ □ □ very difficult to understand

65. Have you heard from him lately?

native-like + □ □ □ □ □ - very foreign

very easy to understand □ □ □ □ □ very difficult to understand

66. This is the goodest cake I have ever tasted!

native-like + □ □ □ □ □ - very foreign

very easy to understand □ □ □ □ □ very difficult to understand

67. I didn't buy nothing at the supermarket.

native-like + □ □ □ □ □ - very foreign

very easy to understand □ □ □ □ □ very difficult to understand

68. She was here for two years ago.

native-like + □ □ □ □ □ - very foreign

very easy to understand □ □ □ □ □ very difficult to understand

69. There is one chair too much.

native-like + □ □ □ □ □ - very foreign

very easy to understand □ □ □ □ □ very difficult to understand

70. He drives badlier than his brother.

native-like + □ □ □ □ □ - very foreign

very easy to understand □ □ □ □ □ very difficult to understand

71. We have just come back from the island Rhodes.

native-like + □ □ □ □ □ - very foreign

very easy to understand □ □ □ □ □ very difficult to understand

72. Came he to the party yesterday?

native-like + □ □ □ □ □ - very foreign

very easy to understand □ □ □ □ □ very difficult to understand

73. When I five years ago visited London, I didn't realize how big it was.

native-like + □ □ □ □ □ - very foreign

very easy to understand □ □ □ □ □ very difficult to understand

74. He is meaning this book, not that one.

native-like + □ □ □ □ □ - very foreign

very easy to understand □ □ □ □ □ very difficult to understand

75. You do good coffee!

native-like + □ □ □ □ □ - very foreign

very easy to understand □ □ □ □ □ very difficult to understand

PLEASE CHECK THAT YOU HAVE ANSWERED ALL THE QUESTIONS (including those on page one)! THANK YOU!